THE CONSTITUTION OF RISK

The Constitution of Risk is the first book to combine constitutional theory with the theory of risk regulation. The book argues that constitutional rulemaking is best understood as a means of managing political risks. Constitutional law structures and regulates the risks that arise in and from political life, such as an executive coup or military putsch, political abuse of ideological or ethnic minorities, corrupt self-dealing by officials, or pathological regulatory decision making by experts. The book claims that the best way to manage political risks is an approach it calls "optimizing constitutionalism" – in contrast to the worst-case thinking that underpins "precautionary constitutionalism," a mainstay of liberal constitutional theory. Drawing on a broad range of disciplines such as decision theory, game theory, welfare economics, political science, and psychology, this book advocates constitutional rulemaking undertaken in a spirit of welfare maximization and offers a corrective to the pervasive and frequently irrational attitude of distrust of official power that is prominent in American constitutional history, theory, and public discourse.

Adrian Vermeule is John H. Watson Professor of Law at Harvard Law School. He is the author or coauthor of seven previous books, most recently *The System of the Constitution* (2011). He was formerly Bernard D. Meltzer Professor of Law at the University of Chicago, and he was elected to the American Academy of Arts and Sciences in 2012.

The Constitution of Risk

Adrian Vermeule

Harvard Law School

CAMBRIDGE
UNIVERSITY PRESS

CAMBRIDGE
UNIVERSITY PRESS

32 Avenue of the Americas, New York, NY 10013-2473, USA

Cambridge University Press is part of the University of Cambridge.

It furthers the University's mission by disseminating knowledge in the pursuit of education, learning, and research at the highest international levels of excellence.

www.cambridge.org
Information on this title: www.cambridge.org/9781107618978

© Adrian Vermeule 2014

First published 2014

Printed in the United States of America

A catalog record for this publication is available from the British Library.

Library of Congress Cataloging in Publication data
Vermeule, Adrian.
The constitution of risk / Adrian Vermeule, Harvard Law School
    pages   cm
Includes bibliographical references and index.
ISBN 978-1-107-04372-5 (hardback)
    1. Constitutional law – United States.   2. Risk management – Political aspects – United States.   I. Title.
KF4550.V366   2013
342.73–dc23   2013027300

ISBN 978-1-107-04372-5 Hardback
ISBN 978-1-107-61897-8 Paperback

Contents

"One of the chief advantages derived by the present generation from the improvement and diffusion of philosophy, is deliverance from unnecessary terrours, and exemption from false alarms.... The advancement of political knowledge may be expected to produce, in time, the like effects. Causeless discontent, and seditious violence, will grow less frequent and less formidable, as the science of government is better ascertained, by a diligent study of the theory of man."

Samuel Johnson, "The False Alarm," 1770

Introduction

I have two claims to offer. One is that constitutional rulemaking is best understood as a means to regulate and manage political risks. The other is that an approach I will call "optimizing constitutionalism" is the best approach to constitutional risk regulation. It will take a book to flesh out these claims, but let me at least introduce them.

CONSTITUTIONS AS RISK-MANAGEMENT DEVICES

What do constitutions do? Legal and political theory offer several answers. Constitutions create and empower government by coordinating expectations and thereby creating institutions of lawmaking;[1] constitutions tie the hands of majorities in ways that protect majorities from their own predictable excesses and pathologies;[2] constitutions protect the rights of discrete and insular minorities;[3] constitutions further moral principles of equality, freedom, and human dignity;[4] and, most generally, constitutions "design democracy."[5]

---

[1] *See generally* RUSSELL HARDIN, LIBERALISM, CONSTITUTIONALISM, AND DEMOCRACY (2003) (arguing that social coordination for mutual advantage constitutes the core of effective liberal constitutionalism).

[2] *Compare* JON ELSTER, ULYSSES AND THE SIRENS: STUDIES IN RATIONALITY AND IRRATIONALITY (1979) (advancing this suggestion), *with* JON ELSTER, ULYSSES UNBOUND: STUDIES IN RATIONALITY, PRECOMMITMENT, AND CONSTRAINTS (2000) (critiquing it).

[3] *See generally* JOHN HART ELY, DEMOCRACY AND DISTRUST: A THEORY OF JUDICIAL REVIEW (1980) (arguing that the Constitution should be interpreted so as to ensure that discrete and insular minorities are able to participate in the political process, thereby reinforcing the principles of democratic self-government).

[4] RONALD DWORKIN, FREEDOM'S LAW (1997).

[5] CASS R. SUNSTEIN, DESIGNING DEMOCRACY: WHAT CONSTITUTIONS DO (2001).

None of these answers is wrong, exactly. The problem is to determine whether and how they fit together. Each of the answers identifies a value or good promoted by constitutionalism, but those goods may work at cross-purposes to one another and, under certain conditions, trade off against one another. Empowering popular control through a coordinated set of lawmaking institutions creates a risk of majoritarian oppression; in turn, creating a set of insulated institutions, such as courts, to protect the rights of minorities risks undermining democracy and political equality; and so on. In these cases, the tensions between and among the values of constitutionalism are best understood not as contradictions, but as competing risks and tradeoffs. Our problem is not that we have no good theories of constitutionalism, but that we have too many, with too little understanding of how the plural aims and values of constitutionalism relate to one another under the conditions of uncertainty that bedevil constitutional rulemaking. None of the stock theories of constitutionalism provides an overarching analytic framework for addressing risk-saturated tradeoffs among constitutional goods.

In what follows, I attempt to provide such a framework. I claim that *constitutions, and public law generally, are best understood as devices for regulating and managing political risks.* Whoever and wherever we are, we inevitably have a "constitution of risk," in the sense that constitutional law structures and regulates the risks that arise in and from political life. Constitutional theory and public discourse is fraught with debates, arguments, and worries about political risks – risks ranging from the large-scale and episodic, such as an executive coup or military putsch, to the small-scale and chronic, such as political abuse of ideological or ethnic minorities, ambient low-level corruption, and official incompetence.

This claim draws on a large and diverse set of insights developed in disciplines such as decision theory, game theory, welfare economics, political science, and psychology. The resulting framework goes under the heading of "risk analysis" or "risk management."[6] In what follows, I will arbitrage the insights of risk regulation into constitutional law and theory. The key to this approach is to understand constitutions and public law as devices for regulating *political* risks, rather than risks arising from the environment, the market, or technology. Constitutions, whether designed or grown, may be justified and criticized as more or less successful devices for managing

---

[6] For a comprehensive overview, see Daniel M. Byrd III & C. Richard Cothern, Introduction to Risk Analysis: A Systematic Approach to Science-Based Decision Making (2000).

a range of risks that arise in and from politics, including tyranny and dictatorship, self-dealing by officials, akratic decision making by majorities, exploitative oppression of minorities, and various forms of bias or corruption in adjudication, regulation, and political decision making.

The risk-regulation lens is, if anything, even more suitable for public law and political risks than it is for the sorts of health, safety, and environmental risks typically addressed by ordinary regulation. Given the poverty of our causal theories about the large-scale and long-run effects of constitutional arrangements, constitutional rulemakers inevitably act under conditions of profound uncertainty. They must identify and cope with a set of worries ("risks") that may or may not materialize, are potentially quite harmful if they do materialize, and that quite possibly compete with one another, because the measures taken to prevent one risk may exacerbate a different risk, or may even exacerbate the target risk itself. This is just the type of decision-making environment that the modern theory of risk management provides tools to comprehend and address.

Although I substantiate this claim by offering examples drawn primarily from the history of constitutional law and theory in the United States, I draw on a broad transnational discourse of liberal-democratic constitutionalism and political theory to motivate the argument and to give depth to the picture. And throughout, I offer local comparisons to the constitutional rules of other polities where appropriate.

POLITICAL RISKS AS SECOND-ORDER RISKS

Why focus on political risks, rather than risks to health, safety, the environment, and other goods? And what counts as a "political" risk anyway? The ordinary risks addressed by administrative risk regulation may be called *first-order risks*, which are dealt with by substantive governmental policies. Some of these risks arise as the unintended consequence of human action, as when the uncoordinated actions of financial firms create systemic risks to the economy. Some arise as the intended result of human action, exemplified by the risks of terrorist activity. Some arise from the interaction between human action and the forces of nature, as in risks of flooding, which is the joint product of exogenous natural conditions and human decisions about where to locate people and buildings.

By contrast, constitutional law addresses *second-order risks* that arise from the design of institutions, from the allocation of power across institutions to make first-order decisions, and from the selection of officials to staff institutions. Constitutional law structures the power of government and allocates it in complex ways to a set of institutions, themselves constituted by the same law. Any such structure creates the chance of various good or bad political consequences, just as any policy for regulating nuclear power creates the chance of various good or bad environmental and economic consequences. Constitutional rulemakers will have to assess and then somehow compare and balance the goods and bads that might arise from various institutional designs and allocations of power across institutions – precisely the sort of decision that risk analysis addresses.

By defining political risks as second-order risks, I do not at all mean to imply that constitutional rulemakers do or should focus solely on the harms that may flow from official abuses, rather than the harms of "private" action that officials may prevent. On the contrary, I will argue, in contrast to the approach taken by Antifederalists and some other members of the founding generation, that official abuses should not be minimized, but rather optimized – in other words, that some positive rate of official abuse is optimal, as the unavoidable byproduct of a regime that optimizes the net overall risks of action and inaction, of abuses and neglect, on the part of both officials and powerful nongovernmental actors. As we will see, some of the founders attended solely to one side of the ledger – the harms of official abuses, especially at the federal level – without paying sufficient attention to the benefits of vigorous governmental action, especially at the federal level. In other cases, however, founders and early commentators widened the lens to include all relevant risks.

Nor do I mean to imply that constitutions or the rules of public law can never, or do never, focus on the sort of health, safety, and environmental risks typically addressed in the modern theory of risk regulation. In recent years, some constitutions have inscribed principles of health and safety regulation in the fundamental laws of their polities. An example is the Constitution of France, which mandates that regulation honor a version of the environmental "precautionary principle," to be discussed in chapters 1 and 2.[7] By and large, however, what is distinctive about constitutions is that they offer second-order rules, which create institutions and allocate

---

[7]   1958 CONST. CHARTER FOR THE ENVIRONMENT Art. 5 (Fr.) ("When the occurrence of any damage, albeit unpredictable in the current state of scientific knowledge, may seriously and irreversibly harm the environment, public authorities shall, with due respect for the principle of precaution and the areas within their jurisdiction, ensure the implementation of procedures for risk assessment and the adoption of temporary measures commensurate with the risk involved in order to deal with the occurrence of such damage.").

official power to and across institutions; it follows naturally that the main subject of constitutionalism is political risk.

WHO ARE THE REGULATORS?

I have been speaking of "constitutional risks" and their "regulation." Who are the regulators of constitutional risks? Are only constitutional founders and designers who establish new constitutional orders at issue, or might other actors be included, such as officials who act within a constitutional system that is already up and running?

I mean to include and to address any actors who make constitutional rules, whether at the stage of constitutional design or at the stage of constitutional "interpretation" and implementation. The scare quotes are to indicate that in most mature systems of written constitutionalism, there is substantial leeway for interpreting the fundamental document one way or another, so interpretation often amounts to constitutional rulemaking *de facto*. (An analogous point holds with at least equal force for unwritten, conventional constitutions.) Certainly this is notoriously true in the United States, given the age, vagueness, generality, and downright opacity – the Delphic character – of many of its constitutional provisions. But it holds to greater or lesser degree in many other constitutional orders as well.

This is not to say that written constitutions are completely plastic, or that there is no difference between writing and interpreting constitutional texts. The upstream choices of the text-writers will sometimes, to some degree, constrain the downstream discretion of the text-interpreters. Justice Holmes famously observed that "judges do and must legislate, but they can do so only interstitially; they are confined from molar to molecular motions."[8] Within that constrained discretion, however, interpreters make constitutional rules in a straightforward sense.

Put differently, constitutional provisions either will or will not clearly dictate what sort of attitude in-system officials must take toward particular constitutional risks. If the relevant provisions are clear, then it is the constitutional designers who have made the relevant choices about constitutional risk-regulation, and we may ask whether their choices were good ones. If the relevant provisions are ambiguous or silent, then in-system interpreters will have to make the relevant choices about constitutional risk-regulation, and we may instead evaluate the interpreters' choices. The arguments and considerations I will offer are applicable at either stage.

---

[8]   *S. Pac. Co. v. Jensen*, 244 U.S. 205, 221 (1917) (Holmes, J., dissenting).

Whether through constitutional design or constitutional interpretation, then, some actor or other will make constitutional rules. Whenever they do so they will have to engage in the regulation of constitutional risks, like it or not. They may do so heedlessly or thoughtfully, but there is no escaping the fact that their choices about rules will structure the risk environment of the constitutional order – will help to determine, if only in small measure, whether and when constitutional risks materialize. Any and all constitutional rulemakers, to whatever extent they indeed have discretion to make rules, are thus the audience for and the subject of the claims I will discuss.

RISK AND UNCERTAINTY

A clarifying word about "risk" is necessary. The term "risk" has a colloquial sense that includes, under one large umbrella, well-defined decision-theoretic concepts such as risk, uncertainty, and ignorance. I generally mean to use the colloquial sense, except where the context of particular problems otherwise requires.

Strictly speaking, risk, uncertainty, and ignorance all have distinct technical meanings. In decisions made under risk, the decision maker can identify a discrete set of possible outcomes and assign to each outcome both a probability of occurring and a utility consequence if it does occur. In decisions under uncertainty, the possible outcomes can be specified and utilities attached to them, but probabilities cannot be assigned to the outcomes, or at least the probability assignments have no epistemic credentials – they are ungrounded hunches that need not hook up to anything real in the world. Under ignorance, even the range and nature of possible outcomes is itself unclear.

Risk, uncertainty, and ignorance form a sort of intellectual arena in which various camps of decision theorists, game theorists, and statisticians have fought epic battles. Within the normative branch of rational choice theory, the issues include not only the question how decisions under uncertainty are to be made, but whether there exists genuine uncertainty at all. Some Bayesian statisticians, and their fellow travelers in economics and political science, deny that there is any such thing as true uncertainty, on the ground that some probability assignment can always be elicited from the decision maker, even for unique, one-time events. In response, critics of the Bayesian view suggest that probability assignments can vary with the procedure for eliciting them, a clue that such assignments lack epistemic credentials in at least some cases.

Insofar as possible, I mean to stay well away from this contested terrain. In what follows, I will sometimes offer both a risk-based interpretation of relevant constitutional arguments, and sometimes an uncertainty-based interpretation. The loose injunction to design constitutions to avoid the "worst-case scenario," for example, is irreducibly ambiguous. On the one hand, it can be interpreted in an uncertainty model as a *maximin strategy* for designing institutions: where the probability of various harms is unknown, act so as to maximize the minimum payoff, or to bring about the best worst-case outcome. On the other hand, the injunction can instead be interpreted in a risk model as a choice that embodies a high degree of risk aversion; in the latter case, probabilities are used but bad outcomes are treated as producing higher expected costs than good ones produce expected benefits. Overall, I will attempt to take account of both risk and uncertainty as appropriate perspectives, in different cases and situations. To some limited degree, of course, that itself represents a choosing of sides, insofar as it betrays a belief that genuine uncertainty does sometimes exist, and that the strict Bayesian approach is misguided. To that extent, I plead guilty.

STRATEGIC AND NONSTRATEGIC RISKS

There is a tempting contrast between first-order risks and second-order risks that goes as follows. Some of the time or even much of the time, first-order risks are simply given ("exogenous"). They arise from Nature with an emphatic capital N, or from the scientific structure of the world as it really is. From the standpoint of the regulator, the fixed character of (some or many) first-order risks makes their regulation a problem in decision theory, which is the theory of noninteractive, nonstrategic decisions. On the other hand, the comparison continues, second-order risks are inherently strategic and interactive. The risks that arise from the allocation of power across officials and institutions are risks that occur because of the strategic behavior of people within institutions, who choose their behavior in light of what they anticipate that others will do. On this view, second-order political risks must be addressed with the tools of game theory rather than decision theory.

It is surely the case that strategic risks are an important part of political risk regulation, and that game-theoretic tools are an important weapon in the arsenal of the constitutional analyst, and indeed the constitutional rulemaker. At various points in what follows I will point to constitutional arguments with an implicitly game-theoretic structure, decades or centuries *avant la lettre*. That said, the contrast between first-order and second-order risks is overblown. Almost all first-order risks can be described as strategic and interactive, and not just the ones that arise from intentional action by public enemies, such as the risk of terrorism. The reason that first-order risks can almost uniformly be characterized in interactive terms is that decisions by regulated parties and by officials jointly determine the nature and magnitude of almost all first-order risks. Health and safety risks arising from economic production, for example, are the result of a complex multiparty strategic interaction between producers, employees, unions, consumers, and a potpourri of administrative agencies. Even risks that seem to come from Nature herself, such as hurricane damage, are pervasively shaped by the prior decisions of many parties – in the case of hurricanes, the citizens who live on flood plains and the legislature and agencies that subsidize them to do so.

Conversely, despite their pervasively strategic character, some first-order risks can be treated, for purposes of risk analysis, *as though* they are fixed and exogenous for the time being, and can thus be addressed with the tools of decision theory. Once citizens have bought houses on flood plains, the risks of hurricane damage are largely fixed in the short run, and thus the decision whether an emergency management agency should forcibly evacuate residents in the face of an impending hurricane of uncertain strength and trajectory can be viewed as a problem of decision theory. In the constitutional setting, as we will see, many arguments about the regulation of political risks have an implicitly decision-theoretic structure. Where institutions or patterns of behavior are costly to change in the short run, this can be a perfectly valid treatment, even if the problem is a strategic one in some long-run sense.

POLITICAL RISK, PROPERTY, AND CONTRACT

My broad definition of political risk is somewhat nonstandard, but I hope in a useful way. Literatures in the economics of international development, international law, and business strategy define "political risk" narrowly, to refer to "the risk that a government will expropriate property or violate a contract without providing adequate compensation."[9] In these literatures, political risk management is undertaken by firms contemplating

---

[9]   Stephen J. Choi, G. Mitu Gulati, & Eric A. Posner, *The Evolution of Contractual Terms in Sovereign Bonds*, 4 JOURNAL OF LEGAL ANALYSIS 131 (2012).

ventures or joint ventures in developing nations that are politically or legally unstable. Such firms attempt to gauge the risk of expropriation and to adopt measures – contractual, political, or economic – to minimize that risk. Insofar as the constitutional law of the host country enters the picture, its major or indeed only role is to provide rights protections for investors; here rights serve as a credible signal that the host government is committed to economic development and will not myopically seize investors' assets for short-run gain.[10] The function of constitutional law as a credible commitment to property protection also underlies a classic account of the political economy of the development of capitalism. On this account, the Glorious Revolution in England in 1688–1689 amounted to a regime change that deprived monarchs of arbitrary power to confiscate property, creating incentives to invest in economic enterprises and making possible the economic development of the eighteenth and nineteenth centuries.[11]

These literatures are useful so far as they go, but they do not go very far. They address only a narrow subset of the second-order risks that arise from the design of institutions and the allocation of powers across institutions. Expropriation of property or arbitrary interference with contract rights is one of those risks, but there are many others that have nothing to do with property or contract, and instead involve risks to liberty, equality, or democracy. In general, the literature on political risks in international development is useful for multinational firms and for a slice of the problems that interest constitutional analysts, but its definition of political risks is too cramped for my purposes.

Accordingly, in what follows, I will generally focus on risks to goods other than property or contract rights; that focus will allow me to explore largely uncharted terrain. This is not to say, however, that I will ignore property rights altogether. Throughout, I use the Supreme Court's highly controversial 2005 decision in *Kelo v. City of New London*[12] to structure questions about the optimal constitutional regulation of "takings" – government appropriations of property through the power of eminent domain.

Kelo allowed a "taking" of private property that was then transferred to another private party for economic redevelopment of an economically

---

[10] *See, e.g.*, Daniel Farber, *Rights as Signals*, 31 J. LEGAL STUD. 83, 84 (2002) (arguing that "legal reform is a good signal of being truly committed to economic reform").

[11] *See* Douglass C. North & Barry R. Weingast, *Constitutions and Commitment: The Evolution of Institutional Governing Public Choice in Seventeenth-Century England*, 49 J. ECON. HIST. 803, 815–16 (1989).

[12] 545 U.S. 469 (2005).

depressed urban area; the decision triggered suffered a barrage of criticism from libertarian advocates of constitutional property rights. Takings generally require "just compensation" to the owner, but there are also restrictions on when government may engage in taking private property at all, most prominently that the taking must be for "public use."[13] The libertarian critics hotly denied that a transfer of property to a private party, in the interests of economic redevelopment, could count as a public use. In *Kelo*, however, the Supreme Court offered an expansive definition of the public-use requirement, and allowed a wide range of governmental takings; as we will see, that approach fits comfortably with the argument I will develop. The libertarian critiques of *Kelo* focus to excess on one type of political risk – the risk that the power of eminent domain will be abused by officials in the service of interest groups or private-regarding agendas – while neglecting countervailing risks.

But now I have arrived at my second, quite distinct claim; let us turn to that.

PRECAUTIONARY CONSTITUTIONALISM AND OPTIMIZING CONSTITUTIONALISM

The book's overarching theoretical claim is that constitutions and public law are best understood as devices for regulating second-order political risks. But how in fact should such risks be managed? As to that separate question, I offer a separate, narrower claim: *optimizing constitutionalism* is the best approach to constitutional regulation of political risks. Optimizing constitutionalism trades off all relevant political risks, giving them their due weight in the circumstances, without any systematic skew or bias against any particular type of political risk. This second claim is partially independent of the first as a logical matter: one may subscribe to the macro-idea that constitutional law manages political risks without accepting the narrower claim that optimizing constitutionalism is the best approach.

To understand the second claim, some background is necessary. The history of constitutional law and theory has witnessed a running contest between two (families of) competing views. The first view I will call *precautionary constitutionalism*. Precautionary constitutionalism is my construct, as opposed to a label that its proponents have self-consciously

---

[13] U.S. Const. amend. V, cl. 5 ("nor shall private property be taken for public use, without just compensation").

adopted. Yet I hope the construct is a useful one that captures something shared among disparate proponents in disparate contexts. It holds, roughly speaking, that constitutional rules should above all entrench precautions against the risks that official action will result in dictatorship or tyranny, corruption and official self-dealing, violations of the rights of minorities, or other political harms of equivalent severity. On this view, constitutional rulemakers and citizens design and manage political institutions with a view to warding off the worst case. The burden of uncertainty is to be set against official power, out of a suspicion that the capacity and tendency of official power to inflict cruelty, indignity, and other harms are greater than its capacity and tendency to promote human welfare, liberty, or justice.

In ordinary risk management there is a continuum of more or less precautionary approaches; so, too, precautionary constitutionalism may take stronger or weaker forms, along a continuum. The weakest form is a rebuttable presumption, or even just a tiebreaking rule, to the effect that precautions against political risks should be observed unless there is some apparent reason to depart from them. In the strongest form, precautionary constitutionalism encodes a powerful presumption of distrust, holding that if it is possible for officials to abuse their powers, then constitutional rulemakers should act as if those officials will be certain to do so – an approach that focuses strictly on the harm of the worst-case scenario, as opposed to the probability of its occurrence. I will call this extreme form of the precautionary approach *maximin constitutionalism*, after the maximin strategy in decision theory: roughly, where the probabilities of possible harms are unknown, choose the course of action that maximizes the minimum payoff – the action with the best worst-case scenario.[14] This is equivalent to treating the worst as sure to happen;[15] given certain further premises, it amounts to an infinite aversion to political risks. As I shall discuss, maximin constitutionalists tend to focus on the *fat-tail risks of politics* – possible political outcomes that are highly unlikely to occur, but are more likely than in a normal distribution of risk, and that would inflict grievous harms on the values protected by constitutionalism if they did occur.[16]

---

[14] *See* R. DUNCAN LUCE & HOWARD RAIFFA, GAMES AND DECISIONS: INTRODUCTION AND CRITICAL SURVEY 278–279 (1957).

[15] *See id.* at 280.

[16] For an introduction to the idea of fat-tail risks, with applications to international investing and geopolitical risks, see IAN BREMMER & PRESTON KEAT, THE FAT TAIL: THE POWER OF POLITICAL KNOWLEDGE IN AN UNCERTAIN WORLD (2010). For regulatory applications, and an argument that rational risk management should focus on avoiding truly catastrophic outcomes, see Michael P. Vandenbergh and Jonathan A. Gilligan, *Macro-*

Under uncertainty, maximin is not the only coherent approach; other decision rules are also possible. One is maximax, which maximizes the pay-off from the best case rather than the worst case.[17] A maximax approach to political risk would emphasize the hope of upside gains from constitutionalism. One might even assemble a set of maximally optimistic constitutional arguments emphasizing the promise of official power rather than its perils – something like *utopian constitutionalism*. However, I will set aside that alternative and give it only incidental consideration here. In the major constitutional democracies, it is just an observable fact about those who engage in constitutional theorizing that utopian constitutional argument is far less pervasive, far less central, than is the distrustful maximin perspective or its weaker precautionary relatives.

This dominance of distrust surely has something to do with liberalism (in the political-theory sense). Both in the United States and elsewhere, the historical core of constitutional argument has been liberal constitutional argument. Liberalism comes in many shapes and sizes, but a major strand in the tradition of liberal constitutional argument – one of its hallmarks – is pessimism about power and fear of the abuse of power, especially by officials enjoying monopoly control over the state's instruments of coercion. For my purposes, relevant landmarks in this tradition include Karl Popper's argument that the question "who should rule?" should be replaced by the question "how can we so organize political

---

Risks: The Challenge for Rational Risk Regulation, 21 DUKE ENVTL. L. & POL'Y F. 165 (2011). The most famous regulatory application involves climate change. *See* Martin L. Weitzman, *On Modeling and Interpreting the Economics of Catastrophic Climate Change*, 91 REV. ECON. & STAT 1, 2 (2009).

[17] *See* LUCE & RAIFFA, *supra* note 14, at 280–86; Kenneth J. Arrow & Leonid Hurwicz, *An Optimality Criterion for Decision Making Under Ignorance*, *in* UNCERTAINTY AND EXPECTATIONS IN ECONOMICS (C.F. Carter and J.L. Ford eds., 1972); Richard T. Woodward & Richard C. Bishop, *How to Decide When Experts Disagree: Uncertainty-Based Choice Rules in Environmental Policy*, 73 LAND ECON. 492 (1997). Weighted combinations of the extremes are also rational. Woodward & Bishop, *supra*, at 496 n.7. That possibility just underscores, in a framework of uncertainty rather than risk, that more or less pessimistic responses to the possibility of harm may all be compatible with rational decision-making. *See* David Kelsey, *Choice Under Partial Uncertainty*, 34 INT'L ECON. REV. 297 (1993). Despite occasional assertions in the literature that pessimism has a kind of natural or commonsense priority, standard frameworks for decisionmaking under uncertainty do not by themselves support such a view – unless the particular model at issue builds in further, pessimistic assumptions. An example is Itzhak Gilboa & David Schmeidler, *Maxmin Expected Utility with Non-Unique Prior*, 18 J. MATHEMATICAL ECON. 141 (1989). The "maxmin" criterion the authors develop, which can range between standard maximin and expected utility maximization, is derived from an axiom of uncertainty aversion, *see id.* at 144; the axiom itself is not a requirement of rationality, and other axioms might be used instead.

institutions that bad or incompetent rulers can be prevented from doing too much damage?,"[18] and Judith Shklar's "liberalism of fear," which supposes that political liberals should "be less inclined to celebrate the blessings of liberty than to consider the dangers of tyranny and war that threaten it."[19] That Popper and Shklar are very different theorists underscores the point: distrust of official power is at least arguably a common element across liberal theories of law and constitutionalism. Across eras and controversies, and along the continuum of stronger or weaker versions, precautionary constitutionalists share a language whose deep structure is fear of official abuses; in this regard, precautionary constitutionalism is law's analogue to a powerful strain of distrust and worst-case thinking in liberal political theory.

The second, competing view of constitutional risk regulation is what I will call optimizing constitutionalism or, equivalently, "the mature position" – a pointedly tendentious phrase coined by Albert Hirschman in the different, but related, context of the political theory of reform.[20] The following chapters offer a sustained critique of precautionary constitutionalism and maximin constitutionalism, and a sustained argument for optimizing constitutionalism and the mature position. Optimizing constitutionalism holds that all relevant political risks matter, and that a systematically precautionary and distrustful approach to the constitutional allocation of power is a mistake. For one thing, precautions must be incentive-compatible. If they rest on a jaundiced diagnosis of official motivations and then simply prescribe, by fiat, public-spirited action or public-regarding constraints that are inconsistent with those motivations, the precautions will be futile and ineffective. Furthermore, precautions may neglect the benefits of official action, which must be weighed in the balance along with the risks and harms of abuses; one of the relevant benefits is that official power may be wielded to prevent or remedy abuses of political, economic, or social power by nongovernmental actors. Finally, and crucially, precautions against official abuses can actually create or exacerbate the very risks they are intended to prevent; where that occurs, precautions will be perversely self-defeating.

Political risks, including the risk of abuse of power, lie on all sides of the critical questions of constitutional rulemaking. In that sense, optimizing

[18] Karl Popper, *The Paradoxes of Sovereignty, in* POPPER SELECTIONS 320 (David Miller ed., 1985) (emphasis omitted).
[19] Judith N. Shklar, *The Liberalism of Fear, in* POLITICAL THOUGHT AND POLITICAL THINKERS 3, 9 (Stanley Hoffmann ed., 1998).
[20] ALBERT O. HIRSCHMAN, THE RHETORIC OF REACTION (1991).

constitutionalism can more justly lay claim to the mantle of being the sys-
temically minded approach;[21] precautionary constitutionalism focuses
myopically on just a particular target risk or set of target risks, while
neglecting countervailing risks, or so I will suggest. In light of predictable tradeoffs among the competing goods that constitutional rulemaking
properly aims to secure, there is no alternative to considering all relevant
risks, with no systematic skew or bias against official power (or for that
matter in favor of it). Optimizing constitutionalism, then, adopts mature –
meaning well-rounded and balanced – case-by-case judgments about
risks and harms, both those avoided and those created by constitutional
precautions.

THE LIMITS OF OPTIMIZING CONSTITUTIONALISM – AND ITS NEGATIVE VALUE

Optimizing constitutionalism thus rejects rigidly precautionary presumptions or rules, except – and this is an important qualifier – to the extent
that in some particular domain, such rules are themselves the best response
in light of all relevant risks. In particular domains, that is, it may turn out
that in light of the limited rationality or distorted incentives of front-line
decision makers, the best course of action is to restrict official power to
a certain domain, or through certain procedures. Yet the crucial methodological point is that one must not adopt such an approach *a priori*;
constitutional precautions are valid only when and to the extent that they
happen to fall out naturally, as the byproduct of a mature analysis of all
relevant political risks.

The only general positive counsel I offer, then, is that constitutional rulemakers should consider all relevant risks, on all sides of relevant questions.
As a *positive* counsel this is obviously thin, even banal. But its value lies in
its *negative* aspect.[22] It is a placeholder for, and a summary reminder about,
a rich variety of ways in which constitutional rulemakers can go badly
wrong. I provide a taxonomy of these mistakes, with detailed illustrations,
throughout the succeeding chapters. The common theme is that constitutional rulemakers may become obsessed with a particular risk (a so-called
target risk), thereby neglecting questions about the incentive-compatibility

---

[21] For the importance of systemic thinking in constitutional analysis and design, see ADRIAN
VERMEULE, THE SYSTEM OF THE CONSTITUTION (2011).

[22] In this regard, it is somewhat in the spirit of JON ELSTER, SECURITIES AGAINST MISRULE:
JURIES, ASSEMBLIES, ELECTIONS (2013), which argues that the main aim of institutional
design should be negative: to filter out distorting influences on decision makers.

of precautions against that risk, neglecting countervailing risks, or – the worst possibility – overlooking that the obsession may perversely bring about the very risk the rulemakers dread. At bottom, optimizing constitutionalism offers a master principle of *avoiding obsession with particular risks*, and it arms rulemakers with a breviary that lists and illustrates the ways in which such an obsession may come into being.

Two corollaries deserve mention. First, because precautionary constitutionalism and optimizing constitutionalism lie on a continuum, the arguments have a sliding-scale quality. The stronger the version of precautionary constitutionalism, the stronger the mature critiques become. Conversely, weaker forms of precautionary constitutionalism, such as rebuttable presumptions and tiebreaking rules, are less exposed to those critiques. The price of this reduction in intellectual exposure, however, is that the force of the precautionary stance must itself be diluted; in the limit, the precautionary stance becomes so watered-down that it shades imperceptibly into mature analysis. Where this occurs, I have no further quarrel to press.

Second, the argument for optimizing constitutionalism – the mature position – is compatible with, and derives from, the overarching claim that political risk-regulation is the best framework within which to manage and reconcile the multiple purposes of constitutionalism. Yet it bears repeating that the two claims are logically independent. Anyone who subscribes to the overarching claim need not commit herself to the mature position; as a logical matter it is perfectly possible to hold that the central concern of constitutionalism is indeed political risk regulation, yet also to reject all the argument in favor of optimizing constitutionalism, in favor of a systematically precautionary outlook. Although I will argue against that combination of views, it cannot be rebutted on strictly logical grounds. Rather, it fails on substantive grounds, because precautions may prove futile, may do more harm than good, or may prove perverse. As we will see, the constitutional and institutional risks that a precautionary strategy is aimed to prevent may appear on all sides of the relevant questions; indeed, those risks may be exacerbated by the very precautions taken to prevent them.

THE ROLE OF OTHER RISK MANAGEMENT PRINCIPLES

The precautionary and optimizing approaches do not exhaust the suite of decision-making principles that have been discussed in the literature on ordinary first-order risks. There is no agreed-on list, but standard treatments may mention "BAT" (Best Available Technology), in which the risk manager mandates that firms or other agents must adopt the best available technology to reduce a particular target risk;[23] feasibility analysis, which says that regulation should minimize a target risk to the extent "feasible," which in turn may mean either technologically feasible or economically feasible;[24] and "tolerable" risk levels,[25] in which the risk manager in essence satisfices, rather than optimizing.[26] Other principles could be mentioned as well.

I will not discuss these other principles directly or at length, although my analysis will have obvious implications for them and applications to them. For one thing, as we will see, the main debates in constitutional law and theory center on precautionary and optimizing approaches. For another thing, some of these principles are even less well-defined, even spongier, than the precautionary approach; for that reason some of them, on the briefest analysis, quickly reduce to either the precautionary or the optimizing approach.

Most important, to spell out the analysis of these subsidiary principles would be otiose given the main line of my argument, which applies fully to whatever extent these principles differ from optimizing constitutionalism. Just as precautionary constitutionalism goes wrong to the extent that it makes matters worse overall, by focusing excessively on a target risk while neglecting or exacerbating countervailing risks, so too with these lesser rivals of optimization. Under feasibility analysis, for example, a myopic focus on a target constitutional risk may reduce *that* risk to the extent "feasible," while creating or exacerbating countervailing risks. If so, it will fail the test of the mature position. The argument generalizes to the other principles as well.

---

[23] *See, e.g.,* Charles Yoe, Primer on Risk Analysis: Decision Making under Uncertainty 83 (2012).

[24] For a detailed analysis and critique, see Jonathan Masur and Eric Posner, *Against Feasibility Analysis,* 77 U. Chi. L. Rev. 657 (2010); for an attempted rehabilitation, see David M. Dreisen, *Two Cheers for Feasible Regulation: A Modest Response to Masur and Posner,* 35 Harv. Envtl. L. Rev. 313 (2011).

[25] Yoe, supra note 23, at 84.

[26] Roughly speaking, the satisficing decision maker tries to attain an aspiration level – here, a level at which the target risk is tolerable – rather than trying to attain the optimal state of affairs. The distinction stems from Hebert Simon and has spawned an enormous literature. See Reva Brown, *Consideration of the Origin of Herbert Simon's Theory of 'Satisficing' (1933–1947),* 42 Management Decision 1240–1256 (2004); Satisficing and Maximizing: Moral Theorists on Practical Reason (Michael Byron ed.) (2004).

ARGUMENTS AND CHOICES: A CAUTION

Having stated the main claims, several definitions and assumptions should be made explicit. The book is a study in the theory of constitutional argument. I aim to identify, critique, and evaluate two major strategies of constitutional argument that have not previously been identified or evaluated as such – precautionary constitutionalism, on the one hand, and the mature position, on the other. I do not at all attempt to lay out what a desirable constitution would look like, as a substantive matter. So long as we think maturely about what the constitutional rules should be, there can be no wholesale objection in principle to whatever set of rules results (although of course one might well have objections at retail, based on substantive views about constitutional rulemaking in particular domains, with respect to particular problems).

Put conversely, although I will sharply critique precautionary constitutionalism in its various guises, the rules for which precautionary constitutionalists argue may or may not turn out to be defensible on mature grounds; what matters for these purposes is the rationale, not the rule. Indeed, as Chapter 2 explains at length, it is even possible that in particular domains, for particular problems, a mature analysis of political risks will end up supporting precautionary decision-procedures for a given constitutional official or institution, within that domain. So long as the higher-level analysis is itself mature, there is nothing objectionable about such an outcome. What would be objectionable is an approach to constitutional rulemaking that systematically picks the rules at issue on one-sided precautionary grounds, rather than on the basis of an evenhanded risk assessment.

CONSTITUTIONAL LAW AND PUBLIC LAW

Although I will sometimes, for brevity, speak only of constitutions, I mean throughout to use constitutionalism in its widest sense to include the whole body of public legal rules – public law being the body of legal rules that structures the relationships between and among officials wielding legal authority, and between officials and citizens (whereas "private" law, on a conventional definition, addresses the legal relationships between and among citizens). Constitutions manage political risks, but so do quasi-constitutional statutes embedded in the framework of a polity's public law, and whose repeal would violate unwritten norms of the constitutional order, even if it would be legal in the strict sense.

In American public law, a leading example of such a statute is the Administrative Procedure Act (APA), a trans-substantive statute that regulates the procedures through which agencies act. In tandem with constitutional rules and other structural statutes like the Federal Advisory Committee Act, the APA regulates political risks posed by agencies and the experts who advise them. As we will see in Chapter 6, structuring the relationship between expert advisory bodies and agencies is an enterprise in trading off various uncertain harms and benefits that may arise from different allocations of authority to make first-order policies – in other words, an exercise in the regulation of political risks.

FUNCTIONALISM, EVOLUTION, AND THE INTENTIONS OF RULEMAKERS

One final caution, methodological in nature: "constitutions" do nothing. Only people can produce or regulate political risks. The claim that constitutions regulate political risks, then, must be shorthand for some claim about what people do. There are three possibilities:

1. The risk-regulation function of constitutions may be just an observation about their effects, untethered from any claim about who does the regulating.
2. Without anyone intending it, some selection process may weed out constitutions that fail to manage political risks successfully. In this sense constitutions "evolve" into more or less successful risk-regulation devices, as a result of human action but not of human design.
3. Constitutional rulemakers sometimes intentionally create constitutional rules with a view to regulating political risks.

I offer only the third claim, rather than either of the first two. The first is a bad sort of functionalism that posits no mechanism to explain why and how constitutions have the effects attributed to them; it leaves the genesis of the risk-regulation function mysterious.[27] The second is possible, just wildly implausible. As I have argued elsewhere, there is no extant account of institutional selection that would support such a grandiose claim; the mechanisms posited in such accounts are far too fragile, and the environment in which constitutions operate generally changes too rapidly,

---

[27] *See* Jon Elster, Explaining Social Behavior: More Nuts and Bolts for the Social Sciences 14–15 (2007).

to believe that bodies of constitutional rules have time to evolve toward, let alone to, efficient or successful states.[28]

The third approach has the virtue that it is supported by evidence. As I will attempt to detail at length in the chapters that follow, constitutional rulemakers from the founding era to recent times have articulated arguments that are best interpreted and understood in terms of the modern theory of risk regulation. Although the arguments were not cast in modern terms, many constitutional rulemakers have, like Monsieur Jourdain, spoken the prose of risk analysis all their lives without knowing it. The third position does not imply that constitutional rulemakers always design rules with a view to regulating political risks, or that they always succeed in regulating such risks intelligently even when they attempt to do so. That said, however, I do claim to show that actual constitution-makers constantly wrestle with problems of political risk-regulation, in substance if not explicitly in terms.

PLAN OF THE BOOK

So much for the main claims, the main assumptions, and the main limits and qualifications. The structure of the book is as follows. Part I encompasses Chapters 1 and 2, the theoretical core of the book. Chapter 1 lays out the principal targets, precautionary constitutionalism and its hypertrophic form, maximin constitutionalism. In order to dispel any concern that these targets are built of straw, I begin by documenting the extensive history of precautionary constitutionalism and even maximin constitutionalism in American legal rulemaking and commentary. American political culture is pervasively distrustful of official power, and this distrust reaches a zenith in constitutional discourse. In the founding era, both Antifederalists and, to a surprising degree, Federalists as well, expressed pervasive fear of official "abuses" and offered precautionary remedies to be embodied in the constitutional design. In later times, precautionary constitutionalism has taken new and different forms. As we will see, one of the leading theoretical rationales for the massive and highly libertarian body of free-speech jurisprudence in America is an explicitly precautionary notion: Vincent Blasi's idea of the "pathological perspective," which holds that rules of free speech should be designed with a view to preventing the worst-case scenario of political abuses by incumbent officials. And modern precautionary constitutionalists like Bruce Ackerman have argued for constitutional

---

[28] ADRIAN VERMEULE, LAW AND THE LIMITS OF REASON 97–122 (2009).

or quasi-constitutional rules and structures intended to minimize the risks of presidential or military abuses or even dictatorship.

Chapter 2 lays out the main criticisms of precautionary constitutionalism, and details the alternative view. I identify a series of legal actors and commentators who have provided withering critiques of precautionary constitutionalism. These predecessors range from Alexander Hamilton, Joseph Story, and other early figures, to New Dealers such as Felix Frankfurter and Robert Jackson. Their basic view, although not their terminology, is captured by Hirschman's mature position. Chapter 2 also provides an analytic taxonomy of methods for undermining precautionary constitutionalism. Fusing some of Hirschman's ideas with the modern theory of risk regulation, I will identify several major strategies of anti-precautionary argument: the *futility thesis*, which posits that a given precautionary rule of constitutional law will fail the test of incentive-compatibility and thus prove ineffectual; the *jeopardy thesis*, which posits that the risk of abuses is more than compensated by the benefits of vigorous official action; the *perversity thesis*, which argues that constitutional precautions will exacerbate the very risks they are intended to prevent; and the *argument for ex post remedies*, a distinctive and important case of the jeopardy thesis, which claims that relevant harms can best addressed after they materialize, rather than by means of anticipatory precautions.

Part II turns from theory to applications. Chapters 3 through 6 offer case studies at descending levels of generality, from largest to smallest. All are intended to substantiate, illustrate, complicate, and extend my theoretical claims about precautionary and optimizing constitutionalism. Taken together, the applications cover the gamut of basic features of constitutionalism: checks and balances, federalism, and judicial review; structures of legislative, executive, administrative, and judicial decision making; procedures of deliberation in all these institutions; and, in a more modern vein, procedures for incorporating technical expertise into the decision making of constitutional institutions.

Chapter 3 begins with the macro-level, taking up several of the most distinctive large-scale features of the American constitutional order: checks and balances, the extended federal republic, and the robust norm of free political speech. I focus on James Bryce's brilliant but neglected analysis, which underscores the regulatory mistakes of the framers, particularly Madison. In Bryce's view, the framers were obsessed with taking precautions against unconstrained popular majoritarianism, and attempted to check the power of majority opinion through complicated governmental structures. Those precautionary structures, however, proved perversely self-defeating: far from constraining the power of mass public opinion, they exacerbated its force. The dominance of mass public opinion in American constitutionalism, on this view, actually results from the perverse failure of a precautionary strategy advocated by constitutional rulemakers.

The consequence is that in America, mass public opinion governs. On Bryce's view, this places both an upper bound and a lower bound on the performance of the American constitutional order. In his striking formulation, "the American democracy is not better just because it is so good."[29] Although this outcome is tolerable and reasonably stable, the framers failed to foresee the causal pathways by which it came about; in that sense, the eventual stability of the regime they set up was fortuitous. Here as elsewhere, precautionary strategies of constitutionalism, intended as a hedge against uncertainty and unforeseen consequences, themselves generate unforeseen consequences. As advocates of the mature position point out, uncertainty lies on all sides of constitutional choices.

Chapter 4 descends one step on the scale of generality, taking up a single fundamental precept of constitutionalism: the maxim that "no man may serve as judge in his own cause" (*nemo iudex in sua causa*). The maxim is a mainstay of precautionary constitutionalism; it warns against a risk – the risk of self-interested decision making – that much constitutional discourse assumes should be prevented or avoided at all costs.

I attempt to show that the maxim is overblown, in ways that illuminate my broader thesis. The maxim embodies a strict precaution against self-dealing by officials or institutions, yet self-dealing is merely one bad among many. Likewise, the value of impartiality that underpins the maxim is merely one good among many. Both the bad and the good trade off against a host of other considerations, such as the autonomy of decision makers and institutions, the energy or activity levels of officials, and the value of the information and expertise that biased adjudicators systematically tend to possess. Moreover, in some cases, precautions against self-dealing create perverse countervailing risks of self-dealing by other officials or institutions.

Impartiality, in other words, creates risks of its own – both risks to other values and indeed to impartiality itself. Accordingly, in practice, constitutional framers and later constitutional rulemakers have fundamentally compromised the *nemo iudex* maxim by allowing legislators to set their own salaries and create their own districts; allowing judges to decide cases

---

[29]   2 JAMES BRYCE, THE AMERICAN COMMONWEALTH 1256 (Liberty Fund 1995) (3d ed. 1941).

brought to raise their own compensation; and by allowing administrative agencies to fuse legislative, executive, and judicial power, deciding cases they themselves have initiated, under rules of their own creation. These structures tolerate risks of impartiality because there are cogent arguments that other goods will be obtained by doing so, or that precautions against impartiality will be futile or self-defeating.

Chapter 5 turns to another pillar of constitutionalism, namely procedural precautions against hasty and ill-considered decision making. In many settings, constitutional rulemakers create *second-opinion mechanisms* that attempt to safeguard against the risk that decision makers will act precipitately or with inadequate deliberation, and that add an extra filter against bad legislation or policies (somehow defined). This idea, too, is a mainstay of precautionary constitutionalism, and thus warrants treatment here. Constitutional theorists, especially in the liberal tradition, overwhelmingly tend to warn against governmental "panic" and "overreaction" to perceived problems, and go on to counsel strong precautions against those pathologies.

I will suggest, however, that second-opinion mechanisms can create countervailing risks, either because they add to the direct costs and opportunity costs of lawmaking, or even because they can themselves reduce the quality of decisions. The latter risk can arise because second-opinion mechanisms create a risk of epistemic free-riding, by causing front-line decision makers to invest too little in acquiring information and in deliberating about their choices. Precautions against the risks of ill-considered decision making, then, trade off against other risks and can prove perverse under some circumstances.

Chapter 6 expands the lens beyond constitutional law properly so-called, to include public law more generally. I focus on administrative law, and the problems and opportunities posed by expert decision making. Precautions against corrupting political influences on technocratic expertise are a mainstay of the *de facto* or unwritten constitution of the administrative state, as are precautions against the excessive autonomy of experts. All too frequently, however, proponents of one or the other set of precautions focus myopically on the target risk that most concerns them, neglecting countervailing risks.

In the administrative state, panels of experts wield a large and constantly growing share of political power, and one of administrative law's central tasks is to manage the competing risks posed by experts and by political decision making. On the one hand, legal rules mandating that administrative agencies consult experts are a widespread precaution against the risks of "capture" and politicized administration, in which agencies choose suboptimal policies under the pressure of legislators, interest groups, or politically selected officials in the executive branch. As always, however, there are countervailing risks: expert decision making is subject to a number of known pathologies, including various forms of epistemic free-riding and reputational influences; these risks are especially serious when experts make decisions in groups.

Trading off these risks under various conditions, I argue that administrative law should generally use a simple decision-rule: a majority vote of experts prevails, unless administrative officials have some valid and articulable second-order reason for believing that the expert panel has arrived at its decision on epistemically suspect grounds. Such an approach is not theoretically unimpeachable, but has pragmatic virtues when the costs of implementation and the failings of alternative approaches are taken into account.

In the Conclusion, I weave together the threads spun throughout the preceding chapters and attempt to capture the virtues – emphatically *negative* virtues – of the optimizing approach to constitutionalism. On this approach, law's equivalent of the mature position, constitutional rulemakers should approach their tasks without prejudices or obsessions. Enlightened rulemakers will not be systematically concerned either to constrain or to expand governmental power; either to protect or curtail individual rights; either to take precautions against political risks, or not to do so. Everything depends on what the balance of risks turns out to be, in particular domains, and with respect to particular problems.

Again, it might turn out that with respect to certain problems, and for certain types of decision makers within the constitutional system, a precautionary approach may *itself* just be the optimizing strategy in a second-order sense, in light of the limited rationality or harmful incentives of the first-order decision makers. To that extent, the optimizing approach includes and embraces the precautionary one. But I do not at all think this empties the optimizing approach of significance; indeed this utter plasticity is its significance. The point of the optimizing approach is cautionary, ironically enough. It is to warn rulemakers about a number of ways in which obsession with particular target risks can damage or defeat their enterprise.

What is at issue, at bottom, is whether constitutional rulemaking will be undertaken in a *systematic* spirit of distrust and caution or instead – and this is what I advocate – in a spirit of welfare-maximization that may sometimes happen to counsel caution but that need not do so, and that will not do so where caution is itself harmful in expectation. The negative virtue of the optimizing approach is that it does not commit itself, *a priori*, to any precautionary maxim such as "better safe than sorry" or "in matters of constitutional design, assume the worst." At the highest level of analysis, and to the extent possible for ordinary humans, constitutional rulemakers should lack any systematic predilections or leanings, should have no favorite moves or characteristic concerns – no obsessions. Constitutional rulemakers, I suggest, should have no style.

In this way, optimizing constitutionalism offers a corrective to the pervasive and frequently irrational attitude of distrust of official power that is so prominent a feature of American constitutional history and discourse. Although that attitude has rarely been more powerful than it is today, I will attempt to show that an optimizing and thoroughly rational approach to constitutional rulemaking has actually prevailed at certain critical points in American constitutional history, including some partial successes in the founding era and even greater successes in the New Deal and the early 1940s. We may be of good cheer; there is reason to hope that the wheel will turn again.

Part I

Theory

1

Precautionary Constitutionalism

In the regulation of financial, environmental, health, and safety risks, "precautionary principles" state, in their most stringent form, that new instruments, technologies, and policies should be rejected unless and until they can be shown to be safe.[1] Examples include requirements that new drugs pass stringent tests of safety before they are licensed for sale; requirements that nuclear power plants pass stringent tests of design safety before coming into operation; and the Bush administration's "one percent" doctrine, which held that even a miniscule risk of terrorism warranted precautionary countermeasures.[2] Such principles come in many shapes and sizes, and with varying degrees of strength, but the common theme is to place the burden of uncertainty on proponents of potentially unsafe technologies and policies. Critics of precautionary principles urge that the status quo itself carries risks, either on the very same margins that concern the advocates of such principles or else on different margins; more generally, the costs of such principles may outweigh the benefits.

Although this debate is a relatively new one in the theory of regulation, it is a venerable one in constitutional law debates about second-order

[1] *See, e.g.*, Peter L. deFur, *The Precautionary Principle: Application to Polices Regarding Endocrine-Disrupting Chemicals, in* Protecting Public Health and the Environment: Implementing the Precautionary Principle 337, 345–46 (Carolyn Raffensperger & Joel Tickner eds., 1999) ("As described in the Wingspread Statement on the Precautionary Principle, the applicant or proponent of an activity or process or chemical needs to demonstrate to the satisfaction of the public and the regulatory community that the environment and public health will be safe."). For an overview of the massive literature on precautionary principles in various regulatory domains, see Implementing the Precautionary Principle: Perspectives and Prospects (Elizabeth Fisher et al. eds., 2006).

[2] *See* Ron Suskind, The One Percent Doctrine: Deep Inside America's Pursuit of Its Enemies Since 9/11 (2006) ("If there's a 1% chance that Pakistani scientists are helping al Qaeda build or develop a nuclear weapon, we have to treat it as a certainty in terms of our response." (quoting former Vice President Richard Cheney)).

political risks, or so I will claim. At the wholesale level, many theorists defend a master principle according to which constitutions should be designed to take precautions against political risks arising from the design of institutions and the allocation of power among officials. At the retail level, many constitutional rules and structures have been justified as precautions against the risk of abuse of power by incumbent officials or other constitutional actors, the risk of tyrannous majorities, or other political pathologies. Although later chapters will critique precautionary justifications for constitutional rules, the aim of this one is to reconstruct such arguments in charitable terms, in order to put them in their best possible light.

PRECAUTIONARY PRINCIPLES AND POLITICAL RISKS

In the domain of risk regulation, precautionary principles come in many different forms. One count shows no less than nineteen versions of "the precautionary principle"[3] – or nineteen different precautionary principles, related only by a vague family resemblance. As we will see, constitutional precautionary principles are equally heterogeneous. The principal dimensions of variation include the following:

> *Scope.* To what political risks does the principle apply? The leading ones I will discuss are "abuse of power" or self-dealing by officials, "tyranny" in the sense of legislative[4] or executive dictatorship,[5] majoritarian oppression,[6] minoritarian oppression, the death of federalism or the abolition of the states,[7] and various forms of biased policymaking by agencies and biased judging. All these have the second-order character that is the hallmark of political risks; they arise from particular allocations of decision-making power across officials and institutions.

> *Weight.* How strong is the principle within its scope? What sort of showing or what sort of reasons suffice to defeat it?

---

3   Jonathan B. Wiener, *Precaution in a Multirisk World, in* HUMAN AND ECOLOGICAL RISK ASSESSMENT: THEORY AND PRACTICE 1509, 1513 (Dennis J. Paustenbach ed., 2002) (citing Per Sandin, *Dimensions of the Precautionary Principle*, 5 HUM. ECOL. RISK ASSESS. 889 (1999)).

4   *See* THE FEDERALIST NO. 47, at 300–08 (James Madison) (Clinton Rossiter ed., 1961).

5   *See* Youngstown Sheet & Tube Co. v. Sawyer, 343 U.S. 579, 650–53 (1952).

6   *See* United States v. Carolene Prods. Co., 304 U.S. 144, 152 n.4 (1938).

7   *See* Brutus XV, *in* 2 THE COMPLETE ANTI-FEDERALIST 437, 437–42 (Herbert J. Storing ed., 1981).

Timing. When does the constitutional rule intervene to ward off an uncertain threat? How far in the future must or may the threat arise?

Justification. Why should there be ex ante precautions at all, as opposed to ex post remedies?

Overall, in both regulatory and constitutional domains, it is best to envision a continuum of precautionary principles, varying both in their stringency and in the timing of their application.[8] "On these sliding-scale dimensions, regulation is more 'precautionary' when it intervenes earlier and/or more stringently to prevent uncertain future adverse consequences."[9] In the weakest form, precautionary principles may be cast as mere considerations, tiebreakers, or easily rebuttable presumptions, but we will see that constitutional actors have often argued for much stronger versions of precautionary measures against political risks.

The inherent messiness of the subject creates a dilemma about what to include. Constitutional arguments offered by framers and other constitutional actors may appear precautionary, in some broad sense, but those actors are not decision theorists or game theorists and they rarely specify the precautionary principle that underlies the argument, or whether the constitutional rules at issue might instead be justifiable on nonprecautionary grounds. I have opted to lump before splitting. Rather than narrowing the focus at the outset, I will begin by canvassing a broad range of seemingly precautionary or quasi-precautionary arguments.

For ease of exposition, I will arrange the examples along two axes. First, precautionary arguments may be addressed to constitutional designers or else to interpreters of an established constitution. Second, such arguments may be pitched at wholesale, as master principles, or at retail, as justifications for particular constitutional rules and structures. Collating these two distinctions yields four cases, which I will take up in turn. With these in hand, I will distinguish constitutional precautionary principles from some near relations.

WHOLESALE PRINCIPLES OF CONSTITUTIONAL DESIGN

In his *Life of George Washington*, John Marshall described a precautionary mindset widespread among Antifederalists of the founding era: "*That power might be abused, was, to persons of this opinion, a conclusive argument against its being bestowed*; and they seemed firmly persuaded that

---

[8] Wiener, *supra* note, at 1514.
[9] *Id.*

the cradle of the constitution would be the grave of republican liberty."[10] Robert Yates, writing as the Antifederalist pamphleteer Brutus, went so far as to offer "an axiom in politic[s]," to the effect that "the people should never authorize their rulers to do any thing, which if done, would operate to their injury"[11] – a principle that, like the maximin criterion, seemingly took no account of the probability of the harm occurring, as opposed to the consequences of its occurrence. Brutus in effect offered a precautionary master principle of constitutional design aiming to preclude even the possibility that constitutional power would be abused.

The most obvious predecessor, and perhaps ancestor, of this approach was David Hume's maxim that "in contriving any system of government, and fixing the several checks and controls of the constitution, every man ought to be supposed a knave, and to have no other end, in all his actions, than private interest."[12] Hume's "knavery principle" is best understood not as a factual claim that all men are so motivated, but rather a claim that constitutional design will work best if all men are presumed to be so motivated. Later theorists have advanced a cluster of justifications for a presumption of that sort; for our purposes, most relevant is the idea that the knavery principle represents a kind of "precautionary exercise"[13] that is useful for constitutional designers, despite its counterfactual character.

Suppose that each office-holder who is a bad type does damage that outweighs the benefits supplied by an office-holder who is a good type. In a risk model, the designers may decide to act in a risk-averse fashion, discounting their estimate of the probability that good types will hold power by the disproportionate harm that bad types inflict.[14] Alternatively, suppose that the designers face genuine uncertainty about the proportion of knaves in the pool of potential office-holders, a question on which they simply have no epistemically justified estimate of probabilities. The designers may then do best to maximize the minimum payoff from constitutional arrangements by supposing that all office-holders will be bad types, and by

---

[10] 5 John Marshall, The Life of George Washington: Commander in Chief of the American Forces, during the War which Established the Independence of His Country, and First President of the United States 131 (Philadelphia, C.P. Wayne 1807) (emphasis added).

[11] Brutus VIII, *in* 2 The Complete Anti-Federalist, *supra* note, at 405, 406.

[12] David Hume, *Of the Independency of Parliament, in* 1 Essays and Treatises on Several Subjects 37, 37 (London, A. Millar 1764) (emphasis omitted).

[13] Geoffrey Brennan & James M. Buchanan, The Reason of Rules: Constitutional Political Economy 52 (1985).

[14] *See id.* at 54–59.

adopting rules designed above all to preclude the harms of the worst-case scenario – a type of maximin constitutionalism.

RETAIL PRINCIPLES OF CONSTITUTIONAL DESIGN

At the retail level, many rules and structures of the Constitution of 1787 were designed and chosen on explicitly precautionary grounds. At the Philadelphia convention and in the subsequent debates over ratification, both Federalists and Antifederalists often cast their arguments in precautionary terms:

> In the Virginia debates, Henry Lee correctly observed that "the opposition continually objected to possibilities with no consideration of probabilities." Madison, too, objected to the supposition that "the general legislature will do every thing mischievous they possibly can." At the same time, in the Pennsylvania debates James Wilson defended the document by claiming that "we were obliged to guard even against possibilities, as well as probabilities."[15]

This tendency to treat worst-case political possibilities as though they are certain to occur is, in effect, the maximin approach to constitutionalism.

The unitary executive. At the Convention, a main thread in the debate over a unitary executive centered on the question whether a unitary or multiple executive was a better precaution against the risk of despotism. On the one hand, Edmund Randolph "strenuously opposed a unity in the Executive magistracy. He regarded it as the foetus of monarchy."[16] On the other hand, Wilson argued that "Unity in the Executive instead of being the fetus of Monarchy would be the best safeguard against tyranny."[17] Although the two had contrasting views of the merits of the institutional question, the aim of choosing the right precautions against monarchical despotism was common to both.

Separation of powers; checks and balances. In a similar vein, Federalists and Antifederalists were united on the view that the separation of powers, and various structures of checks-and-balances, were best justified as precautions against abuse of power. In New York, Melancton Smith put the argument in starkly precautionary form by claiming that "because there

---

[15] Jon Elster, Securities Against Misrule: Juries, Assemblies, Elections 46–47 (2013) (internal citations omitted).

[16] 1 The Records of the Federal Convention of 1787, at 66 (Max Farrand ed., 1911).

[17] *Id.*

would eventually be corruption in Congress, '[i]t is wise to multiply checks to a greater degree than the present state of things requires.'"[18] Even if there is no present problem, in other words, the prudent constitutional designer will take precautions against a risk that is likely to materialize at some unknown future point. For Madison, in Federalist 51, the principal justification for both separation of powers and checks-and-balances was that these mechanisms would serve as "auxiliary precautions": precautions against the concentration of all powers in the hands of the legislative department that were auxiliary to elections (direct or indirect), which were an inadequate safeguard.[19]

Standing armies and military appropriations. One of the most contentious elements of the proposed constitution, and one of the most difficult points for its supporters to defend, was the explicit grant of power to Congress to "raise and support armies," subject only to the limitation that no military appropriation last longer than two years.[20] Picking up a longstanding theme of libertarian argument in English constitutionalism, Antifederalists and others worried about the risk that a standing army would become a tool of despotism, whether monarchical or oligarchic. The general argument was that "the liberties of the people are in danger from a large standing army," either because "the rulers may employ [the army] for the purposes of supporting themselves in any usurpation of power, which they may see proper to exercise," or because of the "great hazard, that any army will subvert the forms of the government, under whose authority, they are raised, and establish one, according to the pleasure of their leader."[21] In light of these hazards, Antifederalists criticized the proposed constitution on the ground that it took insufficient precautions. Their preferred alternative was a provision that barred standing armies in times of peace, perhaps with exceptions for minimal garrisons at arsenals and borders, and for raising armies when an imminent threat of foreign invasion appeared.[22]

The Bill of Rights. More generally, and more successfully, the Antifederalists articulated a theory of constitutional rights as precautions, and criticized the proposed document for its failure to include a bill of rights of the sort that many state constitutions set out. Thus, Brutus found

---

[18] MEN OF LITTLE FAITH: SELECTED WRITINGS OF CECELIA KENYON 102 (Stanley Elkins, Eric McKitrick & Leo Weinstein eds., 2002).

[19] THE FEDERALIST No. 51, at 290, 322 (James Madison) (Clinton Rossiter ed., 1961).

[20] U.S. CONST. art. I, § 8, cl. 12.

[21] Brutus X, *in* 2 THE COMPLETE ANTI-FEDERALIST, *supra* note, at 413, 413.

[22] See the clause proposed in Brutus X, *id.* at 416.

it "astonishing, that this grand security to the rights of the people is not to be found in this Constitution."[23] Bills of rights were necessary, he argued, for the "security of life," the "security of liberty," and "for securing the property of the citizens."[24] The main political risk against which bills of rights were directed, on the Antifederalist theory, was agency slack – the abuse of power by "rulers" insufficiently constrained by elections or by the constitutional enumeration of governmental powers.[25] Because "rulers have the same propensities as other men ... the same reasons which at first induced mankind to associate and institute government," a fear of the predatory impulses of their fellows "will operate to influence them to observe this precaution."[26]

Presidential power, military power, and emergencies. Retail-level precautionary arguments about constitutional and institutional design are by no means confined to the remote past. I will illustrate by reference to some arguments for institutional precautions against excessive presidential power or excessive military power, or both. A leading proponent of such arguments is Bruce Ackerman, who discerns, in contemporary institutional and political trends, an appreciable possibility of either a presidential or military coup in the American future – possibilities sufficiently grave that Ackerman fears (in the title of one work) "The Decline and Fall of the American Republic."[27] This is a kind of a fat-tail problem in politics; although the chance of a presidential or military coup is exceedingly remote, there is an uncertain possibility that it is higher than a normal distribution of risk would indicate, and the resulting harms to constitutionalism would be severe.

At the stage of solutions, Ackerman has little faith in the courts, primarily because they are reactive rather than precautionary; courts wait too long to intervene, if they do at all. "Since the Supreme Court won't intervene early enough to check [executive] abuses in the future, the only remaining option is to create a new institutional mechanism that will put a brake on the presidential dynamic before it can gather steam."[28] Among the precautionary mechanisms that Ackerman suggests are a "Supreme

---

[23] Brutus II, *in* 2 THE COMPLETE ANTI-FEDERALIST, *supra* note, at 372, 374.

[24] *Id.* at 374–75.

[25] *See* John Francis Mercer, *Address to the Members of the Conventions of New York and Virginia, in* 5 THE COMPLETE ANTI-FEDERALIST, *supra* note, at 102, 105 ("Against the *abuse* and *improper* exercise of these sacred powers, the [p]eople have a right to be secured by a sacred Declaration....").

[26] Brutus II, *supra* note, at 374.

[27] BRUCE A. ACKERMAN, THE DECLINE AND FALL OF THE AMERICAN REPUBLIC (2010).

[28] *Id.* at 143.

Executive Tribunal," empowered to issue binding rulings on legal questions internal to the executive branch,[29] and a framework statute to govern
emergencies, whose central feature would be a "supermajoritarian escalator" – a provision requiring approval of presidential emergency powers by successively larger supermajorities of Congress.[30] These and other
mechanisms are explicitly pitched as safeguards against pathological political risks of presidential and military power. These are risks in the colloquial sense; Ackerman does not clearly specify whether the "threats" he
discerns should be analyzed in a framework of risk or instead a framework
of uncertainty. But the precautionary intent is clear.

WHOLESALE PRINCIPLES OF CONSTITUTIONAL
INTERPRETATION

Once a constitution is in place, actors will propose competing master principles of constitutional interpretation. Among the possible principles, some
will take a precautionary form, urging that the constitution be "strictly" or
"narrowly" construed to prevent political risks. In the history of American
constitutionalism, precautionary master principles have taken two main
forms: one based on federalism, and the other on individual rights. These
two forms are by no means mutually exclusive. Where national regulatory
action is at issue, a coalition between libertarians and proponents of states'
rights will often form, claiming that precautions against overreaching by
the national government protect individual liberty.[31]

A recent example involves the coalition of libertarians and proponents
of states' rights who challenged the constitutional power of Congress to
enact an individual mandate to buy health insurance. The Supreme Court
upheld the individual mandate as a valid exercise of Congress' taxing powers, but issued *dicta* – judicial statements not necessary to the result in the
case at hand – warning that the mandate may lie beyond Congress' powers
to regulate interstate commerce. Part of the Court's commerce analysis
invoked the purported risks to individual liberty of expansive congressional power to regulate commercial transactions. If the individual mandate
were upheld as a commerce regulation, the Chief Justice claimed in the

---

[29] *Id.* at 143–52.
[30] *Id.* at 168–69.
[31] This is a prominent theme in the jurisprudence of Justice Anthony Kennedy of the U.S.
Supreme Court. *See, e.g.*, Bond v. United States, 131 S. Ct. 2355, 2364 (2011) ("By deny-
ing any one government complete jurisdiction over all the concerns of public life, federalism protects the liberty of the individual from arbitrary power.").

leading opinion, "Congress could address the diet problem by ordering everyone to buy vegetables."[32] I will examine the states' rights strand and the libertarian strand separately, but in practice their proponents exploit the interaction between the two for increased rhetorical effect.

States' rights precautionary principles. The states' rights precautionary principle advocates strict construction of national powers. The early-nineteenth-century commentator St. George Tucker urged that the Constitution "is to be construed strictly, in all cases where the antecedent rights of a *state* may be drawn in question."[33] The basis of "Tucker's Rule"[34] was a mix of consent theory and precaution:

> [A]s every nation is bound to preserve itself, or, in other words, [its] independence; so no interpretation whereby [its] destruction, or that of the state, which is the same thing, may be hazarded, can be admitted in any case, where it has not, in the *most express terms*, given [its] consent to such an interpretation.[35]

Here the political "hazard" is that national power will "destroy" the independence of what Tucker took to be the sovereign and independent nation-states of the American confederation; such states must be strongly presumed to take proper precautions for their own survival, and must therefore be presumed not to chance their own destruction unless their consent to assume such a risk is unmistakable. For Tucker and other early states-rights commentators, the master principle of strict or narrow construction of national powers was embodied in the Tenth Amendment, which provides that "[t]he powers not delegated to the United States by the Constitution, nor prohibited by it to the States, are reserved to the States respectively, or to the people."[36]

Libertarian precautionary principles. Tucker and other early proponents of states' rights had another string to their bow, however: the Ninth Amendment, rather than the Tenth Amendment. The former provides that "[t]he enumeration in the Constitution of certain rights shall not be

---

[32] Nat'l Fed'n of Indep. Bus. v. Sebelius, 132 S. Ct. 2566, 2588 (2012) (opinion of Roberts, C.J.).

[33] St. George Tucker, *View of the Constitution of the United States, in* 1 St. George Tucker, Blackstone's Commentaries: With Notes of Reference, to the Constitution and Laws, of the Federal Government of the United States; and of the Commonwealth of Virginia 140, 151 (St. George Tucker ed., Lawbook Exch. 1996) (1803).

[34] Kurt T. Lash, *"Tucker's Rule": St. George Tucker and the Limited Construction of Federal Power*, 47 Wm. & Mary L. Rev. 1343 (2006).

[35] Tucker, *supra* note, at 423.

[36] U.S. Const. amend. X.

construed to deny or disparage others retained by the people,"[37] and has been portrayed as a master principle of constitutional interpretation – an interpretive presumption in favor of "individual liberty."[38] On this view, individuals are conceived to have natural liberty rights, and constitutional courts must review governmental action under a presumption of liberty, itself taken to be embodied in the written constitution.

In both early and recent formulations, this presumption of liberty is often cast in explicitly precautionary terms. For Tucker, the point of the Ninth Amendment was "to guard the people against constructive usurpations and encroachments on their rights," and the combination of the two amendments entailed that "the powers delegated to the federal government are, in all cases, to receive the most strict construction that the instrument will bear, where the rights of a state or of the people, either collectively, or individually, may be drawn in question."[39] More recently, a prominent constitutional libertarian writing in the Tuckerian tradition grounds judicial review of the constitutionality of governmental measures on the need to protect natural liberty from "legislative or executive abuses."[40]

Judicial review. As the last argument shows, judicial review of statutes for constitutionality has itself been justified as a precautionary principle, in the sense that it provides a beneficial safeguard against an uncertain propensity to rights-violations by legislative and executive actors. On this justification, even if courts are not systematically better than legislatures or other actors at identifying the correct scope of constitutional rights (according to some theory or other), it is beneficial to add another veto-point to the lawmaking system. Doing so has the marginal precautionary effect of reducing one type of error, the underprotection of rights.[41] Admittedly, judicial review might itself create another type of error by overprotecting rights, but proponents of this view offer a judgment that the former type of error is more harmful than the latter, so that "it [is] better to err on the side

---

[37] U.S. CONST. amend. IX.

[38] RANDY E. BARNETT, RESTORING THE LOST CONSTITUTION: THE PRESUMPTION OF LIBERTY 242 (2004).

[39] Tucker, *supra* note, at 154.

[40] BARNETT, *supra* note, at 267.

[41] *See* Frank B. Cross, *Institutions and Enforcement of the Bill of Rights*, 85 CORNELL L. REV. 1529, 1577–78 (2000) ("the more institutions that possess a veto over government action, the more costly that action will become and the more likely the action will be struck down"); Richard H. Fallon, Jr., *The Core of an Uneasy Case for Judicial Review*, 121 HARV. L. REV. 1693, 1695 (2008) ("legislatures and courts should *both* be enlisted in protecting fundamental rights [and] both should have veto powers over legislation that might reasonably be thought to violate such rights").

of too much rather than too little protection of rights,"[42] which is essentially a precautionary claim.

RETAIL PRINCIPLES OF CONSTITUTIONAL INTERPRETATION

Although precautionary principles of constitutional interpretation are sometimes stated in general terms, they are other times stated so as to have a limited domain, applying to particular classes of problems or controversies, to particular clauses of the written constitution, or to particular governmental powers.

State taxing power. McCulloch v. Maryland,[43] Chief Justice Marshall's great opinion on structural constitutionalism, is famous for its expansive construction of the national government's enumerated powers, in direct opposition to the states' rights precautionary principle advocated by Tucker. Indeed Marshall himself announced a precautionary principle that narrowly construed state power to tax federal instrumentalities. Flipping on its head Tucker's concern that an expansive construction of national power would "hazard" the "destruction" of the independent sovereign states, Marshall argued that an expansive construction of state taxing power risked the same denouement for federal instrumentalities, because "the power to tax involves the power to destroy."[44] Unless the federal government possessed the power to immunize its chartered instrumentalities from state taxation, the consequences might be dire:

> If we apply the principle for which the State of Maryland contends, to the constitution, generally, we shall find it capable of changing totally the character of that instrument. We shall find it capable of arresting all the measures of the government, and of prostrating it at the foot of the states. The American people have declared their constitution and the laws made in pursuance thereof, to be supreme; but this principle would transfer the supremacy, in fact, to the States.[45]

Like Brutus, only with the opposite political valence, Marshall slips with lightning speed from the premise that a political risk is "capable" of occurring to the conclusion that it *must* be guarded against.[46] In the words Marshall had used to mock the Antifederalists, "that power might

[42] Fallon, *supra* note, at 1708.
[43] 17 U.S. 316 (1819).
[44] *Id.* at 431.
[45] *Id.* at 416.
[46] *Id.* at 432.

be abused, was, to persons of this opinion, a conclusive argument against its being bestowed."[47]

Federal spending power. As historians of constitutional federalism have shown, Tuckerian principles enjoyed a revival during and after the 1830s.[48] The tradition of precautionary states'-rights argument continued strongly for another century, although of course with varied fortunes. The final crisis of the old order in the 1930s witnessed a vigorous assertion of precautionary narrow construction of national powers. Perhaps the clearest example is *United States v. Butler*,[49] the 1936 decision in which the Court invalidated the New Deal's scheme, in the Agricultural Adjustment Act, for granting subsidies to farmers who would agree to curtail production. The issue was whether Congress might use spending to indirectly accomplish an aim that, under the contemporary law, Congress lacked the constitutional power to accomplish through direct legislation. The Court announced a precautionary principle against such uses of the federal spending power, one explicitly justified as a safeguard against political abuse:

> If, in lieu of compulsory regulation of subjects within the states' reserved jurisdiction, which is prohibited, the Congress could invoke the taxing and spending power as a means to accomplish the same end, clause 1 of § 8 of Article I would become the instrument for total subversion of the governmental powers reserved to the individual states. ... If the act before us is a proper exercise of the federal taxing power, evidently the regulation of all industry throughout the United States may be accomplished by similar exercises of the same power. ... [T]he general welfare of the United States ... might be served by obliterating the constituent members of the Union. But to this fatal conclusion the doctrine contended for would inevitably lead.[50]

Presidential power and counterterrorism. Earlier, we saw a set of institutional-design proposals by Bruce Ackerman, intended as precautions against the risk or uncertain possibility of a presidential or military coup, or of executive abuses more generally. Ackerman is pessimistic about the capacity of courts to do anything to constrain executive power. Other theorists, however, urge courts to accept (or to make explicit that they have already been practicing) a set of judicial doctrines that will safeguard against the risks of executive abuses of civil liberties in the war on terror.

---

[47] MARSHALL, *supra* note, at 240–41.
[48] Lash, *supra* note, at 1382–89.
[49] 297 U.S. 1 (1936).
[50] *Id.* at 75–78.

Cass Sunstein, Samuel Issacharoff, and Richard Pildes all suggest that courts should require a clear statutory statement of legislative authorization for executive action in emergencies.[51] On this view, although it is too much to expect robust substantive review from courts during times of national crisis, courts can at least install democratic checks on executive overreaching through clear-statement rules. The motivation for this requirement is explicitly precautionary. The idea is that clear-statement rules will hedge against the chance that hot emotions that produce widespread public fear, and cold cognitive mechanisms like the availability heuristic, will combine to produce excessive regulatory responses to low-probability risks of terrorist activity.[52] The precautions, then, are precautions against pathological decision making by the executive branch – a distinctively political risk.

Recess appointments. In 2013, the federal court of appeals for the District of Columbia circuit – widely thought to be the nation's second most prominent court – decided an important case about presidential power to make "recess appointments," or appointments that are made while the Senate is not in session, and thus bypass the usual process of Senate consent. The relevant clause of the Constitution provides that "[t]he President shall have Power to fill up all Vacancies that may happen during the Recess of the Senate, by granting Commissions which shall expire at the End of their next Session."[53] One of the main issues in the case – *Noel Canning v. NLRB*,[54] conventionally known as *Canning* – was whether that clause allows the president to make "intrasession" recess appointments, when the Senate takes a recess *during* a given session of Congress, or instead allows only "intersession" recess appointments, when the Senate takes a recess *between* sessions of Congress. The court held that the latter, narrower interpretation was correct; it said that intrasession recess appointments are prohibited. (There was also another holding, not relevant here.)

The court's initial arguments for this conclusion drew on the text and original understanding of the constitutional clause. "[T]he Recess," according to the court, could only mean, and at the time of the Constitution's ratification did mean, an intersession recess. Despite that textualist and originalist beginning, however, the heart of the court's opinion was a long,

---

[51] *See* Samuel Issacharoff & Richard H. Pildes, *Between Civil Libertarianism and Executive Unilateralism: An Institutional Process Approach to Rights During Wartime*, 5 THEORETICAL INQ. L. 1 (2004); Cass R. Sunstein, *Minimalism at War*, 2004 SUP. CT. REV. 47.

[52] *See* Sunstein, *supra* note, at 74–75.

[53] U.S. CONST. art. II, sec. 2, cl. 3.

[54] 705 F.3d 490 (D.C. Cir. 2013), cert. granted, U.S. (June 24, 2013).

impassioned treatment of the functional effects and broad purposes of the constitutional structure. And the nub of the court's reasoning was precautionary. Intrasession recesses must be excluded from the scope of the recess appointment power as a precaution against the risk of presidential aggrandizement, or even presidential despotism. In the court's words:

> To adopt the [government's] proffered intrasession interpretation of "the Recess" would wholly defeat the purpose of the Framers in the careful separation of powers structure reflected in the [appointments provisions of the Constitution]. As the Supreme Court observed ... "The manipulation of official appointments had long been one of the American revolutionary generation's greatest grievances against executive power, because the power of appointment to offices was deemed the most insidious and powerful weapon of eighteenth century despotism."[55]

Recess appointments are hardly the stuff of which tyranny is made, because of their inherently limited duration, expiring at the end of the next congressional session. So one might see all this talk of aggrandizement and despotism as a rhetorical flourish in support of the textual arguments. Yet the opposite is closer to the truth. The court was quite candid that the point of its textual arguments was to establish a firm rule as a precaution against presidential aggrandizement:

> We must reject ... vague alternative[s] in favor of the clarity of the intersession interpretation. As the Supreme Court has observed, when interpreting "major features" of the Constitution's separation of powers, we must "establish high walls and clear distinctions because low walls and vague distinctions will not be judicially defensible in the heat of interbranch conflict." ... Allowing the President to define the scope of his own appointments power would eviscerate the Constitution's separation of powers.[56]

Canning is best understood to adopt a rigid and narrow interpretation of the recess appointment power, excluding all intrasession recess appointments, as a precaution against the risk of presidential despotism. The judges were haunted by a slippery-slope risk – the risk that, unless a clear line were drawn, the president would end up with "free rein to appoint his desired nominees at any time he pleases, whether that time be a weekend, lunch, or even when the Senate is in session and he is merely displeased with its inaction."[57] Analytically, there is no necessary connection between

---

[55] 705 F.3d at 503 (internal citation omitted).
[56] 705 F.3d at 504 (internal citation omitted).
[57] 705 F.3d at 504.

precautionary arguments and slippery-slope arguments, as I explain later, but the two rest on similar anxieties and often appear together.

Canning is not, of course, a final decision from the Supreme Court. As of now, the Court will hear the case in the Fall of 2013, and might well decide to overturn the decision below or, at a minimum, to modify its holding or rationale. Yet the point of discussing *Canning* is not to cite it for its binding legal authority; even if it is eventually overturned, the decision still aptly illustrates the precautionary approach to interpretation of particular constitutional provisions. As I will show later, there are other equally plausible, but less precautionary, interpretations of the recess appointment power. The *Canning* decision rests on contestable choices about the risks of presidential aggrandizement, and about the proper judicial response to those risks.

Free speech. On the "rights" side of the conventional structure-rights divide, precautionary arguments are if anything even more common. Vincent Blasi's influential account of free speech urges judges to devise free speech doctrine by taking a "pathological perspective," in which constitutional rules are geared to preventing the worst-case scenario – abuses targeted at the speech of political minorities, dissenters, or opponents of the regime.[58] Blasi's argument calls for a type of constitutional risk aversion, or, if one prefers to think in terms of uncertainty, a type of constitutional maximin.

Here there is a stock contrast between two cases that both address subversive political speech; one illustrates an expected-risk approach, the other a precautionary approach. In a case involving subversive advocacy by Communist organizations, *Dennis v. United States* held that courts should evaluate the risk that advocacy of overthrow of the government will lead to very severe harms, even if in the remote future, under a test formulated by Learned Hand: "In each case (courts) must ask whether the gravity of the 'evil,' discounted by its improbability, justifies such invasion of free speech as is necessary to avoid the danger.'"[59] Some passages in the Court's opinion might be interpreted, in isolation, as advocating a precautionary approach to the risk of subversive violence; free speech and the doctrinal requirement of a "clear and present danger" cannot, the Court said, mean that "before the Government may act, it must wait until the putsch is about to be executed, the plans have been laid and the signal is

---

[58] Vincent Blasi, *The Pathological Perspective and the First Amendment*, 85 COLUM. L. REV. 449, 449–50 (1985).

[59] 341 U.S. 494, 510 (1951) (quoting United States v. Dennis, 183 F.2d. 201, 212 (2d Cir. 1950) (Hand, J.)).

awaited."[60] Reading the opinion as a whole, however, its centerpiece was Hand's analysis, which considers all relevant risks and thus implies optimal rather than maximal precautions.

In contrast to this straightforward expected-harm calculus, *Brandenburg v. Ohio* held that "the constitutional guarantees of free speech and free press do not permit a State to forbid or proscribe advocacy of the use of force or of law violation except where such advocacy is directed to inciting or producing imminent lawless action and is likely to incite or produce such action."[61] The latter holding attempts to build a doctrinal barrier against politically motivated restrictions on speech and other worst-case political pathologies, and thus exemplifies Blasi's precautionary approach. Similar justifications have been offered for other free-speech principles and doctrines, such as the strong presumption against "prior restraints" that regulate speech before it actually occurs – a precautionary principle against government regulation that might "chill" protected expression.[62]

"Takings" and property rights. The Takings Clause of the Fifth Amendment, which applies to the states through the Fourteenth Amendment, provides that "private property [shall not] be taken for public use without just compensation."[63] Among the many controversies that attend this provision, the sharpest one in recent years has involved the requirement that takings (the exercise of "eminent domain" by the government) must be for "public use." That requirement is independent of, and cumulative with, the requirement that the government pay "just compensation" for takings that are otherwise permissible.

On a narrow construal, the public use requirement means that takings may only be used to transfer property from private to public hands, as when private land is converted into public parkland or is given to common carriers open to general public use, such as railroads.[64] The Supreme Court has, however, emphatically rejected that narrow reading. In the 2005 *Kelo* decision,[65] the Court upheld the taking of private residential property as part of a city's economic redevelopment plan, under which the property would be transferred to private commercial entities. "For public use," according to the Court, means "for a public purpose," and legislatures

[60] *Id.* at 509.
[61] 395 U.S. 444, 447 (1969).
[62] See Jonathan Remy Nash, *Standing and the Precautionary Principle*, 108 COLUM. L. REV. 494, 516–17 (2008).
[63] U.S. CONST. amend. V, cl. 5.
[64] Kelo v. City of New London, 545 U.S. 469, 479–80 (2005).
[65] *Id.*

should receive a large dollop of judicial deference in determining what counts as a public purpose.[66]

The dissenters, and a legion of critics, argued for a bright-line rule that economic development can never count as public use. The main argument for that rule was precautionary. Suggesting that "the specter of condemnation hangs over all property" as a result of the Court's decision, Justice O'Connor argued that excluding economic development from the category of public use was necessary to "ensure stable property ownership by providing safeguards against excessive, unpredictable, or unfair use of the government's eminent domain power – particularly against those owners who, for whatever reasons, may be unable to protect themselves in the political process against the majority's will."[67] Here the relevant risk is a public-choice concern that legislatures influenced by private commercial interests will exercise the takings power in ways that benefit those interests while harming overall welfare, in part by making all property rights uncertain, while offering pretextual justifications about economic development. As O'Connor put it, "[t]he beneficiaries [of the Court's holding] are likely to be those citizens with disproportionate influence and power in the political process, including large corporations and development firms."[68] O'Connor's argument failed at the Court, but after *Kelo* a number of state legislatures enacted statutes barring takings for purpose of economic development.[69] For present purposes, all that matters is that the critics of *Kelo* stand squarely in the tradition of precautionary constitutionalism.

Due process and an impartial tribunal. The constitutional law of due process requires a neutral adjudicator where protected interests are at stake. Among the various threats to neutrality – corruption, bias, or ideology, protean words all – which should be policed by due process? The structure of the problem is that it is difficult to prove, in particular cases, whether the various decision-making distortions operated and affected the outcome; consequently, the way in which the default rules or burdens of proof are set will often prove dispositive. Thus the Supreme Court, and the lower courts, have developed a series of rules that are explicitly geared to prevent risks of decisional distortions that are difficult to observe directly. One series of cases develops a precautionary principle

[66] *Id.* at 480.
[67] *Id.* at 496 (O'Connor, J., dissenting).
[68] *Id.* at 505.
[69] *See* Ilya Somin, *The Limits of Backlash: Assessing the Political Response to Kelo*, 93 MINN. L. REV. 2100, 2138–43 (2009) (collecting state statutes).

against adjudication by officials with a personal pecuniary stake in the case at hand.[70] Such an interest need not be direct, and its biasing effect need not be proved in particular cases; it suffices, as the Court once put it, that there is a "possible personal interest."[71] Both later and in Chapter 4, I will take up the underlying ideal of impartial decision making at greater length; suffice it to say that one strand in due process law is precautionary.

Reasonable doubt rule. In criminal trials, one relevant risk is conviction of the innocent. Because there is rarely an independent benchmark of guilt or innocence apart from the trial itself, that risk is inherently difficult to gauge. The reasonable doubt rule can then be understood as a precautionary principle that seeks to erect safeguards against the possibility of convicting the innocent.[72] In Blackstone's formulation, the rule's premise is that it is better for ten guilty men to go free than for one innocent to be convicted.[73] More generally, the reasonable doubt precautionary principle says that in criminal trials the ratio of false negatives (acquittals of the guilty) to false positives (convictions of the innocent) should be N to 1, where N has been specified by various courts and commentators as ranging not only up to 10, but also as high as 100 or even more.[74] This approach might or might not be consistent with an expected-utility calculus, but is not usually justified in such terms. For instance, classical arguments for the reasonable doubt rule do not typically consider the countervailing risk that the guilty who are set free will go on to commit crimes against innocent third parties[75] – a point I take up later. Rather, the basic intuition behind the reasonable doubt rule

---

[70] *See, e.g.,* Tumey v. Ohio, 273 U.S. 510, 523 (1927) ("[I]t certainly violates the Fourteenth Amendment and deprives a defendant in a criminal case of due process of law to subject his liberty or property to the judgment of a court, the judge of which has a direct, personal, substantial pecuniary interest in reaching a conclusion against him in his case.").

[71] Gibson v. Berryhill, 411 U.S. 564, 579 (1973) ("those with substantial pecuniary interest in legal proceedings should not adjudicate these disputes").

[72] See Peter Joy, *The Relationship Between Prosecutorial Misconduct and Wrongful Convictions: Shaping Remedies for a Broken System,* 2006 WIS. L. REV. 399; Jonathan Remy Nash, *The Supreme Court and the Regulation of Risk in Criminal Law Enforcement,* 92 B.U. L. REV. 171 (2012).

[73] 3 WILLIAM BLACKSTONE, COMMENTARIES 352 (1769).

[74] *See* Alexander Volokh, *Guilty Men,* 146 U. PA. L. REV. 173, 178 (1997) (for example, Maimonides "interpreted the commandment of *Exodus* as implying a value of $n = 1000$ for the purpose of an execution").

[75] *See* Larry Laudan, *The Elementary Epistemic Arithmetic of the Law,* 5 EPISTEME 282–294 (2008).

is vaguely precautionary: the burden of risk or uncertainty should be resolved in favor of protecting the innocent.

Prophylactic rules. Finally, precautionary arguments also underpin many so-called prophylactic rules of constitutional doctrine. The stock example is *Miranda v. Arizona*,[76] which, in effect, requires police to inform suspects of their constitutional rights as a precondition for using the suspects' voluntary statements as evidence. In the stock justification,[77] *Miranda* warnings were said not to be required by the Constitution itself: the constitutional requirement is just that waivers of rights be "knowing and voluntary," all things considered. Instead, *Miranda* warnings are a judicially created adjunct doctrine that overprotects constitutional interests, in part because of the difficulties of case-by-case determination of whether a suspect's waiver of rights was indeed voluntary. In other words, one might protect suspects through ex post remedies, involving case-specific determinations of whether police have abused their position of power; but judges think that approach inadequately protective, and thus have created auxiliary ex ante precautions in the form of *Miranda* warnings. More recently, the Supreme Court confused matters by overturning a federal statute that purported to overturn *Miranda*, and the Court suggested that *Miranda* has some sort of constitutional status; yet it did not quite say that *Miranda* warnings are directly required by the Constitution.[78] Whatever the details here, the conceptual point is clear enough.

CONSTITUTIONAL PRECAUTIONARY PRINCIPLES AND NEAR RELATIONS

Given the multidimensional variation of constitutional precautionary principles, it is important to compare and contrast them with several near relations – conceptual structures or modalities of constitutional argument that in some way or another attempt to regulate the risks of politics by building some form of bias or skew into constitutional rules. No sharp distinctions are possible, but I will try to indicate some rough lines of

---

[76] 384 U.S. 436 (1966).

[77] *See, e.g.*, Evan H. Caminker, *Miranda and Some Puzzles of "Prophylactic" Rules*, 70 U. CIN. L. REV. 1, 4–5 (2001) ("the Court had justified its decision to do so on the ground that the *Miranda* rule was merely 'prophylactic' rather than an interpretation of the Fifth Amendment itself").

[78] See *Dickerson v. United States*, 530 U.S. 428 (2000). For a close analysis, see Caminker, *supra* note 77.

demarcation that draw a blurry boundary around the category of constitutional precautions.

Constitutional clear statement principles. In several areas of constitutional law and doctrine, actors have argued for clear statement principles
for interpreting the Constitution. In the setting of separation of powers,
Madison stated in the First Congress that the legislative and executive
powers "must [be] suppose[d] … intended to be kept separate in all cases
in which they are not blended."[79] Chief Justice Taft endorsed a similar
principle in *Myers v. United States.*[80] And, as we have seen, Tucker's rule
of strict construction of national powers amounts to a clear statement
rule that presumes against national power unless it has been expressly
granted. These clear statement principles of constitutional interpretation
are different from constitutionally inspired clear-statement principles for
interpreting statutes; an example of the latter is the proposed requirement
of clear legislative authorization for presidential emergency measures, as
previously mentioned.[81]

Clear statements principles for interpreting the Constitution may or
may not count as precautionary principles, depending on how they are
justified. Such principles might be justified as a precaution against political
risks, but then again they might be justified on other grounds. Thus Tucker's
Rule – ultimately founded on the "hazard" that national power will be
used to "destroy" the putative independent sovereignty of the States – is
explicitly precautionary. The Madison-Taft principle, by contrast, is not
clearly precautionary. Although Madison did suggest that a conflation of
powers would "abolish at once that great principle of unity and responsibility in the executive department, which was intended for the security of
liberty and the public good,"[82] the main thrust of the argument was simply
that a clear statement rule of separation of powers was the best interpretive
inference from the structure of the new Constitution.

Slippery-slope arguments. Constitutional clear statement principles
may or may not be precautionary; in turn, constitutional precautionary principles may or may not rest on slippery-slope arguments. The

[79] 2 Jonathan Elliot, The Debates in the Several State Conventions on the
Adoption of the Federal Constitution 380 (Philadelphia, J.B. Lippincott & Co.
1881) (1836).
[80] 272 U.S. 52 (1926).
[81] For more general treatments of clear-statement rules in statutory interpretation, see
John F. Manning, *Clear Statement Rules and the Constitution,* 110 Colum. L. Rev. 399
(2010); and William N. Eskridge, Jr. & Philip P. Frickey, *Quasi-Constitutional Law: Clear
Statement Rules as Constitutional Lawmaking,* 45 Vand. L. Rev. 593 (1992).
[82] *Myers,* 272 U.S. at 160.

argument in *United States v. Butler* – allowing federal spending for the purpose of circumventing limits on federal regulatory power would license a sequence of events ending in the abolition of state independence – takes a slippery-slope form.[83] By contrast, the Antifederalist concern over standing armies did not necessarily have a slippery-slope element. Rather, standing armies were seen as a standing risk that could or would eventually produce a tyrannical *coup d'état*, but that risk could be understood as a constant hazard rather than as the end-state of a predictable slide down a slippery slope.

The difference is that the *Butler* argument has the dynamic or intertemporal element that is a hallmark of slippery-slope arguments.[84] In this dynamic, a precedent at Time 1, perhaps unobjectionable in itself, triggers one or more causal mechanisms[85] that make it more likely that a more expansive precedent will be set at Time 2, and so on, until the bottom of the slippery slope is reached. Each step in the sequence increases the probability that the next step will occur, and it is this feature that makes the slope slippery. By contrast, the underlying risk model might have no inherently dynamic features at all. The actor might fear that the distribution of risks has a fat tail, such that extreme undesirable outcomes are surprisingly possible at any given time. The actor might then argue for taking precautions in light of the high variance of this distribution. Yet draws from a distribution of that sort might be entirely independent of one another, so that whether the risk does or does not materialize at Time 1 has no effect on whether it materializes at Time 2, and there is no slippery slope in the picture. I conclude that, although precautionary arguments might be and sometimes are predicated on slippery-slope risks, they need not be; slippery slopes are not a necessary feature of precautionary arguments, but merely one of several possible justifications for taking precautions.

PRECAUTIONARY CONSTITUTIONALISM: THEMES AND CONCERNS

The assemblage of precautionary principles, structures and doctrines is heterogeneous. The arguments come from different actors in very different historical eras and situations. Moreover, as I have emphasized, there

---

[83] 297 U.S. 1 (1936).
[84] Frederick Schauer, *Slippery Slopes*, 99 HARV. L. REV. 361, 381–382 (1985).
[85] Eugene Volokh, *The Mechanisms of the Slippery Slope*, 116 HARV. L. REV. 1026, 1029 (2003).

is a continuum or spectrum of precautionary stances, from the extreme of maximin constitutionalism to weaker rebuttable presumptions or tie-breaking rules. Nonetheless, it is possible to identify some common themes and concerns that underpin precautionary constitutionalism, and that will help us to reconstruct it in the best possible light before we turn to critiques in the next chapter.

If power can be abused, it will be. As John Marshall pointed out, distrust of the motivations of officials is a major theme of precautionary constitutionalism. Underpinning many of the arguments we have seen is an implicit account of what officials maximize: power and the enjoyment of the fruits of power. On this account, grants of discretion to governmental officials will inevitably be abused, as officials use their discretion to pursue self-regarding aims or to further the welfare, not of the citizenry as a whole, but of interest groups and narrow political coalitions. Shklar's liberalism of fear "regards abuses of public power in all regimes with equal trepidation" and "worries about the excesses of official agents at every level of government."[86] Precautionary constitutionalism shares this central concern and translates it into the language and institutional structures of the law.

If institutions can expand their power, they will do so. Transposing this account of motivations from the individual to the collective level, precautionary constitutionalists implicitly portray structured groups of officials – political institutions – as power-maximizers. The further assumption is that institutions maximize power through empire-building[87] – by expanding their jurisdiction or the scope of their discretion to encompass an ever-greater terrain. Where this comes at the expense of other institutions, the assumption is one of aggrandizement.

If a risk materializes, it may be too late to do anything about it. A hallmark of precautionary constitutionalism is the concern that unless safeguards are installed before the fact, abuses will be irremediable. In the extreme case – a transition to dictatorship, perhaps through a presidential or military coup – legal and political institutions may be swept away or else left in place as a sham. Even in lesser cases, official abuses or remorseless institutional aggrandizement may create a new status quo that law and politics will find it excessively costly to alter. Plutarch

[86] Judith N. Shklar, *The Liberalism of Fear, in* POLITICAL THOUGHT AND POLITICAL THINKERS 3, 9–10 (Stanley Hoffmann ed., 1998).

[87] Daryl J. Levinson, *Empire-Building Government in Constitutional Law,* 118 HARV. L. REV. 915, 916 (2005).

captures this aspect of precautionary constitutionalism in his account of measures taken by the Roman consul Publicola, after the overthrow of the Tarquin kings:

> He enacted a law by which any one who sought to make himself tyrant might be slain without trial, and the slayer should be free from blood-guiltiness if he produced proofs of the crime. For although it is impossible for one who attempts so great a task to escape all notice, it is not impossible for him to do so long enough to make himself too powerful to be brought to trial, which trial his very crime precludes. He therefore gave any one who was able to do so the privilege of anticipating the culprit's trial.[88]

Consider fat-tail risks in politics. In finance, climate change, and other policy areas, important recent work has focused on "fat-tail risks" – risks that are exceedingly unlikely to materialize, but more likely than in a normal distribution, and that are exceedingly damaging if they do materialize.[89] Under certain types of probability distributions ("fat tail distributions"), such risks will have an important role in the decision-making calculus; here the crucial mistake is to assume that the relevant risk is normally distributed, such that exceedingly damaging outcomes are effectively impossible.

In politics and law, by analogy, we might understand precautionary constitutionalists and maximin constitutionalists as alert to the possibility of fat-tail distributions of political outcomes. The risk that a constitutional democracy might suddenly slide into dictatorship, for example, is exceedingly remote, but such an event might also be exceedingly harmful to constitutional values if it did occur. Moreover – and this is what the fat tail means – the risk of an extreme catastrophic harm might be significantly higher than the rulemaker appreciates, if the rulemaker wrongly assumes that the risk is normally distributed. On this view, although it is easy to scoff at alarmist fears about dictatorship and other miniscule probabilities, it would actually be a serious mistake to exclude such possibilities from consideration by focusing, myopically, on their low probability of occurrence while ignoring the possibility of fat-tail risks, with enormous potential for harm. A sensible rulemaker will take into account the possibility that political risks are not normally distributed.

---

[88] 1 PLUTARCH, PLUTARCH'S LIVES 533 (Bernadotte Perrin trans., 1914).

[89] For accessible introductions to the issues, see Martin L. Weitzman, *Fat-Tailed Uncertainty in the Economics of Catastrophic Climate Change*, 5 REV. ENVTL. ECON. & POL'Y 275–92 (2011); NASSIM NICHOLAS TALEB, THE BLACK SWAN: THE IMPACT OF THE HIGHLY IMPROBABLE (2d ed. 2010).

Safeguards should be redundant and robust. To the precautionary constitutionalist, safeguards against abuses should display two properties: redundancy and robustness. Although these terms are given several somewhat different definitions in the literature on mechanism design, for present purposes simple definitions will do. Redundancy means that no single safeguard should bear all the weight; rather, there should exist a series of filters that, taken as a system, will catch all attempts at abuse of official power before they materialize. Robustness means that the system of successive filters cannot easily be undermined or subverted by the very officials or institutions constrained by the system. For legal rules, robustness is ensured in part by clarity; clear and specific delineations of power will alert citizens and other institutions if some one institution is exceeding the bounds of its authority.

Limit the downside. Perhaps the simplest intuition behind precautionary constitutionalism is that it is best if rulemakers attempt to limit the downside risks of politics, eschewing ambitious attempts to maximize the possible upside gains of politics.[90] This kind of systematic attitude of constitutional risk-aversion has seemed attractive to many political theorists. As I mentioned in the Introduction, for example, Karl Popper's political theory emphasizes that a liberal society should "[w]ork for the elimination of concrete evils rather than for the realization of abstract goods."[91] Popper here captures an important strand in liberal theory, which sees the state as a standing danger to individual freedom, and which attempts to circumscribe the state's powers so as to "minimize the danger that these powers will be misused."[92] Concretely, Popper proposes, the master "principle of a democratic policy" should be to "create, develop and protect political institutions for the avoidance of tyranny."[93]

In later chapters I will argue at length that a systematically precautionary approach to constitutionalism is misguided. Yet it is important to appreciate that precautionary constitutionalism does not rest on any simple mistake or transparent fallacy. Its highly distrustful account of official and institutional motivations is widespread and time-honored; its emphasis

---

[90] *Cf.* David Wiens, *Prescribing Institutions Without Ideal Theory*, 20 J. POL. PHIL. 45, 46 (2012) (arguing for an "institutional failure analysis approach," which "takes its primary design task to be obviating or averting social failures").

[91] KARL R. POPPER, CONJECTURES AND REFUTATIONS: THE GROWTH OF SCIENTIFIC KNOWLEDGE 485 (2d ed. 2002).

[92] *Id.* at 472.

[93] Karl Popper, *The Paradoxes of Sovereignty, in* POPPER SELECTIONS 324 (David Miller ed., 1985).

on prevention, rather than remediation, of constitutional abuses resonates with the paramount place of constitutional rules in the legal system; and it offers a plausible account of the benefits of robustness and redundancy in the design of constitutional safeguards. The arguments against precautionary constitutionalism face an uphill struggle. Let us now turn to those arguments to see whether they succeed.

2

Optimizing Constitutionalism: The Mature Position

The last chapter defined and illustrated precautionary constitutionalism, attempting to put that approach in its best light. This chapter turns to criticisms of constitutional precautions offered by early proponents of national power such as Hamilton, Marshall, and Story, and by New Dealers such as Frankfurter and Jackson. These critics argued that precautionary constitutionalism might prove futile for lack of incentive-compatibility; might jeopardize other values, resulting in greater risks overall; might prove perversely self-defeating, if and because the precautions create or exacerbate the very risks they were intended to prevent; and might prove unnecessary, given the availability of after-the-fact remedies against materialized risks. As we will see, these criticisms of precautionary constitutionalism parallel the criticisms of precautionary principles in the theory of regulation. Critics of precautionary regulation are following a path that the critics of precautionary constitutionalism have already traveled.

I argue that the modern theory of risk regulation has arrived at a conclusion that is structurally equivalent to Hirschman's mature position.[1] On this view, the goal of regulators should simply be to take optimal precautions, according to a calculus that weighs all relevant risks of action and inaction. As it turns out, however, constitutional theorists such as Publius and Story already endorsed the mature position, arguing in their own language for a resolutely optimizing approach to constitutionalism. What's new is, in this case at least, very old.

Once the historical and interpretive work is complete, I offer an argument that the mature position is the best approach to constitution-making. I identify a strictly negative but nonetheless valuable function of the mature

---

[1] ALBERT O. HIRSCHMAN, THE RHETORIC OF REACTION 153–54 (1991).

position, which improves the processes of constitutional design and interpretation by laundering out one-sided arguments and thereby placing all relevant risks before decision makers. The mature position is sometimes criticized on second-order or indirectly consequentialist grounds, the argument being that even if the mature position is the ideal decision procedure, precautionary principles are necessary to compensate for predictable biases or distortions in regulatory decision making. I trace a parallel argument through the constitutional debates and also outline a rejoinder, applicable to both ordinary risk regulation and the regulation of political risks more specifically. Because relevant biases and distortions appear on all sides of the issues, the second-order argument for precautions, based on the capacities of decision makers, neglects tradeoffs and can prove self-defeating in precisely the same fashion as first-order arguments for precaution. In some cases, localized precautions may fall out naturally from a mature, even-handed assessment of all relevant political risks, but the set of constitutional rules will not be generally and systematically precautionary. Even if particular rules end up being precautionary, a mature assessment should govern at the highest level of analysis.

Let me caution again that this is a study in the theory of constitutional argumentation, not a treatise on constitutional design or interpretation. I aim to critique precautionary arguments for constitutional rules, not to evaluate the ultimate merits of those rules. Where particular precautionary arguments fail, the rules they were offered to justify may or may not be independently justifiable under the mature position. If we get the analysis right, the set of constitutional rules that will result is not my concern here.

COUNTERING PRECAUTIONARY ARGUMENTS

If constitutional law, history, and theory provide a wide array of precautionary justifications for legal rules, they also provide a repertoire of counterarguments. In various eras, framers, judges, and other actors have attempted to undermine the arguments for precaution. At the stage of constitutional design, such actors offer arguments to block the formulation of precautionary constraints. At the stage of constitutional interpretation, the point of the arguments is to prevent narrow construction of powers already granted.

Although anti-precautionary arguments appear in many eras and in many diverse contexts, I suggest they fall into recurring structural patterns. Adapting a set of categories from Albert Hirschman's analysis of political rhetoric,[2] supplemented by the modern theory of risk regulation, I will sort the arguments into four groups:

(1) *Futility arguments*, in which the opponent argues that a given precautionary principle will fail to attain its ends.

(2) *Jeopardy arguments*, in which the opponent argues that a given precaution will produce net costs in light of countervailing risks on other margins.

(3) *Perversity arguments*, in which the opponent argues that a given precaution will prove self-defeating because of countervailing risks on the *same* margin – in other words, because it actually exacerbates the very risk that the precaution attempts to prevent.

(4) *Arguments for ex post remedies*, in which the opponent acknowledges the risk but argues that the correct mechanism to address it is not a general ex ante precaution. Instead, the correct mechanism is an ex post remedy applied case-by-case, after the relevant risk has actually materialized. Strictly speaking, this can be described as a special case of jeopardy, but it is an important special case that warrants separate treatment.

FUTILITY: "PARCHMENT" PRECAUTIONS AND COMMITMENT PROBLEMS

One rejoinder to a proposal for constitutional precautions is that the proposal may fail the criterion of incentive-compatibility.[3] The very conditions that make the precaution necessary also ensure that the actors against whom precautions are taken will have incentives to undermine or ignore it, and no other actors will have incentives to enforce the precaution against its violators.[4] Where this is so, the benefits of the precaution are zero and the proposal is futile.

Checks and balances; standing armies. The *locus classicus* of futility argument in constitutional theory is Madison's reference to "parchment

---

[2]   *Id.* at 7.

[3]   For summaries of and citations to the relevant literatures in political economy, see Daryl J. Levinson, *Parchment and Politics: The Positive Puzzle of Constitutional Commitment*, 124 HARV. L. REV. 657, 670–80 (2011); MARK TUSHNET, TAKING THE CONSTITUTION AWAY FROM THE COURTS 95–128 (2000). A particularly clear treatment is Daron Acemoglu, *Why Not a Political Coase Theorem? Social Conflict, Commitment, and Politics*, 31 J. COMP. ECON. 620, 639–48 (2003).

[4]   *See* ADRIAN VERMEULE, JUDGING UNDER UNCERTAINTY: AN INSTITUTIONAL THEORY OF LEGAL INTERPRETATION 118–52 (2006).

barriers" in Federalist 48. The general line of his argument, which extends over Federalist 47, 48, and 51, is that formal specification of electoral accountability and separated powers in the constitution will be inadequate to contain legislative tyranny unless checks-and-balances mechanisms are added as "auxiliary precautions" and unless those mechanisms are made incentive-compatible by tying "[t]he interest of the man" to "the constitutional rights of the place [i.e., the institution]," so that "ambition [can] be made to counteract ambition." [5]

Yet the claim that parchment precautions are futile first appears in the Federalist Papers in connection with the debate over standing armies, not checks-and-balances, and was made by Hamilton, not Madison. Internal insurrections within Pennsylvania and Massachusetts, Hamilton observed, had compelled both states to raise and maintain standing forces, the general lesson being "how unequal parchment provisions are to a struggle with public necessity." [6] Hamilton's futility critique of precautionary prohibitions on standing armies in peacetime thus took the form of an argument in the alternative. One possibility would be that the exception for war or insurrection would be interpreted, in operation, so as to nullify the prohibition, because "the national government, to provide against apprehended danger, might in the first instance raise troops, and might afterwards keep them on foot as long as they supposed the peace or safety of the community was in any degree of jeopardy.... [A] discretion so latitudinary as this would afford ample room for eluding the force of the provision." [7] If, alternatively, the prohibition were seriously thought to prevent even the raising of armies in time of peace, it would simply be ignored or violated when apparent risks of invasion or insurrection so required. Whether evaded by interpretation or violated outright, the prohibition would prove futile.

None of this is to say that Hamilton's argument was in fact correct. But as noted earlier, the federal constitution did not ultimately embody the stringent precautions against standing armies that the Antifederalists desired. Even without such precautions, standing armies did not become a regular feature of the federal establishment until after the Civil War, suggesting at a minimum that the Antifederalists' preferred precautions were unnecessary. As for the broader issues surrounding the checks and balances of the federal lawmaking system, I take them up at length in Chapter 3. James Bryce, as we will see, argued that both checks and balances, and also

[5] THE FEDERALIST NO. 51, at 290, 322 (James Madison) (Clinton Rossiter ed., 1961).
[6] THE FEDERALIST NO. 25, at 167 (Alexander Hamilton) (Clinton Rossiter ed., 1961).
[7] *Id.* at 165.

the extended federalist republic, amounted to self-defeating constitutional precautions.

Free speech. In modern terms, the "parchment barriers" argument offered by Hamilton and then Madison points to the difficulties of commitment. As there is no agent external to society who can enforce the terms of constitutional commitments,[8] some indirect incentive-compatible mechanism must be called into play to make such commitments stick, and the existence of such a mechanism cannot be assumed.[9] The commitment problem only partially overlaps the issue of constitutional precautions: not all precautions suffer from commitment problems, while, conversely, those problems may also beset constitutional rules and structures not justified in precautionary terms.

An example of the area of overlap is the precautionary "pathological perspective" on free speech doctrine, under which "the overriding objective at all times should be to equip the first amendment to do maximum service in those historical periods when intolerance of unorthodox ideas is most prevalent."[10] The pathological perspective underwrites doctrines that attempt to create an intertemporal commitment: judges will commit themselves, or their successors, to clear speech-protective rules that will provide a bulwark against majoritarian oppression or other political pathologies. As we have seen, the stock example is the rule of *Brandenburg v. Ohio*,[11] under which government may not ban speech to preserve public order unless there has been advocacy that is intended to produce and likely to produce an imminent violation of the law.

However, the pathological perspective by itself provides no mechanism to make doctrinal restrictions of this sort stick when pressing exigencies arise. The predictable result has been that when an impressionistic judicial calculus of expected harms shows the existence of a grave threat to public order that the *Brandenburg* test would disable government from addressing, it is the test that has given way.[12] The main objection to the

---

[8] *See* JON ELSTER, ULYSSES UNBOUND: STUDIES IN RATIONALITY, PRECOMMITMENT, AND CONSTRAINTS 88–174 (2000); Acemoglu, *supra* note, at 622–23.

[9] *See* Levinson, supra note, at 663.

[10] Vincent Blasi, *The Pathological Perspective and the First Amendment*, 85 COLUM. L. REV. 449, 449 (1985).

[11] 395 U.S. 444 (1969).

[12] *See* ERIC A. POSNER & ADRIAN VERMEULE, TERROR IN THE BALANCE: SECURITY, LIBERTY, AND THE COURTS 232–34 (2007); Frederick Schauer, *A Comment on the Structure of Rights*, 27 GA. L. REV. 415, 417 (1993) (arguing that the pre-*Brandenburg* test of "clear and present danger" implicitly persists, in modified form, in contexts such as national

"pathological perspective" argument for a precautionary approach to free speech law is simply that precautions will systematically tend to prove futile when they would prevent government from taking action against apparently dangerous threats.

Clear statement requirements and emergency powers. Similar problems afflict the idea that presidential action in emergencies can be constrained by a doctrinal requirement of clear statutory authorization. The judges who are charged with enforcing the requirement may themselves be swept away by the sense of crisis, and when they are, they will tend to find the requirement satisfied so long as there is any plausibly relevant statute in the picture. In the words of political scientists Terry Moe and William Howell:

> The Court can issue rulings favorable to presidents, but justify its decisions by appearing to give due deference to the legislature.... Congress's collective action problems, combined with the zillions of statutes already on the books, make it entirely unclear what the institution's "will" is – and this gives the Court tremendous scope for arguing that, almost whatever presidents are doing, it is consistent with the "will of Congress."[13]

The upshot is that during conditions of perceived war, crisis or emergency, the judges' track record has been extremely forgiving; judges have frequently found "clear" authorization under statutes whose terms were hardly pellucid.[14] The judges do this in part because they have powerful incentives to do so at the time; when a perceived crisis occurs, judges who are aware of the limits of their own knowledge rationally fear the security consequences of holding that an executive measure lacks statutory authorization, and thus are powerfully tempted to read statutes for all they are worth, rather than enforcing a clear-statement requirement. Even if such a requirement is announced in prior legal doctrine, there is little incentive on the part of later judges to enforce it, and the requirement will prove incentive-incompatible. As with other precautionary measures, clear-statement restrictions on presidential emergency powers and war powers suffer from severe commitment problems.

---

security, and allows speech rights to be "outweighed" even where they apply); *see also, e.g.*, United States v. Progressive, Inc., 467 F. Supp. 990 (1979) (granting an injunction against a magazine article that provided instructions for building a hydrogen bomb, with no plausible showing of intent to produce imminent harm).

[13] Terry M. Moe & William G. Howell, *The Presidential Power of Unilateral Action*, 15 J.L. ECON. & ORG. 132, 152 (1999).

[14] POSNER & VERMEULE, *supra* note, at 48.

JEOPARDY: OTHER-RISK TRADEOFFS

In many settings, the most forceful argument against precautions is simply that the optimal level of the target risk is not zero, and that some degree of expected harm from the target risk is necessary to obtain other goods. This jeopardy response invokes other-risk tradeoffs. Faced with a precautionary argument aimed at preventing a target risk, the opponent points to a distinct countervailing risk whose expected costs will be increased by the precaution.[15] If the opponent instead argues that the precaution will exacerbate the target risk itself, the appeal is to a same-risk tradeoff, and the response is one of perversity.

To illustrate the distinction, Hamilton (as Publius) deployed both types of argument against a precautionary rule that would prohibit the raising of standing armies in times of peace. Under such a prohibition,

> [a]ll that kind of policy by which nations anticipate distant danger and meet the gathering storm must be abstained from, as contrary to the genuine maxims of a free government. We must expose *our property and liberty* to the mercy of foreign invaders, and invite them by our weakness to seize the naked and defenseless prey, because we are afraid that rulers, created by our choice, dependent on our will, might endanger that liberty by an abuse of the means necessary to its preservation.[16]

Here, Hamilton argues both that a prohibition against standing armies in peacetime, justified as a precaution to protect liberty, would create a countervailing risk on a different margin – the seizure of property by foreign invaders – and that it would perversely create a risk to liberty itself, because a foreign invasion would destroy liberty as surely as would domestic despotism.

National governmental powers. If there is a main line of argument to the Federalist Papers, jeopardy is it. Although Publius employs memorable futility arguments and perversity arguments as well – we have seen some of the former and will soon see some of the latter – the overall structure of the Federalist Papers frames a large-scale jeopardy argument: the status quo under the Articles of Confederation poses intolerable

---

[15] For the terms "target risk" and "countervailing risk," see, for example, Jonathan B. Wiener, *Precaution in a Multirisk World, in* HUMAN AND ECOLOGICAL RISK ASSESSMENT: THEORY AND PRACTICE 1509, 1520 (Dennis J. Paustenbach ed., 2002).

[16] THE FEDERALIST NO. 25, at 165–66 (Alexander Hamilton) (Clinton Rossiter ed., 1961) (emphasis added).

countervailing risks on multiple dimensions apart from liberty, such as public order, strong national defense, and the security of property. Liberty-protecting precautions against the power of the Union will hamper the strong national government needed to protect against those risks; therefore the ratifiers should be willing to trade off some risks to liberty against other goods.

In Federalist 41, Publius offered his most general rebuttal to the general Antifederalist argument for precautions against abuse of power:

> It cannot have escaped those who have attended with candor to the arguments employed against the extensive powers of the government that the authors of them have very little considered how far these powers were necessary means of attaining a necessary end. They have chosen rather to dwell on the inconveniences which must be unavoidably blended with all political advantages; and on the possible abuses which must be incident to every power or trust of which a beneficial use can be made.... [C]ool and candid people will at once reflect, that the purest of human blessings must have a portion of alloy in them; that the choice must always be made, if not of the lesser evil, at least of the GREATER, not the PERFECT, good; and that in every political institution, a power to advance the public happiness involves a discretion which may be misapplied and abused.[17]

Quite remarkably, given the contemporary political context, the passage blandly observes that some abuse of power is the inevitable byproduct of cost-justified grants of governmental discretion; the optimal level of political abuse is therefore greater than zero.

Recess appointments. We have seen that the *Canning* decision, from the federal court of appeals for the District of Columbia Circuit, articulated a precautionary rule against presidential power to make intrasession recess appointments. It can be argued that the decision was myopic, in the sense that the *Canning* court focused selectively, even to the point of obsession, on a particular target risk, while ignoring countervailing risks, including risks generated by the precautions themselves.

---

[17] THE FEDERALIST No. 41, at 255–56 (James Madison) (Clinton Rossiter ed., 1961). For a version of the argument that emphasizes the paranoid or otherwise nonrational cognition of those who worry in general terms about governmental "abuse," see 1 JOSEPH STORY, COMMENTARIES ON THE CONSTITUTION OF THE UNITED STATES 408 (Boston, Hilliard, Gray & Co. 1833): A power, given in general terms, is not to be restricted to particular cases, merely because it may be susceptible of abuse, and, if abused, may lead to mischievous consequences. This argument is often used in public debate; *and in its common aspect addresses itself so much to popular fears and prejudices, that it insensibly acquires a weight in the public mind, to which it is no wise entitled* (emphasis added).

One countervailing risk is that a narrow interpretation of the recess appointment power interferes with the major purpose of recess appointments, the purpose that caused the framers to insert the power in the first place: to "keep important offices filled and the government functioning," as another circuit court put it.[18] That purpose has the same constitutional status as the concern the *Canning* court focused on exclusively, the constitutional provision for a senatorial check on appointments. If Congress as a whole has used its undoubted constitutional powers to create an office and mandates that it be filled; the president has tried to fill it; yet the tug-of-war over appointments within the Senate keeps the office empty for a protracted period, the result is a problem of *constitutional* stature, not just a policy problem. All provisions of the Constitution, and indeed the document's very existence, implicitly presuppose that a functioning government is a worthy aim of constitutional interpretation.

Furthermore, the only reason the recess appointments issue even arises, as a practical matter, is the toxic interaction between appointments and the Senate practice of the filibuster, which requires sixty votes for approval of relevant business, including appointments. If the majority in the Senate –at present, a Democratic majority – could just approve regular appointments under majority rule, no problem would occur. So the *Canning* court's narrow interpretation of the recess appointments power indirectly promotes the power of a blocking minority in the Senate.

Madison assumed in Federalist 10 that the risk of oppression by entrenched minorities was low, because "the republican principle ... enables the majority to defeat [a minority faction's] sinister views by regular vote."[19] But if the principle of majority rule is disabled, as it is by the filibuster, then the risk of presidential aggrandizement has to be weighed against the risk of minoritarian factional oppression. (We have learned since Madison's time that it can be just as oppressive to prevent government from operating as to hijack its positive operation for factional ends.) A very clear and narrow interpretation of the recess appointment power minimizes the aggrandizement risk, but also increases the risk and harms of factionalism in the Senate. Precautions on one margin can themselves create new risks on other margins.

Reasonable doubt rule. For an example conventionally treated under the rubric of "rights," consider the justification of the reasonable doubt rule as a precautionary principle against a certain type of political

[18] *Evans v. Stephens*, 387 F.3d 1220, 1224 (CA 11 2004).
[19] THE FEDERALIST No. 10 (Clinton Rossiter ed. 1961).

risk – erroneous conviction of the innocent. Such justifications usually overlook the countervailing risks of false negatives, when those actually guilty are erroneously set free. If those actually guilty of crime can, as a class, be expected to create more far dangerous risks than the average citizen, then a precautionary perspective might even be invoked in favor of the opposite rule – better to convict ten innocents rather than let one guilty man go free. Thus it has been argued, tongue in cheek, that because "[v]iolence is a problem of public risk and public health [, i]n this context, the precautionary principle would favor earlier and more stringent intervention to prevent the 'future dangerousness' of persons who may, with considerable uncertainty, be forecast to commit violence in the future."[20]

This exemplifies a jeopardy argument because the risk against which the reasonable doubt rule takes precautions – unjustified deprivation of liberty through the criminal law – is not the same as the countervailing risk to which the critic of the reasonable doubt rule points – here, "public risk and public health."[21] If the criticism is that the violence to be anticipated from letting the guilty go free will itself deprive third-party innocents of their liberty, suitably defined,[22] then the liberty of innocents appears on both sides of the balance, and a same-risk tradeoff or perversity argument would arise.[23]

In light of these countervailing risks, the reasonable doubt rule and the traditional ten to one ratio are abrogated, quite sensibly, when the costs of false negatives seem higher than usual, according to some impressionistic judicial calculus – a pattern that also illustrates the commitment problems with precautionary judicial doctrines, discussed earlier under the heading of futility and parchment barriers. In *Hamdi v. Rumsfeld*,[24] for example, a plurality held that in hearings to determine enemy combatant status, the burden of proof could be placed on the alleged enemy combatant to disprove the government's evidence.[25] Here the costs of mistakenly releasing an enemy are high; not a few detainees released from Guantanamo have reappeared as jihadis in Iraq or Afghanistan.[26] So the judges relax the

---

[20] Wiener, *supra* note, at 1517.
[21] *Id.*
[22] *See* Adrian Vermeule, *A New Deal for Civil Liberties: An Essay in Honor of Cass R. Sunstein*, 43 Tulsa L. Rev. 921, 922–28 (2008).
[23] *Cf.* Cass R. Sunstein & Adrian Vermeule, *Is Capital Punishment Morally Required? Acts, Omissions, and Life-Life Tradeoffs*, 58 Stan. L. Rev. 703, 745 (2005).
[24] 542 U.S. 507 (2004).
[25] *Id.* at 534.
[26] Alissa J. Rubin, *Bomber's Final Messages Exhort Fighters Against U.S.*, N.Y. Times, May 9, 2008, at A14.

reasonable doubt rule, even though the cost of a mistaken positive finding of combatant status is indefinite preventive detention of the innocent – arguably worse, from the standpoint of a risk-averse innocent, than a term certain with the equivalent expected duration. Decisions of this sort rest on a kind of implicit and unsystematic risk analysis that belies the precautionary principle embodied in the reasonable doubt rule.[27] That rule might or might not be optimal in light of all relevant risks, depending on the value of N, but a precautionary perspective does not structure the questions the right way.

Free speech. A structurally similar point has been made by Frederick Schauer in the setting of free speech.[28] Robust protections for free speech, on Schauer's account, may prevent government from taking precautions against an uncertain possibility or risk of catastrophic harms, such as terrorist attacks. On the other hand, those protections may themselves be seen as precautions against a different harm, "the large-scale restriction of speech."[29] The consequence of this view is that free speech analysis should embody a "decision-theoretic approach"[30] that takes into account countervailing risks and harms on all sides of speech protections and speech restrictions – in other words, a mature analysis of speech-related problems.

The administrative state and the combination of functions. In the protracted rear-guard action fought by various legalists and libertarians against the advance of the administrative state, one of the main arguments has been that combining rulemaking, prosecution, and adjudication in the hands of the same administrative agencies effects a violation of core norms of separation of powers, and thus creates an unacceptable risk of biased agency action. The agency that makes rules and prosecutes violators, the claim runs, cannot possibly adopt an impartial perspective in adjudicating violations of its rules. Accordingly, the Court has periodically been urged to declare the combination of functions in the administrative state a *per se* violation of due process.

The Court, however, has consistently rejected this sort of claim.[31] In *Withrow v. Larkin*, the Court acknowledged that the vast and varied federal

---

[27] *See* Esmail v. Obama, 639 F.3d 1075, 1077–78 (Silberman, J., concurring).

[28] See Frederick Schauer, *Is it Better to be Safe than Sorry? Free Speech and the Precautionary Principle*, 36 PEPP. L. REV. 301 (2009).

[29] *Id.* at 305.

[30] *Id.* at 314.

[31] *See* Marcello v. Bonds, 349 U.S. 302 (1955); FTC v. Cement Inst., 333 U.S. 683 (1948). In *Wong Yang Sung v. McGrath*, 339 U.S. 33 (1950), the Court more or less endorsed the requirements of the Administrative Procedure Act (APA) as constitutionally sufficient. The APA requires separation of functions at the lower level of initial agency adjudication,

administrative state would grind to a halt if the combination of functions – a routine feature of federal administrative agencies – were declared *per se* unconstitutional on precautionary grounds.[32] This is an implicit jeopardy argument: the administrative state supplies so many valued goods that the risk of administrative bias is a constitutionally tolerable byproduct. I will return to this issue later.

Takings and public use. We have seen that critics of the Court's 2005 *Kelo* decision argued for a rule that economic development cannot count as a public use that justifies a taking of private property – a precautionary stance based on the concern that interest groups might cause legislatures to abuse the power of eminent domain for private ends. One of the Court's main responses, along the very lines of Publius's argument in Federalist 41, was simply that all governmental power can be abused:

> Speaking of the takings power, Justice Iredell observed that '[i]t is not suf-ficient to urge, that the power may be abused, for, such is the nature of all power – such is the tendency of every human institution: and, it might as fairly be said, that the power of taxation, which is only circumscribed by the discretion of the Body, in which it is vested, ought not to be granted, because the Legislature, disregarding its true objects, might, for visionary and useless projects, impose a tax to the amount of nineteen shillings in the pound. We must be content to limit power where we can, and where we cannot, consis-tently with its use, we must be content to repose a salutary confidence.'[33]

Like the taxing power, in other words, the power to take property for purposes of economic development is justified despite the possibility of abuses, because the gains are greater still. By focusing myopically on a par-ticular target risk – the public-choice concern about interest-group influ-ence – the critics of *Kelo* overlook the possibility that some level of abuse is optimal, in the sense that it is a necessary byproduct of a constitutional grant of power that is cost-justified overall.

PERVERSITY: SAME-RISK TRADEOFFS

Perversity arguments are particularly useful and attractive to opponents of precautions when there is a dominant constitutional value in the culture

---

but explicitly permits combination of functions at the top level of agency decision mak-ing, and combined arrangements are the norm in most federal agencies.

[32] *See* Withrow v. Larkin, 421 U.S. 35, 52 (1975) ("The incredible variety of administrative mechanisms in this country will not yield to any single organizing principle").

[33] Kelo v. City of New London, 545 U.S. 469, 487 n. 19 (2005).

of the day – a value that has become sacralized, making it unacceptable to argue that the value should be traded off against other goods. Under conditions of that sort, perversity arguments effect a kind of intellectual jiu-jitsu, turning the value against itself and seizing the high ground.

Standing armies. We have seen that in the debate over standing armies, Publius offered a straightforward jeopardy argument based on the goods of public order and national security from foreign invasion. Yet Publius also attempted to turn the Antifederalist argument on its head by suggesting that a prohibition on a national standing army would itself endanger liberty. The jewel of Hamilton's brilliant series of papers on the issue[34] was the crushing Federalist No. 8, titled "The Effects of Internal War in Producing Standing Armies and Other Institutions Unfriendly to Liberty,"[35] which offered a sustained case that the Antifederalist stance against standing armies would exacerbate the very risk that it sought to prevent.

If Antifederalists blocked ratification of the proposed constitution as a precaution against a national standing army, Hamilton warned, the consequence would be to create a European world of warring polities on the North American continent. Such a world would itself inevitably produce an array of standing armies. Moreover, the militarization of the states would result in systematic expansion of executive authority, "in doing which their [i.e., the state] constitutions would acquire a progressive direction towards monarchy.... Thus we should, in a little time, see established in every part of this country the same engines of despotism which have been the scourge of the old world.... [O]ur liberties would be a prey to the means of defending ourselves against the ambition and jealousy of each other."[36] The Antifederalists' error was to focus on the risks of the proposed constitution, while neglecting the countervailing risks of the steadily deteriorating status quo and the accelerating collapse of the Articles of Confederation regime.

Executive power and dictatorship. Along similar lines, Hamilton argued throughout the founding era that precautionary restrictions on the power of the executive would have the perverse result of causing the executive to slip off the bonds of constitutionalism altogether. The general problem, which Hamilton's Federalist No. 20 diagnosed by reference to the history of the Netherlands, was that

---

[34] Most directly, see THE FEDERALIST NOS. 23–28, at 152–82 (James Madison) (Clinton Rossiter ed., 1961), as well as the somewhat more general diagnoses of the faults of the Articles of Confederation in THE FEDERALIST NOS. 2–10,(Clinton Rossiter ed., 1961).
[35] THE FEDERALIST No. 8, at 66–71 (Alexander Hamilton) (Clinton Rossiter ed., 1961).
[36] *Id.* at 68, 71.

[a] weak constitution must necessarily terminate in dissolution for want of proper powers, or the usurpation of powers requisite for the public safety. Whether the usurpation, when once begun, will stop at the salutary point, or go forward to the dangerous extreme, must depend on the contingencies of the moment. Tyranny has perhaps oftener grown out of the assumptions of power called for, on pressing exigencies, by a defective constitution, than out of the full exercise of the largest constitutional authorities.[37]

Although this passage in isolation might be taken to refer to government generally, Hamilton elsewhere made it pellucid that the dynamic of excessive weakness turning into excessive strength applied especially to the executive. As he warned the Philadelphia Convention, "establish a weak government and you must at times overleap the bounds. Rome was obliged to create dictators."[38]

Modern Hamiltonians point to similar possibilities. As against the precautionary view that a reinvigorated or reinforced separation of powers is necessary, in the United States today, to prevent a possible presidential or military coup,[39] it may be that the separation of legislative and executive powers is itself a risk factor for dictatorship. For one thing, the separation of powers may reduce civilian control of the military by allowing the military to foment or exploit conflicts between civilian institutions[40] – a type of divide-and-conquer strategy. Thus one comparative study of civil-military relations finds that civilian control is greater in the United Kingdom than in the United States.[41]

Furthermore, the separation of powers might increase the stability of the system in normal times while creating a risk or uncertain chance that the system will become radically unstable in abnormal times.[42] Suppose that in a system with an independently elected president, constitutional rulemakers set up elaborate vetogates, legislative and judicial oversight, and other checks and balances, all with an eye to minimizing the risks of executive dictatorship. However, these checks and balances create gridlock and

---

[37] The Federalist No. 20, at 136–37 (James Madison) (Clinton Rossiter ed., 1961).
[38] 1 The Records of the Federal Convention of 1787, at 329 (Max Farrand ed., 1911).
[39] *See* Bruce A. Ackerman, The Decline and Fall of the American Republic 141–79 (2010).
[40] Samuel P. Huntington, The Soldier and the State: The Theory and Politics of Civil-Military Relations 177–84 (1957).
[41] Deborah D. Avant, Political Institutions and Military Change: Lessons from Peripheral Wars 21–49 (1994).
[42] This paragraph is adapted from Eric A. Posner & Adrian Vermeule, *Tyrannophobia*, in Comparative Constitutional Design (Tom Ginsburg ed. 2012).

make it difficult to pass necessary reforms. Where the status quo becomes increasingly unacceptable to many, as in times of economic or political crisis, the public demands or at least accepts a dictator who can sweep away the institutional obstacles to reform.[43] Here the very elaborateness of the designers' precautions against dictatorship creates pent-up public demand that itself leads to dictatorship. Comparative politics provides (contested) evidence for this story, especially from Latin America.[44] The New Deal, a "constitutional moment" of higher lawmaking, can be understood as our brush with the Latin American scenario, in which Roosevelt achieved near-dictatorial stature precisely because he seemed the best hope for overcoming the excessive status quo bias of the Madisonian constitution.[45]

The comparative evidence on which these mechanisms rest is uncertain. But that very uncertainty, coupled with the severity of the resulting harms if they do materialize, implies that on a precautionary perspective weakening the separation of powers might itself be the best safeguard against dictatorship. At a minimum, there are uncertainties on all sides of the issue; under certain conditions, the separation of powers may represent a self-defeating precaution.

Presidential emergency powers. Similar issues arise in recent constitutional theory, a prime example being Ackerman's proposals for constraining presidential emergency powers. Ackerman's "supermajoritarian escalator" proposes a framework statute that requires legislative authorization of emergency powers by successively larger supermajorities. Yet this framework fails to account for the reactions of legislators who themselves are aware of the rules.[46] Legislators will know, by virtue of the framework's escalating requirements, that a vote to authorize emergency powers at any

---

43 *See, e.g.,* Jonathan Hartlyn, *Presidentialism and Colombian Politics, in* The Failure of Presidential Democracy 294, 294–96 (Juan J. Linz & Arturo Valenzuela eds., 1994).

44 *See id.* at 294–96; Juan J. Linz, *Presidential or Parliamentary Democracy: Does It Make a Difference?, in* The Failure of Presidential Democracy, *supra* note 43, at 3, 6–8; Adam Przeworski et al., *What Makes Democracies Endure?,* J. Democracy, 39, 44–46 (1996). The Latin American evidence is contested in José Antonio Cheibub, Presidentialism, Parliamentarism, and Democracy (2007), which argues that the correlation between presidentialism and dictatorship is merely an artifact of selection effects: polities that are less stable to begin with are more likely to have presidential systems.

45 Along similar lines, recent scholarship suggests a roughly one-in-eight chance that executive term limits perversely tend to increase the risk of executive coups, by removing the incentive of strong executives to continue to play within the system (a final-period problem). Tom Ginsburg, James Melton & Zachary Elkins, *On the Evasion of Executive Term Limits,* 52 Wm. & Mary L. Rev. 1807, 1849–50 (2011).

46 *See* Adrian Vermeule, *Self-Defeating Proposals: Ackerman on Emergency Powers,* 75 Fordham L. Rev. 631, 641 (2006).

given time will be followed by another vote under even more stringent conditions, and this in effect *lowers* the cost to legislators of granting such powers in the present. The result is a type of moral hazard: legislators may be *more* willing to grant emergency powers than they would be in a regime in which, once granted, emergency powers become a new status quo for the indefinite future. In the limit, the result might be perverse; the very mechanism that is intended to constrain presidential emergency powers might cause legislators to grant them more freely.

Recess appointments. Recall that the court in *Canning* barred intrasession recess appointments, at least in part as a precautionary measure against presidential aggrandizement. That holding might actually turn out to be *perverse*, making matters worse on the very same margin the court was worried about. In other words, the court's precaution against presidential aggrandizement might actually increase the overall risk of aggrandizement in the long run.

How would this occur? The main mechanism involves the risk of backlash. Suppose that the combination of the filibuster, other obstructionist tactics in the Senate, and decisions like *Canning* eventually produce so much pent-up public demand for reform of the appointments process that the president offers some radical reinterpretation of the Constitution, one that gives him substantially increased discretion over appointments. Ingenious commentators have already begun to supply such reinterpretations.[47] Should the new position stick as a political equilibrium, then – given the *Canning* court's own concern with safeguards against presidential power – the court might bitterly regret, *ex post*, that it threw up an obstruction that contributed to creating a backlash in the other direction.

The general point is that an enlightened decision maker will do well to consider the systemic, dynamic, and long-run effects of any given precaution, including the long-run risk of backlash resulting in perverse outcomes. True, where information is costly and time is limited, a rational and sophisticated decision maker might decide to ignore all long-run effects, on the theory that the dynamic possibilities are so numerous and varied as to be essentially incalculable. But that would be a different, far more respectable and self-aware sort of myopia than the myopia on display in *Canning*.

The Senate. Antifederalists favored direct and frequent legislative elections and restrictions on the re-eligibility of representatives, as precautions

---

[47] For one possibility, see Matthew C. Stephenson, *Can the President Appoint Principal Executive Officers Without a Senate Confirmation Vote?*, 122 YALE L.J. 940 (2013).

against elected oligarchy, corruption, and abuse of power. For obvious reasons, the indirect election, long terms, and indefinite re-eligibility of the Senate triggered Antifederalist fears. Madison, writing as Publius in Federalist 63, responded with a perversity argument:

> In answer to all these arguments, suggested by reason, illustrated by examples, and enforced by our own experience, the jealous adversary of the Constitution will probably content himself with repeating, that a senate appointed not immediately by the people, and for the term of six years, must gradually acquire a dangerous pre-eminence in the government, and finally transform it into a tyrannical aristocracy. To this general answer, the general reply ought to be sufficient, that *liberty may be endangered by the abuses of liberty as well as by the abuses of power*; that there are numerous instances of the former as well as of the latter; and that the former, rather than the latter, are apparently most to be apprehended by the United States.[48]

Madison's point rests on the sort of precommitment argument that underpins much of liberal constitutionalism: a Senate "may be sometimes necessary as a defense to the people against their own temporary errors and delusions.... What bitter anguish would not the people of Athens have often escaped if their government had contained so provident a safeguard against the tyranny of their own passions?"[49] The sting in the final sentence is the word "tyranny," which emphasizes the perverse threat to political liberty posed by unrestricted popular liberty to direct events.

Free speech.[50] In a liberal legalist culture, the sacrosanct status of free speech principles – understood as precautions against politically motivated abuse of governmental power – implies that such principles are especially likely to become the target of perversity arguments, which attempt to turn such principles against themselves. Two illustrations come from the free speech law of political protest and subversive advocacy. The first is Justice Jackson's dissent in *Terminiello v. City of Chicago*,[51] in which the Court invalidated a conviction of a defrocked Catholic priest, a right-wing demagogue, for breach of the peace. The demagogue had given a speech that caused riotous battles between his supporters and a hostile mob of left-wing activists. Jackson's argument appealed in part to the benefits of

---

[48] THE FEDERALIST No. 63, at 387–388 (James Madison) (Clinton Rossiter ed., 1961) (emphasis added).
[49] *Id.* at 384.
[50] A helpful treatment of the cases and issues discussed in this sub-section is Eugene Volokh, *Freedom of Speech and the Constitutional Tension Method*, 3 U. CHI. L. SCH. ROUNDTABLE 223 (1996).
[51] 337 U.S. 1 (1949).

public order, but argued more pointedly in the vein of perversity: liberty –
in particular the liberty of free political speech – itself requires public order
as a precondition of its existence, so that the Court's short-sighted protection of speech put at risk the very freedom it was intended to protect. As
Jackson put it,

> [i]n the long run, maintenance of free speech will be more endangered if the
> population can have no protection from the abuses which lead to violence.
> No liberty is made more secure by holding that its abuses are inseparable
> from its enjoyment. We must not forget that it is the free democratic com-
> munities that ask us to trust them to maintain peace with liberty and that the
> factions engaged in this battle [Fascists and Communists] are not interested
> permanently in either.[52]

Jackson here implicitly points to the classic liberal dilemma whether liberalism requires toleration of the intolerant. In the long run, the argument
goes, liberalism may undermine itself by tolerating political speech and
participation by groups who would repeal liberal protections if they came
to power. This is a large-perversity argument: liberal freedoms, at least if
pressed too far, put themselves at risk.

That liberal dilemma also underpins the opinion in *Dennis v. United
States*, which upheld a conviction of Communist defendants for conspiring
to organize the Communist Party to advocate and teach the overthrow of
the U.S. government by violence.[53] As we have seen, the majority opinion
by Chief Justice Vinson upheld the conviction by adopting Judge Learned
Hand's expected-harm test for free speech protection, under which courts
"ask whether the gravity of the evil, discounted by its improbability, justifies such invasion of free speech as is necessary to avoid the danger."[54] As
against Justice Black's dissent, which offered a precautionary argument for
free speech protection – "the freedoms [that the First Amendment] guarantees provide the best insurance against destruction of all freedom"[55] – the
majority replied that if the government fell to Communism, all of Black's
freedoms, including free speech, would fall with it:

> Overthrow of the Government by force and violence is certainly a substan-
> tial enough interest for the Government to limit speech. Indeed, this is the
> ultimate value of any society, for if a society cannot protect its very structure

---

[52] *Id.* at 36–37.
[53] 341 U.S. 494 (1951).
[54] *Id.* at 510 (internal quotation omitted) (citing *United States v. Dennis*, 183 F.2d. 201, 212 (2d Cir. 1950)).
[55] *Id.* at 580 (Black, J., dissenting).

from armed internal attack, it must follow that no subordinate value can be protected.[56]

This sort of perversity argument boils down to the claim that liberty itself depends on strong and stable government – the obverse of Benjamin Franklin's civil-libertarian claim that "[t]hose who would give up essential [l]iberty to purchase a little temporary [s]afety, deserve neither [l]iberty nor [s]afety."[57]

Judicial Review. The perversity critique of a precautionary approach to free speech cases can be generalized into a critique of the larger precautionary justification for judicial review. Conditional on certain theories of rights that recognize affirmative claims to governmental aid or support, judicial review can be argued to block legislative or executive measures that are necessary to implement rights or to protect rights against private violation. On this view, the perverse result is that judicial review might increase the overall incidence of rights-violations. "Inserting an additional veto point into the process of obtaining effective legislation *threatens* erroneous underprotection of fundamental rights; it does not provide a 'hedge' against legislative underprotection of fundamental rights."[58]

Judicial review, interest groups, and property rights. Along similar lines, perversity underlies a general critique of interest-group justifications for judicial review.[59] Such theories posit that courts should exercise closer scrutiny of governmental action where there is a risk of interest-group "capture" – a risk that narrow, well-organized groups will exert disproportionate influence over legislatures or agencies, according to some normative conception of proper influence. As we have seen, the capture concern underlies many criticisms of the *Kelo* decision, which allowed governmental takings of private property for purposes of economic development. The critics believe that interest groups will cause government to abuse the takings power in order to confer benefits on private groups, reducing social welfare overall and undermining the security of property rights.

In Chapter 4, I will discuss some of the affirmative "benefits of capture,"[60] which can provide decision makers with specialized information

---

[56] *Id.* at 509 (majority opinion).

[57] Benjamin Franklin, *Pennsylvania Assembly: Reply to the Governor* (Nov. 11, 1755), *in* 6 THE PAPERS OF BENJAMIN FRANKLIN 242 (Leonard W. Labaree ed., 1963).

[58] Mark Tushnet, *How Different are Waldron's And Fallon's Core Cases For and Against Judicial Review?*, 30 OXFORD J. LEGAL STUD. 49, 61 (2010) (emphasis in original).

[59] For an overview and critique of such theories, see Einer R. Elhauge, *Does Interest Group Theory Justify More Intrusive Judicial Review?*, 101 YALE L.J. 31 (1991).

[60] *See* Dorit Rubinstein Reiss, *The Benefits of Capture*, 47 WAKE FOREST L. REV. 569 (2012).

or spur decision makers to take decisions. Even apart from such benefits, however, it has been argued that enhancing judicial scrutiny in order to raise the costs of interest-group capture may have perverse effects. In the words of a leading critic of interest-group justifications for judicial review,

> even if more intrusive judicial review does increase the transaction costs of capture, that can perversely encourage interest group activity by making successful capture harder to undo. [Furthermore], because increasing transaction costs also increases the costs facing large diffuse groups, it may increase the *relative* advantage of small intense groups and thus increase their success.[61]

In other words, the interest-group justifications for judicial review focus myopically on one sort of response to the threat of capture, overlooking that the precautions they advocate may themselves exacerbate that very threat.

Maximin constitutional design.[62] As we have seen, Federalist 41 gives the most general form of the jeopardy argument: precautions that restrict governmental discretion to provide other goods may reduce social welfare overall. The most general form of the perversity argument holds that designing a constitution on worst-case assumptions – maximin constitutional design, loosely speaking – may itself bring about the worst case. In light of that risk, systematic constitutional caution may prove self-defeating.

An example is a critique of Hume's knavery principle, discussed in Part I.A. Anti-Humean critics object that *the expectation of knavery is self-fulfilling*: presuming officials to be knaves will tend to make officials into knaves.[63] One possibility is that official motivations are partly endogenous to the constitutional rules. On this view, "a constitution for knaves crowds out civic virtues,"[64] a possibility that in turn can rest on one of several mechanisms.[65] Constitutional sanctions for self-interested behavior

---

[61] Elhauge, *supra* note, at 88.

[62] For an earlier stab at these issues, see Adrian Vermeule, *Hume's Second-Best Constitutionalism*, 70 U. CHI. L. REV. 421 (2003).

[63] An excellent treatment of these issues is Lewis A. Kornhauser, *Virtue and Self-Interest in the Design of Constitutional Institutions*, 3 THEORETICAL INQ. L. 21 (2002).

[64] *See* Bruno S. Frey, *A Constitution for Knaves Crowds Out Civic Virtues*, 107 ECON. J. 1043, 1044–45 (1997).

[65] For a model of conditions under which laws (here meaning legal sanctions or incentives) and norms act as either substitutes or complements, see Roland Bénabou & Jean Tirole, *Laws and Norms* (Nat'l Bureau of Econ. Research, Working Paper No. 17579, November 2011), *available at* http://ssrn.com/abstract=1954505.

might undermine social norms that would constrain the same behavior; the net effect may then be an increase in self-interested action by officials. Alternatively, sanctions for self-interested behavior might (unintentionally) convey a signal that many other officials are engaged in the behavior that the sanctions aim to eliminate. If so, the net result may be an increase in noncompliance by office-holders, either because they are conformists who adjust their behavior to track what the majority does,[66] or because they are "reciprocal altruists" who would comply with public-regarding norms if others were complying also, but who are afraid of being chumps and are thus unwilling to comply unilaterally.[67]

Even if officials' motivations are not endogenous to the constitutional rules, the Humean presumption of knavery may have selection effects that perversely tend to filter self-interested actors into office while filtering out public-spirited actors. If public-spirited actors experience a cost from being subjected to elaborate monitoring devices based on a presumption of knavery – the cost of frustration, or of operating under a cloud of suspicion – then the presence of such devices will tend, at the margin, to filter out such actors while filtering in actors for whom the presumption of knavery is, in fact, accurate. Although this is merely one possible effect of such devices, the overall result may be that designing a constitution for knaves perversely tends to select knaves into the public sphere.

EX ANTE PRECAUTIONS VS. EX POST REMEDIES: "NOT WHILE THIS COURT SITS"

By their nature, precautions are taken ex ante the materialization of the relevant risk. Accordingly, another argument against precautions is that ex ante safeguards are unnecessary in light of the availability of ex post remedies, such as suits for damages against officers who execute an unconstitutional policy. Technically, this is a special case of jeopardy and could have been covered under that heading. The core of the concern is simply that ex ante precautions that are unnecessary will imposes costs greater than their benefits. Because the temporal dimension is distinctive, however, separate treatment is warranted.

---

[66] Dirk Sliwka, *Trust as a Signal of a Social Norm and the Hidden Costs of Incentive Schemes*, 97 AM. ECON. REV. 999, 1000 (2007).

[67] Joel J. Van der Weele, *The Signaling Power of Sanctions in Social Dilemmas*, 28 J.L. ECON. & ORG. 103–26 (2012).

There is a standard conceptual issue about the distinction between ex ante precautions and ex post remedies, one that crops up in this setting as well. Clearly, the anticipation of an ex post sanction will itself produce ex ante deterrent effects, if the law can make a credible commitment to providing remedies after the fact. Yet it is wrong (here and elsewhere) to assume that there is no difference between ex ante precautionary regulation and a system of ex post sanctions. For present purposes, a key difference is whether the constitutional rule is formulated to ward off an uncertain harm, or instead is formulated to require that the complaining party demonstrate that a harm has already materialized. The latter approach places the burdens of production and proof on the complainant and requires case-by-case assessment of evidence before the tribunal.

Taxation of federal instrumentalities and contractors. As we have seen, Chief Justice Marshall's opinion in *McCulloch* formulated a rule against state taxation of federal instrumentalities, based on the precautionary principle that "the power to tax involves the power to destroy."[68] The rule of *McCulloch* – a "prophylactic per se rule"[69] that still holds today – is that states may not regulate or tax federal instrumentalities without express congressional authorization.

Later cases extended the precautionary zone to bar state taxation of private parties who do business with the federal government.[70] The governing doctrine was that any state regulation or tax that indirectly regulated the federal government's activity was invalid; the point of this doctrine was to create a precautionary buffer to protect the freedom of otherwise valid federal operations. Justice Holmes, by contrast, articulated a competing position: ex post, case-by-case assessment of the destructive effect of state taxation on federal contractors would be enough to protect vital federal interests, without overprotecting those interests to such a degree as to squash the legitimate taxing power of the states.

In the most famous of Holmes's opinions on this issue, a dissent in *Panhandle Oil Co. v. Mississippi ex rel. Knox*,[71] Holmes voted to uphold a state sales tax on oil sold to the United States for the use of the Coast Guard. "The power to tax," Holmes argued, "is not the power to destroy while this Court sits."[72] The Court's ability to review interference with federal operations at retail thus undermined the need for a wholesale

---

[68] 17 U.S. 316, 431 (1819).

[69] Laurence H. Tribe, American Constitutional Law 1223 (3d ed. 2000).

[70] *See, e.g.*, Osborn v. Bank of the United States, 22 U.S. 738, 867 (1824).

[71] 277 U.S. 218 (1928).

[72] *Id.* at 223 (Holmes, J., dissenting).

precautionary principle. Starting in 1937, the Court began to limit the precautionary buffer zone around federal operations, and the opinion from
which Holmes had dissented was eventually overruled.[73] Under current
law, federal contractors can generally be subjected to nondiscriminatory
state taxes and regulations.[74]

Free speech. Holmes's "not while this Court sits" principle later
migrated to other parts of constitutional law, including the law of free
speech. In *Beauharnais v. Illinois*,[75] the Court sustained a criminal statute that prohibited the publication of libelous assertions about groups.
Rejecting the contention that free speech precautionary principles should
be invoked to invalidate the law, Justice Frankfurter wrote for the Court
along Holmesian lines:

> We are warned that the choice open to the Illinois legislature here may be
> abused, that the law may be discriminatorily enforced; prohibiting libel of a
> creed or of a racial group, we are told, is but a step from prohibiting libel of
> a political party. Every power may be abused, but the possibility of abuse is
> a poor reason for denying Illinois the power to adopt measures against crim-
> inal libels sanctioned by centuries of Anglo-American law. 'While this Court
> sits' it retains and exercises authority to nullify action which encroaches on
> freedom of utterance under the guise of punishing libel.[76]

In other words, the political risk that group libel law would be used as a
pretext for the abuse of power could be dealt with through ex post, case-
by-case assessment, rather than through ex ante precautions. Here as elsewhere in free speech law, however, the precautionary approach has largely
prevailed; the consensus is that *Beauharnais* is no longer good law.[77]

Takings and public use. The principle "not while this Court sits"
migrated more successfully to another area, however: constitutional property law. As against the argument for a precautionary rule that economic
development can never count as a "public use," for fear that the takings
power will be abused by interest groups for self-regarding ends, the *Kelo*
Court offered not only a jeopardy response – discussed earlier – but also the
response that welfare-reducing interest-group influence can be discerned

---

73 *See* James v. Dravo Contracting Co., 302 U.S. 134, 151–52 (1937).
74 *See, e.g.*, United States v. New Mexico, 455 U.S. 720 (1982).
75 343 U.S. 250 (1952) (internal citation omitted).
76 *Id.* at 263–64.
77 *See, e.g.*, Anti-Defamation League of B'Nai B'Rith v. FCC, 403 F.2d 169, 174 n.5 (D.C.
    Cir. 1969) ("[F]ar from spawning progeny, *Beauharnais* has been left more and more bar-
    ren by subsequent First Amendment decisions, to the point where it is now doubtful that
    the decision still represents the views of the Court.").

through fact-specific review in particular cases. Quoting Holmes's dictum from *Panhandle Oil*, the Court said that even where there is a "suspicion that a private purpose [is] afoot, the hypothetical cases posited by [the parties challenging the taking] can be confronted if and when they arise. They do not warrant the crafting of an artificial restriction on the concept of public use."[78] On this view, there is no need for a precautionary restriction on the takings power because abuses can be separated from legitimate uses in a case-by-case review.

Due process. We have seen, in the law of due process, a precautionary principle against the risk of biased judgment by adjudicators with a personal financial stake in the controversy, even an indirect one.[79] By contrast, the risk of bias that arises from combination of investigative, prosecutorial, and adjudicative functions in the same hands is remitted to case-by-case assessment and ex post protection. In *Withrow v. Larkin*,[80] the Court upheld a scheme in which a board of physicians was given the authority to investigate and prosecute claims of professional misconduct, and then to adjudicate those claims; the particular case involved proceedings against an abortionist and had more than a whiff of ideological bias to it. The Court refused to apply a precautionary rule against this combination of functions:

> [V]arious situations have been identified in which experience teaches that the probability of actual bias on the part of the judge or decision-maker is too high to be constitutionally tolerable. Among these cases are those in which the adjudicator has a pecuniary interest in the outcome.... [However, there is] no support for the bald proposition ... that agency members who participate in an investigation are disqualified from adjudicating. The incredible variety of administrative mechanisms in this country will not yield to any single organizing principle.... [This holding] does not, of course, preclude a court from determining from the special facts and circumstances present in the case before it that the risk of unfairness is intolerably high.[81]

Despite the Court's reference to "risk" in the final sentence, lower court cases have made clear that once a precautionary principle barring the combination of functions is rejected, the complaining party must make a specific showing – "in the case before it," as the Court instructed – that biased

---

[78] Kelo v. City of New London, 545 U.S. 469, 487 (2005).
[79] *See* Gibson v. Berryhill, 411 U.S. 564 (1973).
[80] 421 U.S. 35 (1975).
[81] *Id.* at 47, 52, 58.

judgment has actually materialized.[82] Earlier, I suggested that the Court's
tolerance for administrative combination of lawmaking, prosecutorial,
and adjudicative functions rests in part on a jeopardy argument, based
on the many goods that the combination of functions supplies; here I add
that the Court has relegated any risks arising from the combination of
functions to ex post, case-by-case assessment, rather than addressing them
through an ex ante precautionary approach.

CONSTITUTIONAL RISK REGULATION:
THE "MATURE POSITION"

Given the arguments for encoding precautions against political risk in constitutional law, and the counterarguments against such principles, what is
to be done? Story addressed the question with reference to the political
risks posed by standing armies:

> Too much precaution often leads to as many difficulties, as too much confi-
> dence.... It may be admitted, that standing armies may prove dangerous to
> the state. But it is equally true, that the want of them may prove dangerous
> to the state. What then is to be done? The true course is to check the undue
> exercise of the power, not to withhold it.[83]

Here Story in effect argues for a position that considers all relevant risks
of all relevant alternatives, including both action and inaction, and then
adopts cost-justified precautions in light of those risks. In all this, Story
was following a path marked out by Publius. Federalist 41 did not deny the
risks of standing armies, but merely argued for balanced risk assessment:

> A standing force, therefore, is a dangerous, at the same time that it may be
> a necessary provision. On the smallest scale it has its inconveniences. On an
> extensive scale, its consequences may be fatal. On any scale, it is an object
> of laudable circumspection and precaution. A wise nation will combine all
> these considerations; and whilst it does not rashly preclude itself from any
> resources which may become essential to its safety, will exert all its prudence
> in diminishing both the necessity and the danger of resorting to one which
> may be inauspicious to its liberties.[84]

---

[82] *See, e.g.*, Alpha Epsilon Phi Tau Chapter Housing Ass'n v. City of Berkeley, 114 F.3d.
840, 845 (9th Cir. 1997); Valley v. Rapides Parish Sch. Bd., 118 F.3d. 1047, 1053 (5th Cir.
1997).

[83] 3 JOSEPH STORY, COMMENTARIES ON THE CONSTITUTION OF THE UNITED STATES 71, 73
(Boston, Hilliard, Gray & Co. 1833).

[84] THE FEDERALIST NO. 41, at 257–58 (James Madison) (Clinton Rossiter ed., 1961) (emphasis added).

Publius and Story here supplied an example of what Hirschman, writing about the political theory of institutional reform, calls the "mature position":

(1) There are dangers and risks in both action and inaction. The risks of both should be canvassed, assessed, and guarded against to the extent possible.

(2) The baneful consequences of either action or inaction can never be known with [certainty].... When it comes to forecasts of impending mishaps or disasters, it is well to remember the saying *Le pire n'est pas toujours sûr* – the worst is not always sure (to happen).[85]

The mature position is structurally parallel, in the domain of political risks, to the position advanced by critics of precautionary principles in health, safety, and environmental regulation. On this view, given the possibility of countervailing risks, the goal of the designer of a regulatory system should be *optimal* precautions rather than *maximal* precautions.[86] The latter is an incoherent goal in any event, because precautions may themselves create risks, and thereby prove self-defeating.[87] The mature calculus, then, posits that "[o]ptimal regulation in the face of a target risk (TR) and a countervailing risk (CR) would take both seriously and strive to maximize their difference ($\Delta TR - \Delta CR$). Uncertainty is not the crucial problem – trade-offs are."[88]

An example. For a simple illustration, let me return to the issue of recess appointments and the *Canning* decision. (The rest of the book will be occupied with providing more extended and complex illustrations.) The *Canning* court barred all intrasession recess appointments as a precaution against presidential aggrandizement, but we have seen that the holding created countervailing risks and harms – both risks of collateral harm to the orderly functioning of government, and the perverse consequence of possibly increasing the long-term risk of presidential aggrandizement itself. Yet there are at least two other alternative constitutional rules. Those alternatives are far less cramped than the court's holding, and would plausibly optimize across the relevant constitutional risks, or at least do better

---

[85] HIRSCHMAN, *supra* note, at 153–154.

[86] Wiener, *supra* note, at 1511.

[87] *See* CASS R. SUNSTEIN, LAWS OF FEAR: BEYOND THE PRECAUTIONARY PRINCIPLE 4 (2005) (the precautionary principle is "literally incoherent" because "[t]here are risks on all sides of social situations" and thus the precautionary principle "forbids the very steps it requires").

[88] Wiener, *supra* note, at 1520.

overall than the rule the court chose, while sufficiently accommodating the court's slippery-slope concerns.

One possibility would be to say that historical practice has liquidated and fixed, within a range, the duration of intrasession recesses within which an appointment may be made. The practice has varied somewhat, but there is a stable basin of attraction in the region of about ten days. Many intrasession appointments have involved longer recesses — *Canning* itself involved a twenty-day recess — while a few such appointments have fallen in recesses slightly shorter than ten days. But we simply do not observe presidents making intrasession appointments when the Senate recesses for five days, let alone for a lunch break. Observable behavior suggests that the slope is not so very slippery after all.

If that seems too vague or elastic, another possibility would be to tie recess appointments to the Adjournments Clause, which prohibits either house of Congress from adjourning for more than three days, during the session, without the other's consent.[89] The law could say that any adjournment of longer than three days counts as a "recess" and thus enables a recess appointment, but that three days or less will not do. That would offer a perfectly determinate and enforceable line.

The *Canning* court rejected this because there is no explicit textual link between the recess appointments power on the one hand and adjournments on the other.[90] So what? The pragmatic point of the court's enterprise, after all, was to find a "clear distinction" that would prove "judicially defensible in the heat of interbranch conflict." The three-day line offers exactly that, but with reduced countervailing harms and risks, compared to the court's rule. Even granting the concern with presidential aggrandizement, the court's highly precautionary holding represents a poor overall treatment of the relevant risks, in light of the problems of jeopardy and perversity that the holding created. And there were feasible alternative rules that illustrate the optimizing approach of the mature position.

The mature position, cost-benefit analysis, and democracy. Having laid out the mature position, let me clarify its limits, both conceptual and political, in the hope of forestalling confusions. First, the mature position does not necessarily entail cost-benefit analysis, depending on how the latter idea is specified. "Cost-benefit analysis" is a protean term[91] that can be

---

[89] U.S. CONST. art. I, sec. 5, cl. 4.
[90] See *Canning*, 705 F.3d at 504.
[91] *See* Amartya Sen, *The Discipline of Cost-Benefit Analysis*, 29 J. LEGAL STUD. 931, 932–33 (2000).

used to encompass everything from informal consequentialism – Charles Darwin's list of the pros and cons of marriage[92] – to a formal, fully monetized analysis of compensating variations based on willingness to pay and to accept.[93] When used as a loose synonym for consequentialism, cost-benefit analysis can encompass a range of theories about what consequences are relevant and what weights to be assigned to them. Although the version of consequentialism that underpins formal monetized cost-benefit analysis attends only to consequences for subjective welfare, nothing inherent in consequentialism so requires. Violations of rights, somehow defined, may themselves count as bad consequences.[94] What the mature position does point out, however, is that rights may appear on all sides of relevant issues; both the jeopardy and the perversity arguments emphasize the possibility of rights-rights tradeoffs, with jeopardy being relevant if different rights are in conflict and perversity being relevant if the same right appears on both sides of the issue.

Second, the mature position does not, by itself, exclude a fully informed democratic decision to depart from optimal precautions. Risk regulation, whether at the first-order or second-order level, is only a part of what societies might properly care about; once democratic decision makers have figured out what the optimal precautions are, there is a separate normative question about what to do, in light of that mature risk assessment. What the mature position does exclude, however, is a decision to depart from optimal precautions for the wrong sort of reasons, or on spurious grounds. Although democratic decision makers might adopt a suboptimal set of precautions, they should do so with their eyes open, after an evenhanded assessment of both target risks and countervailing risks, rather than in the misguided belief that a prudent approach to risk so requires.

Political fat tails and maximin constitutionalism. Another set of issues involves risk, uncertainty, and extreme outcomes that are, in some sense, real but remote possibilities. Although I have been speaking the language of risk, the point is the same whether put in those terms or instead in the language of uncertainty. The precautionary concern with political fat tails and rare but extreme political outcomes, such as a sudden collapse into dictatorship, is compelling in the abstract, at least if the resulting harms to constitutional values would be sufficiently great. The problem is that the

---

[92] 2 The Correspondence of Charles Darwin: 1837–1843, at 443–445 (Frederick Burkhardt & Sydney Smith eds., 1986).

[93] Matthew D. Adler & Eric A. Posner, New Foundations of Cost-Benefit Analysis 166–73 (2006).

[94] Amartya Sen, *Rights and Agency*, 11 Phil. & Pub. Aff. 3, 4–7 (1982).

concern with political fat tails has no particular valence and yields no particular implications for constitutional rulemaking. The basic reason is that *precautions may themselves have fat tails*[95] – both in ordinary policymaking and in constitutional rulemaking. The very constitutional structures that rulemakers set up to safeguard against remote but extremely damaging possibilities may themselves create a remote chance of an exceedingly harmful outcome.

Consider the possibility, discussed earlier, that the separation of executive and legislative powers, erected in part as a precaution against either executive dictatorship or legislative tyranny, is itself a risk factor for dictatorship or tyranny, perhaps because the separation of powers gridlocks the lawmaking system and thus created pent-up public demand for strong extraconstitutional action. That possibility is a remote one, but may prove extremely damaging to constitutionalism if it does materialize. Constitutional precautions, in other words, can be as susceptible to the fat-tail problem as are the political harms the precautions are intended to guard against.

Likewise, maximin constitutionalism fails to the extent that precautions may themselves trigger a worst-case scenario. Suppose – and the earlier examples substantiate these possibilities – that there is some unquantifiable probability that strong free speech protection will trigger a backlash that results in suppression of political speech, or that strong protection for property rights will trigger a backlash that results in a severe curtailment of property rights. It is unclear what the maximin perspective on constitutionalism implies in such cases. Where a worst-case outcome may, with some unquantifiable probability, result from the precautions taken to prevent that outcome, the maximin approach is at odds with itself.

Second-order precautions? In the risk-regulation debates, one critique of the mature position takes a second-order or indirect-consequentialist form. Although balancing of all relevant risks is the ideal, the argument runs, regulators display predictable cognitive biases and motivational distortions that will cause them to make suboptimal decisions under a balancing approach.[96] Regulators may predictably underweight soft or nonquantifiable variables, such as environmental values; may predictably

---

[95] *See* Gary W. Yohe and Richard S.J. Tol, *Precaution and a Dismal Theorem: Implications for Climate Policy and Climate Research, in* RISK MANAGEMENT IN COMMODITY MARKETS 91 (Hélyette Geman ed., 2008).

[96] *See* David A. Dana, *A Behavioral Economic Defense of the Precautionary Principle*, 97 Nw. U. L. REV. 1315 (2003); David A. Dana, *The Contextual Rationality of the Precautionary Principle*, 35 QUEEN'S L.J. 67 (2009).

overweight certain costs, as opposed to uncertain ones; may be excessively optimistic, and thus underestimate the risk that catastrophic harms will occur in the absence of regulation; or may be influenced or politically constrained by self-interested private groups who oppose regulation. Some version of the precautionary principle can compensate for these distortions, and is therefore a pragmatically useful second-best. On these grounds, rulemakers such as legislators and judges might do well, in a long-run and aggregate sense, to embody precautionary principles in statutes or legal doctrines even if such principles would be harmful when applied to constrain the decisions that an ideal regulator would make. In general, second-order or indirectly consequentialist arguments for (some version of) the precautionary principle imply that it is not necessarily best for regulators to attempt to weigh all relevant risks, because they will predictably display certain biases in doing so.

Proponents of the mature position in the risk-regulation debates counter that the rule-utilitarian defense of precautions does not escape the core problem of the precautionary principle. Cognitive biases or motivational distortions on the part of decision makers are just another type of risk; those biases and distortions can themselves appear on all sides of relevant issues.[97] The rule-utilitarian argument, on this rejoinder, replicates the fatally one-sided character of the precautionary principle, just one step removed – in the form of a second-order argument about the capacities of decision makers, rather than a first-order argument about the nature of the risks to be regulated.

In one set of examples, the very *same* bias appears on all sides; this is a second-order version of the perversity critique. If decision makers underweight soft unquantifiable variables, such as environmental values, this need not justify a precautionary principle in favor of regulation, because environmental values may also be harmed by excessive or misplaced regulation as well as by inadequate regulation. By the very logic of the rule-utilitarian argument, decision makers will also underweight the perverse effects of bad or misplaced regulation on soft variables. Likewise, if decision makers are excessively optimistic, the problem is that they may be excessively optimistic about the consequences of regulating as well as the consequences of failing to regulate.

In another set of examples, regulators may display one type of bias that favors inaction or under-regulation, but simultaneously display a different type of bias that favors action or over-regulation (or vice versa). As against

---

97 Sunstein, *supra* note, at 51–53.

the argument that regulators underweight soft variables, for example, it has been argued that "ordinary thinking is actually warped against giving *quantitative* variables their due weight."[98] On this view, decision makers tend to overweigh vivid narratives and underweight pallid background facts of a statistical character.[99] More generally, given the proliferation of findings and putative findings about cognitive and motivational distortions that have emerged from the heuristics-and-biases program in psychology, it will often be the case that plausible arguments for "systematic bias" can be made on all sides of relevant issues.

A second-order version of the mature position, then, will consider all relevant systematic biases, both for and against regulation, that might afflict front-line decision makers. To be clear, a suitably mature second-order analysis might ultimately conclude that some version of the precautionary principle turns out, in fact, to be the best first-order decision procedure for regulators in a certain domain. This defense of precautionary principles has a perfectly valid theoretical structure; hence it cannot be ruled out, or in, on *a priori* grounds. Everything depends on what predictable biases and decision-making distortions regulators actually display. Yet one cannot justify such a conclusion by pointing in a one-sided fashion to the subset of biases that produce inadequate (or excessive) regulation. First-order precautionary decision-procedures can be justified only by second-order decision making that is itself mature, rather than precautionary. As I have argued at length elsewhere, the limits of reason – the information costs, cognitive biases, and other decisional pathologies that afflict first-order decision makers – should be taken into account by institutional designers,[100] but only in a way that considers all relevant limits on reason, not merely some skewed or biased subset of those limits that pull systematically for or against regulation of particular risks.

Structurally parallel points apply, with appropriate modifications, to constitutional law. I will confine myself to one example, the argument that anticipated political pathologies call for clear and strictly enforced rules of content neutrality and viewpoint neutrality in free speech law. Judges fear that in future periods of political pathology, cognitive biases or political pressures will cause their successors on the bench, or their future selves, to override free-speech protections; hence they attempt to precommit to a clear

---

[98] RICHARD A. POSNER, ECONOMIC ANALYSIS OF LAW 403 (7th ed. 2007).

[99] *See* Amos Tversky & Daniel Kahneman, *Judgment Under Uncertainty: Heuristics and Biases*, 185 SCIENCE 1124, 1127–28 (1974).

[100] *See* ADRIAN VERMEULE, LAW AND THE LIMITS OF REASON (2009).

and rigid rule to compensate for the anticipated pathologies. This argument has the structure of the rule-utilitarian argument for precautions.

The parallel problem, however, is that pathologies can appear on all sides of the relevant issues. In particular, the rulemakers – here judges who craft free speech doctrine – may themselves display a *pathological fear of succumbing to pathological fear*, a kind of phobophobia. If so, they will prove pathologically unwilling to bend or break the rules and will decline to craft standards or exceptions that allow the rules to be overridden, even where such exceptions are socially desirable, all things considered.[101] To make things worse, if the judges' phobophobia produces a series of decisions that are so publicly unacceptable that they produce widespread disrespect for free speech protection, then the pathological perspective may prove self-defeating; the judges' concern for protecting free speech in the long run may actually undermine free speech in the long run.

In this light, it is inadequate to say that because there is a risk that judges will react fearfully to subversive advocacy, "second-order balancing" counsels in favor of a "pathological perspective," which in turn requires strong, rule-like precautionary protections in favor of free speech.[102] The problem is that fear can be present on all sides of the relevant issue, at the second level no less than the first. If some judges are irrationally fearful of subversive speech – where "irrationally" means "to a degree not warranted or justified by the evidence" – then other judges are irrationally fearful of governmental attempts to disrupt organizations that threaten force or violence. The latter judges are the mirror-image of the former; they are subject to a kind of "libertarian panic,"[103] driven by the salience of highly salient or lurid governmental abuses in the past, just as the former judges are obsessed by highly salient risks of terrorism or other harms by organized violent groups. The limits of reason appear on all sides of the equation; a mature calculus would weigh both risks and both types of decisional distortions on the part of judges and other officials. It is an open question what the result of that fully mature second-order decision making would be; doubtless the result would be highly contextual, varying with time and

---

[101] *Cf.* Mark Tushnet, *The First Amendment and Political Risk*, 4. J. LEGAL ANALYSIS 103 (2012).

[102] SUNSTEIN, *supra* note, at 218–21.

[103] *See* Adrian Vermeule, *Libertarian Panics*, 36 RUTGERS L.J. 871, 871 (2005) (arguing that "the mechanisms underlying security panics have no necessary or inherent pro-security valence"; rather, "[t]he very same mechanisms are equally capable of producing libertarian panics[, which are] episodes in which aroused publics become irrationally convinced that justified security measures represent unjustified attempts to curtail civil liberties").

circumstances. But it is clear that one cannot, in the abstract, invoke a one-sided analysis of second-order decision-making distortions to support a general precautionary approach to free speech.

Mature institutions and the allocation of decision-making competence. The mature position implies that the institutional system set up to design a new constitution, and the institutional system for interpreting and enforcing the constitution once it is in place, should take into account all relevant limits of reason on the part of first-order decision makers, and all relevant political risks, on all sides of relevant questions. That implication is pitched at a high level of generality; it is thus consistent with a wide range of allocations of decision-making competence across institutions.

To continue the last example, which institution(s) should be charged with considering all relevant risks of protecting or discouraging dangerous political speech, of the sort at issue in the *Dennis* case? Learned Hand's expected-harm test assumes that the judges should take all relevant risks into account, both the risks of prohibition and the time-discounted risks of failing to prohibit. Yet there is nothing inevitable about allocating this task *to judges*, even if one subscribes to the mature position. Another possibility is that judges should defer to the congressional judgment, embodied in the challenged statutes, that one set of risks outweighs the other. On this approach, a standard critique of *Dennis* – that it was too deferential to nonjudicial actors[104] – might get things backwards. Insofar as Hand's test assumes that judges should make an independent assessment of risks and choose optimal precautions, it allocates to the judiciary a power that might be better left in legislative hands.

Nothing in the mature position, of course, entails that a deferential approach in *Dennis* would indeed be superior. Whether that alternative is in fact superior or not will depend on judgments, largely empirical and predictive, about the motivations and epistemic capacities of officials in different institutions. Moreover, there are many possible ways to allocate the competence to assess political risks across institutions. Courts, for example, might be empowered to issue a constitutional decision that the legislature can then override, perhaps through special procedures or with special majorities – the sort of "weak-form judicial review" seen in many constitutional democracies.[105] All this implicates a well-known set

---

[104] *See, e.g.,* EDWIN C. BAKER, HUMAN LIBERTY AND FREEDOM OF SPEECH 26 (1992).
[105] Mark Tushnet, *Weak-Form Judicial Review and "Core" Civil Liberties,* 41 HARV. C.R.-C.L. L. REV. 1, 4–11 (2006).

of debates about how a system of judicial review should be designed,[106] debates that the mature position, by itself, cannot resolve. What the mature position adds is the caution that arguments for any particular allocation of competence to assess political risks should attend to the risks generated by constitutional precautions as well as the risks prevented by them.

The negative function of the mature position. Given all this, the mature position may seem a rather thin or even banal commitment; who can be opposed in principle to weighing all relevant risks? And if the mature position need have no particular implications for the allocation of competence to assess risks across institutions within the constitutional system, what turns on accepting or rejecting it?

I believe, however, that the mature position has an important negative function, both in the domain of ordinary regulation and in the domain of constitutional design and interpretation: it places tradeoffs on the "viewscreen"[107] and thereby excludes unconstrained demands for "maximal safety" or "security" against perceived risks. Proponents of the mature position in risk regulation call this a cognitive justification.[108] I prefer to emphasize its negative character as a filter that strains out certain types of bad arguments and obsessions with particular risks. Such an approach does not dictate any particular outcomes, but merely attempts to launder the inputs to decision making, to avoid obsessions, and thereby to improve the process of regulating (political) risks.[109]

In the domain of ordinary regulation, "availability cascades" based on highly salient risks can produce distorted regulation that focuses to excess on target risks while ignoring countervailing risks.[110] A similar problem arises in the constitutional domain. Episodes of constitution-making often take place after, and in part because of, the occurrence of

---

[106] For references and a position in these debates, see ADRIAN VERMEULE, JUDGING UNDER UNCERTAINTY: AN INSTITUTIONAL THEORY OF LEGAL INTERPRETATION (2006) (arguing that legal interpretation is plagued by empirical uncertainty and, given their limited information and institutional competence, judges should exercise great restraint their interpretive undertakings), and VERMEULE, *supra* note (arguing that legislators, who are more heterogeneous and politically accountable than judges, are better able to create socially desirable results via legal development).

[107] SUNSTEIN, *supra* note, at 118.

[108] *Id.* at 129.

[109] *Cf.* JON ELSTER, SECURITIES AGAINST MISRULE: JURIES, ASSEMBLIES, ELECTIONS (2013), which argues that the main task of institutional design should be the negative one of weeding out self-interest, passion, prejudice and bias, rather than the positive one of producing good outcomes.

[110] Timur Kuran & Cass R. Sunstein, *Availability Cascades and Risk Regulation*, 51 STAN. L. REV. 683, 715–36 (1999)

a highly salient political risk or a highly salient class of political abuses. Under such circumstances, a kind of constitutional availability cascade can occur: the politics of distrust, the hermeneutics of suspicion, and the spread of a paranoid political style[111] can produce ever-more stringent demands for constitutional provisions and structures that will protect the citizenry from recent and highly lurid forms of political risk or abuse, even if the precautions that are demanded would be rejected by any decision procedure that is even mildly sensitive to countervailing risks and collateral costs.[112]

Under such circumstances, the mature position may help to serve as a valuable intellectual corrective, by placing all relevant risks before constitutional designers, constitutional interpreters, and the public who ultimately judges both. The central place of the mature position in Publius's argument is an encouraging example. It shows that at least sometimes, the mature position may even carry the day against widespread, obsessive fears of particular political risks, such as the abolition of the states, tyranny and despotism, an oligarchy of elected representatives, or standing armies – the sort of fears that afflicted the Antifederalists.

To be sure, where constitutional politics reaches a fever pitch of suspicion, it may be that no set of arguments, and indeed no set of institutions, can prevent distorted constitutional regulation of political risks. Yet under imaginable political conditions, the rationality of the mature position – in a broad rather than technical sense of "rationality" – can have outsized influence. If, for example, different groups are obsessed by different target risks, then (under certain voting rules for the adoption of a new constitution) a small subset of mature and balanced risk assessors who attend to countervailing risks can have outsized influence on outcomes, by providing decisive votes for provisions that take optimal rather than "maximal"

---

[111]   Richard Hofstadter, *The Paranoid Style in American Politics*, HARPER'S MAG., Nov. 1964, at 77.

[112]   For classic exposés of the paranoid political style in the founding era, particularly among the Antifederalists, see BERNARD BAILYN, THE IDEOLOGICAL ORIGINS OF THE AMERICAN REVOLUTION (1967); and MEN OF LITTLE FAITH: SELECTED WRITINGS OF CECELIA KENYON (Stanley Elkins, Eric McKitrick & Leo Weinstein eds., 2002). Gordon Wood has observed that conspiracy theorizing and libertarian panic were widespread in the post-Enlightenment world, before it became widely understood that political action is pervasively subject to unintended consequences. *See* Gordon S. Wood, *Conspiracy and the Paranoid Style: Causality and Deceit in the Eighteenth Century*, *in* THE IDEA OF AMERICA: REFLECTIONS ON THE BIRTH OF THE UNITED STATES, 81, 81–125 (2011). Yet this does nothing to undermine the point that those forces were causally efficacious in American political life. Even if they operated elsewhere, they operated here as well.

or distorted precautions – a kind of miracle of aggregation[113] at the stage of constitution-making. This is merely a possibility. The larger point, however, it that it is hard to see how the constitution-making process can go worse overall if there are at least some public voices for the mature position.

TWO WAYS OF REGULATING POLITICAL RISK

In this chapter and the last, I have contrasted two general approaches to constitutional regulation of second-order political risks: precautionary constitutionalism on the one hand, and optimizing constitutionalism on the other. These approaches lie on a continuum, but for expository purposes a stylized contrast between them is useful, and the arguments apply in sliding-scale fashion as one moves along the continuum. I have argued that the theory and practice of constitution-making in the United States display a running debate between the two camps. From their inception, constitutional precautionary principles have faced critiques based on futility, jeopardy, and perversity – in modern terms, based on tradeoffs between and among multiple political risks, whether on the same dimension or on different dimensions. In light of these critiques, constitutional theorists and judges such as Story and Jackson developed a mature position that, in effect, calls for optimizing, balanced assessment of target risks and countervailing risks.

I believe that the mature position is correct, that it leaves open a wide range of institutional arrangements, but that it has a valuable negative function in laundering out bad arguments and in structuring second-order deliberation about the allocation of power across institutions. The public articulation of the mature position is no panacea for the paranoid political style that sometimes crops up in episodes of constitution-making, but it can hardly make things worse, and under imaginable conditions might even make the process of constitution-making better.

---

[113] Philip E. Converse, *Popular Representation and the Distribution of Information, in* INFORMATION AND DEMOCRATIC PROCESSES 385 (John A. Ferejohn & James H. Kuklinski eds., 1990).

Part II

Applications

3

The Framers' Self-Defeating Precautions

Having laid out competing views on the constitutional regulation of political risk, and given the main lines of the argument for the mature position, the next four chapters turn to applications. The case studies are pitched both at the macro-level of large-scale constitutional structures, in this chapter, and at the micro-level of particularly critical constitutional principles, rules, and legal doctrines, in Chapters 4, 5, and 6.

This chapter explains, critiques, and reformulates James Bryce's brilliant large-scale account of the American constitutional order in his neglected classic of constitutional and political analysis, *The American Commonwealth*,[1] first published in 1888. Bryce argues that Madison's precautionary strategy for channeling and containing majoritarian opinions and passions, by means of complex constitutional structures, had perverse results; it strengthened rather than containing the force of public opinion. The Madisonian strategy, shared by other framers, provides a large-scale illustration of self-defeating precautions against political risks, here the risk of populism. The power of mass opinion in America results in part from the very safeguards the framers put into place against it.

The upshot is that in America, public opinion rules. As a normative matter, the results are mixed; once in place, government by public opinion sets both a lower bound and an upper bound on the performance of the American democracy, ensuring that it performs tolerably well but also preventing it from performing better still. Although the precautionary Madisonian strategy eventually produced a tolerable political regime, it did so fortuitously, by causal pathways that Madison and other framers failed to foresee. Ironically, precautionary constitutionalism, often justified as a hedge against the limits of the knowledge and foresight of

---

[1] 2 James Bryce, The American Commonwealth (Liberty Fund 1995) (3d ed. 1941).

constitutional rulemakers, itself produces unforeseen and possibly damaging results. Unforeseen consequences are on all sides of the issues; they can result from the very precautions taken to guard against them.

THE CONSTITUTION AND PUBLIC OPINION

Bryce's claim is not that the structure of the constitutional order is sufficient, by itself, to bring about the dominance of public opinion; as we will see, Bryce's argument hinges on the interaction between constitutional structures and background political, economic and geographic conditions. Nor does Bryce argue (not clearly anyway) that a Madisonian constitutional structure is necessary to bring about the dominance of public opinion. Even without the framers' self-defeating precautions, public opinion might have become dominant in any event. However, even if a causal factor is neither necessary nor sufficient to bring about a result, it may still raise the probability of that result or supply the actual causal pathway by which the result comes to pass. Bryce does clearly argue that the framers' attempts to check and harness public opinion actually helped to make public opinion dominant in the America of his day, and specifies several mechanisms that brought about that result. I will elicit Bryce's claim by reconstructing his analysis of three critical macro-structures of the Constitution: checks and balances, federalism, and free speech, taking the latter in a broad sense that includes a public culture of free political expression.

CHECKS AND BALANCES

In the Madisonian scheme, two main features of the Constitution are intended to constrain and channel public opinion: the elaborate checks and balances of the federal lawmaking system, and the large scale of the extended Republic. On Madison's part, this was a calculated strategy of *divide et impera*: by pitting ambition against ambition in a system of checks and balances, and by increasing the scale of the republic, the formation of harmful majority factions could be suppressed.[2] Bryce thus observes that "[t]hose who invented this machinery of checks and balances were anxious not so much to develop public opinion as to resist and build

[2] Letter from James Madison to Thomas Jefferson (Oct. 24, 1787), *reprinted in* 10 THE PAPERS OF JAMES MADISON 206 (Robert A. Rutland et al. eds., 1977). On Madison's divide-and-conquer tactics, see Eric A. Posner, Kathryn E. Spier & Adrian Vermeule, *Divide and Conquer*, 2 J. LEGAL ANALYSIS 417 (2010).

up breakwaters against it."[3] Writing as Publius in Federalist 63, Madison famously advocated "the total exclusion of the people, in their collective capacity, from any share" in the operation of government, except through the (largely indirect) choice of representatives.[4]

One of Bryce's themes, however, is that the framers' choices, aims, and plans repeatedly misfired. To be sure, the framers had succeeded in their main task, the creation of a functioning political order:

> It must never be forgotten that the main object which the framers of the Constitution set before themselves has been achieved. When Sieyes was asked what he had done during the Reign of Terror, he answered, "I lived." The Constitution as a whole has stood and stands unshaken.[5]

Yet even this minimal success came about *despite* the framers' calculations rather than *because of* them, through causal pathways they did not anticipate. Later constitutional theorists have emphasized that the framers' design failed to foresee the rise of political parties and the passions surrounding slavery, but Bryce goes farther; he argues that "these wisest men of their time did not foresee what strike us now as the specially characteristic virtues and faults of American democracy."[6] In general, the fog of uncertainty is so thick in large-scale matters of government that "beyond the near future – that is to say, beyond the lifetime of the generation which already holds power – no true philosopher will venture."[7]

In this vein, Bryce argues that the Madisonian strategy of dividing government into competing branches perversely increased the force of public opinion. Where "the ordinary functions and business of government … are parcelled out among a number of bodies and persons whose powers are so carefully balanced and touch at so many points … there is a constant risk of conflicts, even of deadlocks."[8] The system of checks and balances, in other words, creates a series of actual or anticipated constitutional showdowns,[9] in which branches of government – perhaps acting at the behest of political parties, perhaps acting out of genuine institutional

---

[3] 2 BRYCE, *supra* note, at 926.

[4] THE FEDERALIST No. 63, at 397 (James Madison) (Henry Cabot Lodge ed., 1888) (emphasis omitted).

[5] 1 BRYCE, *supra* note, at 275.

[6] 2 BRYCE, *supra* note, at 20.

[7] *Id.* at 1541–42.

[8] *Id.* at 925–26.

[9] *See* Eric A. Posner & Adrian Vermeule, *Constitutional Showdowns*, 156 U. PA. L. REV. 991, 1005–10 (2008).

interest[10] – fall into conflict over first-order policies or over second-order rules for the allocation of authority to determine first-order policies. "In such cases there is a stoppage of governmental action which may involve loss to the country."[11]

Yet these deadlocks and showdowns do not usually result in paralysis; they are settled by the overwhelming force of public opinion tilting in favor of one side or another. "The master ... is at hand to settle the quarrels of his servants. If the question be a grave one, and the mind of the country clear upon it, public opinion throws its weight into one or other scale, and its weight is decisive."[12] Crucially, the power of public opinion to resolve showdowns is not just a given; at least in part, it is itself an endogenous product of the system that produces the showdowns. "[A] system of government by checks and balances specially needs the presence of an arbiter to incline the scale in favour of one or other of the balanced authorities, [so] that public opinion must therefore be more frequently invoked and more constantly active in America than in other countries."[13]

Here Bryce's account verges on functionalism in the pejorative sense. It may be that a system of checks and balances has special need for an authoritative arbiter; it does not follow that an arbiter must come into being, or that public opinion will be that arbiter. The microfoundations of the account are thus unclear. Yet Bryce's reference to public opinion being "invoked" hints at a methodologically respectable mechanism. Parties to the deadlock – political parties who control one or another branch of government, or officials pressing individual interests or the institutional interests of the branch they control – have every interest in mobilizing latent public majorities to overawe their opponents with the threat of defeat at re-election. The resulting public opinion will be in part endogenously shaped by the political actors, and in part an exogenous constraint on their behavior.

Bryce also offers a second mechanism, in some tension with the first:

> [T]he efforts made in 1787 to divide authority and, so to speak, force the current of the popular will into many small channels instead of permitting it to rush down one broad bed, have really tended to exalt public opinion above the regular legally appointed organs of government. Each of these

---

[10] Daryl J. Levinson & Richard Pildes, *Separation of Parties, Not Powers*, 119 HARV. L. REV. 2311 (2006).

[11] 2 BRYCE, *supra* note, at 926.

[12] *Id.*

[13] *Id.*

organs is too small to form opinion, too narrow to express it, too weak to give effect to it. It grows up not in Congress, not in State legislatures, not in those great conventions which frame platforms and choose candidates, but at large among the people.[14]

Here the implicit contrast is between a system of separated legislative and executive powers, on the one hand, and a parliamentary system on the other. The latter provides "one broad bed" through which the waters of public opinion may rush, producing the formation of a dominant parliamentary majority. In contrast the separation of powers, by attempting to break up the force of those waters into many channels, causes the flood of public opinion to overflow its banks and act outside of political institutions narrowly conceived. The framers' precautions proved self-defeating because they acted, and could act, only on one margin – the design of governmental institutions – while overlooking that public opinion might escape institutional constraints altogether.

Taking Bryce's logic to an extreme, the elaborate vetogates of the federal constitution might even bring about pressure to subvert the constitution itself, as I discussed in Chapter 2. In times of economic crisis, if there is pent-up popular demand for new policies – such as redistributive measures – whose enactment is thwarted by the supermajoritarian system of checks and balances, the result might not be a stable status quo but instead a populist Caesarism that sweeps aside the institutional barriers to reform.[15] Bryce nowhere suggests this; on the contrary, his view is that "Caesarism is the last danger likely to menace America."[16] It is not clear, however, that anything in Bryce's theory entitles him to stop short of this ultimate possibility.[17] Such a sequence would merely illustrate, in an extreme form, that the measures by which the framers of the federal constitution attempted to constrain and moderate public opinion may themselves induce an aroused public to slip off the bonds of constitutionalism altogether – a version of the Hamiltonian claim that excessive weakness of government has a dynamic tendency to mutate into excessive strength.

---

[14] *Id.* at 926–27 (emphasis added).

[15] For elaboration and citations to comparative evidence pro and con, see Adrian Vermeule, *Regulating Political Risks*, 47 Tulsa L. Rev. 241 (2011).

[16] 2 BRYCE, *supra* note, at 1244.

[17] Here Bryce illustrated his own point that political predictions are highly likely to err; his low estimate of the risks of Caesarism in America rested in part on the belief, spectacularly falsified by the 20th century, that "[n]o political system would offer a greater resistance to an attempt to create a standing army or centralize the administration." *Id.*

THE SCALE OF THE REPUBLIC

For Madison, the large scale of the new republic would be an effective guarantor against majoritarian oppression. As Publius put it, "[e]xtend the sphere [of the republic] and you take in a greater variety of parties and interests; you make it less probable that a majority of the whole will have a common motive to invade the rights of other citizens; or if such a common motive exists, it will be more difficult for all who feel it to discover their own strength and to act in unison with each other."[18] The underlined passage anticipates the theory of pluralistic ignorance[19]: members of a majority who are uncertain of the preferences and beliefs of others may be unaware that they form a majority, and Publius suggests that this becomes more likely as the scale of the republic increases, presumably due to higher costs of information.

Bryce recognizes that geographic scale raises the costs of assembling a majority coalition,[20] but he argues that the extended-republic strategy partially backfires as well, because the very scale of the American polity exacerbates the fatalism of the multitude. Given some antecedent tendency on the part of minorities to surrender to the beliefs and preferences of majorities, then the size of the polity acts as a multiplier:

> The larger the scale on which the majority works, the more potent are these tendencies. When the scene of action is a small commonwealth, the individual voters are many of them personally known to one another, and the causes that determine their votes are understood and discounted.... But when the theatre stretches itself to a continent, when the number of voters is counted by many millions, the wings of imagination droop, and the huge voting mass ceases to be thought of as merely so many individual human beings no wiser or better than one's own neighbors.... It inspires a sort of awe, a sense of individual impotence, like that which man feels when he contemplates the majestic and eternal forces of the inanimate world. Such a feeling is even stronger when it operates, not on a cohesive minority which had lately hoped, or may yet hope, to become a majority, but on a single man or small group of persons cherishing some opinion which the mass disapproves.[21]

---

[18] THE FEDERALIST NO. 10, at 59 (James Madison) (Henry Cabot Lodge ed., 1888) (emphasis added).

[19] FLOYD H. ALLPORT, SOCIAL PSYCHOLOGY 305–09 (1924).

[20] 2 BRYCE, *supra* note, at 1540 ("The spirit of faction has certainly, as Madison expected, proved less intense over the large area of the Union than it did in the Greek republics of antiquity or in the several states from 1776 to 1789.").

[21] *Id.* at 997–98.

Here we may, without stretching too much, read Bryce as suggesting that the pluralistic ignorance on which Publius relied is a double-edged sword. The larger the republic, the less likely it is that minorities know that others share their preferences or beliefs, and the more isolated any given member of a minority feels. The scale of the republic, in other words, has effects on two margins, not merely one: it both makes it more difficult for majorities to organize to oppress minorities (Publius's point), but also make it more difficult for minorities to organize to resist majorities (Bryce's point). The overall effect of these countervailing tendencies is unclear *a priori*, implying that Madison was too confident that a large republic would provide a structural check on majoritarianism. Bryce's contribution is not to overthrow Publius's argument about the effects of the extended republic altogether, but rather to show that the issues are more complex than Publius realized.

FREE SPEECH

Finally, Bryce's views on the freedom of speech – in the broad sense of a culture of free political discussion, rather than its technical legal sense[22] – also warrant mention here. Although not part of the original Madisonian design for managing public opinion through structural means – the enactment of the First Amendment's guarantee of freedom of speech in 1791 was instead a sop to antifederalist concerns – Bryce's account of free speech fits into the larger theme: measures intended to protect minorities from majoritarian oppression may have the perverse effect of exacerbating the fatalism of the multitude, and may thus dampen minorities' ability to oppose majoritarian measures.

Bryce is explicit that "the unbounded freedom of discussion" tends to make the multitude fatalistic, and thus ensures that "[r]arely does anyone hold out and venture to tell the great majority of his countrymen that they are wrong."[23] Far from increasing the expression of dissent by minorities, the unbounded freedom of discussion reduces it. In Bryce's diagnosis, the very absence of majoritarian repression makes it seem hopeless to resist the majority's decision, once taken:

> Under a repressive government, the sense of grievance and injustice feeds the
> flame of resistance in a persecuted minority. But in a country like this, where

---

[22] As of 1890 the Supreme Court had yet to invalidate a single state or federal law on free-speech grounds. Thanks to Mike Klarman for this point.
[23] 2 BRYCE, *supra* note, at 1001.

the freedom of the press, the right of public meeting, the right of association and agitation have been legally extended, and are daily exerted, more widely than anywhere else in the world, there is nothing to awaken that sense. He whom the multitude condemns or ignores has no further court of appeal to look to. Rome has spoken. His cause has been heard and judgment has gone against him.[24]

The argument here is structurally parallel to the argument about the scale of the republic. In the latter context, Bryce showed that the variable relied on by Publius had effects on two margins, not one: increasing scale both makes it more difficult for majorities to organize to repress, and also more likely that minorities will spontaneously submit. Here a similar point applies, albeit with a dynamic wrinkle: free discussion makes it easier for minorities to express their views before democratic mechanisms have reached a decision, but that very freedom of discussion saps the minority's motivation to resist decisions once taken, or to attempt to undo them. Majority views may face more critique, dissent, and resistance on the way to an initial victory, but face less ex post resistance and political reconsideration than in regimes with less freedom of discussion. Here too, the net effect on minoritarian expression of dissent is unclear, but Bryce's argument entails that it is simpleminded to assume that maximizing the freedom of discussion will maximize expressed dissent by minorities.

GOVERNMENT BY PUBLIC OPINION EVALUATED

How well does government by public opinion work? Bryce's basic assessment is paradoxical: "one may say that the American democracy is not better just because it is so good."[25] On this view, as against Voltaire's quip that the best is the enemy of the good,[26] it is also true that the good may be the enemy of the still better;[27] American democracy functions at a tolerably high level, yet its very virtues prevent it from attaining a higher level still. Commentators have said that Bryce "wavers between democratic optimism and aristocratic pessimism" about democracy,[28] but I will suggest

---

[24] *Id.* at 999

[25] *Id.* at 1256.

[26] OXFORD DICTIONARY OF QUOTATIONS 797 (5th ed. 1999).

[27] *Cf.* Cass R. Sunstein, *Free Speech Now*, 59 U. CHI. L. REV. 255, 315 (1992) ("To the economists' plea that 'the perfect is the enemy of the good,' we might oppose Dewey's suggestion that 'the better is too often the enemy of the still better.'" (quoting THE PHILOSOPHY OF JOHN DEWEY 652 (John J. McDermott ed., 1973))).

[28] Francis G. Wilson, *James Bryce on Public Opinion: Fifty Years Later*, 3 PUB. OPINION Q. 420, 430 (1939).

that he has a coherent position: the structural determinants of the quality of American democracy both push it to a moderately high level and also create an upper bound that limits further improvement. The appearance of vacillation is an illusion stemming from the double-edged character of that position.

FAILURES AND SUCCESSES OF PUBLIC OPINION

In one pair of chapters, Bryce discusses the failures and successes of public opinion; in another related pair, he dismisses false claims about the faults of democracy and specifies its true faults. Bryce's discussion is multifaceted, but I will focus on the main lines of this account, at the cost of some oversimplification.

Distilled, Bryce believes that government by public opinion is better at determining social *ends* than is representative government on the Westminster model, yet is worse at determining *means*.[29]

> Since every question that arises in the conduct of government is either a question of ends or a questions of means, errors may be committed by the ruling power either by fixing on wrong ends or in choosing wrong means to secure those ends. It is now, after long resistance by those who maintained that they knew better what was good for the people than the people knew themselves, at last agreed that as the masses are better judges of what will conduce to their own happiness than are the classes placed above them, they must be allowed to determine the ends. This is in fact the essence of free or popular government, and the justification for vesting power in numbers. But assuming the end to be given, who is best qualified to select the means for its accomplishment? To do so needs in many cases a knowledge of the facts, a skill in interpreting them, a power of forecasting the results of measures, unattainable by the mass of mankind. Such knowledge is too high for them. It is attainable only by trained economists, legists, statesmen. If the masses attempt it they will commit mistakes not less serious than those which befall a litigant who insists on conducting a complicated case instead of leaving

---

[29] Bryce is well aware that the distinction between ends and means can become blurry in hard cases. "Often it is one which cannot be sharply drawn, because some ends are means to larger ends, and some means are desired not only for the sake of larger ends, but for their own sakes also." 2 Bryce, *supra* note, at 1251. But he appears to assume, in a pragmatic spirit, that in matters of government there are a good number of easy cases in which the distinction is perfectly intelligible, as when the public desires a certain overall tax burden, and the technical question for policymakers is what type of tax or mix of taxes will implement that burden most efficiently. I will assume that the distinction is basically intelligible across a range of cases.

it to his attorney and counsel. But in popular governments this distinction between ends and means is apt to be forgotten.... Thus we find that the *direct government of the multitude* [i.e., government by public opinion] may become dangerous not only because the multitude shares the faults and follies of ordinary human nature, but also because it is intellectually incompetent for the delicate business of conducting the daily work of government, i.e., of choosing and carrying out with vigour and promptitude the requisite executive means.[30]

Bryce's argument here owes a great deal to Tocqueville's comparison of "democratic" and "aristocratic" government. Tocqueville held that democratic government would often be technically incompetent and thus inefficient, yet had the great virtue that "the majority of citizens 'may be mistaken but cannot be in conflict of interest with themselves.'"[31] Although Bryce is comparing representative government with government by public opinion (as two species of the genus "popular government"), rather than comparing aristocratic with democratic government, Bryce's picture of representative government is more or less a picture of the Westminster system of the Victorian era, featuring a large dollop of aristocratic and elite participation within the framework of popular government.[32] In both comparisons, the argument is that mass democracy tends to prevent governing elites from pursuing their own interests at the expense of the general welfare.

Bryce, however, adds two distinctive twists to Tocqueville. First, there is a negative argument against any claim that in virtue of the power of aggregation (the so-called "wisdom of crowds") or the power of group discussion (deliberative democracy) a large number of mediocre voters might be able to determine means better than a highly competent elite: "There is a sense in which it is true that the people are wiser than the wisest man. *But what is true of their ultimate judgment after the lapse of time sufficient for full discussion, is not equally true of decisions that have to be promptly taken.*" Governments must make a class of decisions as to which both technical competence and speed are desirable; government by public opinion can attain one desideratum or the other, but not both at the same time. Methodologically, this point about the *opportunity costs of democracy* is one that aggregative models of collective wisdom and models of deliberative

---

[30] *Id.* at 1251–52 (emphasis added).

[31] *See* JON ELSTER, ALEXIS DE TOCQUEVILLE: THE FIRST SOCIAL SCIENTIST 146 (2009) (citing ALEXIS DE TOCQUEVILLE, DEMOCRACY IN AMERICA 265 (Arthur Goldhammer trans., 2004)).

[32] At the time of writing *The American Commonwealth*, Bryce himself sat in the House of Commons.

democracy are only beginning to take on board.[33] Substantively, as I will discuss shortly, the more competitive the military, economic, and political environment for a given polity, the more flexibility and rapidity of policy adjustment there must be, and the larger this issue looms.

Second, and more importantly, Bryce emphasizes that the limited technical competence of mass public opinion is not just a given, but is at least in part an endogenous product of the dominance of public opinion itself.

> [T]he habit of trusting its own wisdom and enjoying its own power, in which the multitude is encouraged by its leaders and servants, disposes it to ignore the distinction [between ends and means] even where the distinction is clear, and makes it refer to the direct arbitrament of the people matters which the people are unfit to decide, and which they might safely leave to their trained ministers or representatives.[34]

It is not just that under government by public opinion, the dominant masses enforce technically poor decisions on their representatives, on experts, and on elites generally; they do so because of the mass political psychology created by their very dominance. Here Bryce specifies a mechanism that, I will suggest, underpins his paradoxical assessment of American democracy, which "is not better just because it is so good."

THE GOOD AS THE ENEMY OF THE BETTER

Why does the American democracy attain a moderately high level, yet then become incapable of further improvement? Why does it have the vices of its virtues? Bryce's idea might be interpreted in several different ways. In one interpretation, inspired by evolutionary models of gradient climbing,[35] the system of American democracy circa 1890 had reached a kind of local maximum. On this picture, some evolutionary process both pushed the system to the top of a local peak and also prevented it from descending the slope to explore other peaks, even if doing so might allow the eventual attainment of an even higher global maximum. Although this approach would

---

33 For an effort to incorporate time and opportunity costs into a jury-theoretic model of collective search, see Christian List & Adrian Vermeule, *Independence and Interdependence: Lessons from the Hive* (Harvard Law. Sch., Pub. L. & Legal Theory Working Paper No. 10–44, 2010), *available at* http://papers.ssrn.com/sol3/papers.cfm?abstract_id=1693908.

34 2 BRYCE, *supra* note, at 1251–52.

35 JON ELSTER, EXPLAINING SOCIAL BEHAVIOR: MORE NUTS AND BOLTS FOR THE SOCIAL SCIENCES, at 111–13 (2007); SCOTT E. PAGE, DIVERSITY AND COMPLEXITY 79–127 (2011).

fit with Bryce's quasi-evolutionary account of the development of political regimes, that account is underdeveloped and implausible on its face, as I suggested in Part I. Accordingly, I will offer a different interpretation that does not require positing an evolutionary mechanism. On this account, some combination of background conditions and causal processes simultaneously produces both a lower bound and an upper bound on the performance of the American political and constitutional order. Absent that combination, the system might not perform as well as it does, yet might also be able to attain a higher level than is possible with the bounds in place (such a system is "not better just because it is so good"). The lower bound represents Bryce's "democratic optimism," the upper bound his "aristocratic pessimism," yet both are essential parts of an integrated view.

To be clear, the existence of these bounds might be more desirable than any alternative. The bounds might in effect reduce the variance of political outcomes, reducing the risks of very bad outcomes even while reducing the chance of very good ones. Nothing in Bryce implies that he would reject such an argument. His point is simply that one must not expect too much, or too little for that matter, from the American democracy, because the development of government by public opinion structurally constrains it to display a kind of mediocrity.

The question remains, however, where the lower and upper bounds come from. Bryce never distills his paradox into a single compact discussion; instead he adduces somewhat different causes in different settings. I will sort the causes into three categories: exogenous geopolitical factors, exogenous domestic factors, and endogenous effects of government by public opinion. The third is the most complex and the most important, but I will begin with some brief remarks on the first two.

Exogenous geopolitical factors. Like Tocqueville,[36] Bryce noted the favorable geopolitical situation of the United States, which was located on a large continent without serious military or economic competitors. That situation gave the American democracy the luxury of making mistakes that might be fatal in the more competitive environment of the Old World: "America has hitherto been able to afford to squander her resources, and ... no other state threatens her. With her wealth and in her position she can with impunity commit errors which might be fatal to the nations of Western Europe."[37] This state of affairs is analogous to the economic idea

---

[36] ELSTER, *supra* note, at 147.
[37] 2 BRYCE, *supra* note, at 1256.

of "x-inefficiency"[38]: the American democracy does not exploit its full potential because, in the absence of competition, it is not spurred to do so. "This is why the Americans submit, not merely patiently but hopefully, to the defects of their government. The vessel may not be any better built, or found, or rigged than are those which carry the fortunes of the great nations of Europe. She is certainly not better navigated. But for the present at least – it may not always be so – she sails upon a summer sea."[39]

As the ominous aside in the last sentence suggests, the problem Bryce discerned here is that an excessively forgiving environment may remove any incentive to make improvements that may urgently become necessary in the future. The x-inefficient firm has no reason to make the investments necessary to fully efficient operation, yet when competitors arrive, it may be too late to do so.

Exogenous domestic factors. In addition to America's geopolitical situation, Bryce believed that the mass of the American people possessed intrinsic traits of national character that allowed their democracy to function well – not as well as might be, but well enough – despite its manifold institutional defects.

> The defects of the tools are the glory of the workman. The more completely self-acting is the machine, the smaller is the intelligence needed to work it; the more liable it is to derangement, so much greater must be the skill and care applied by one who tends it.... [T]he American people have a practical aptitude for politics, a clearness of vision and capacity for self-control never equaled by any other nation.... Such a people can work any constitution. The danger for them is that this reliance on their skill and their star may make them heedless of the faults of their political machinery, slow to devise improvements which are best applied in quiet times.[40]

On this account, Americans possess a talent for political improvisation that keeps defective institutions functioning. Yet this talent can, over time, actually harm its possessor by undercutting incentives to improve the institutions themselves. This claim about *self-defeating political capacities* interacts with Bryce's claim about the forgiving nature of the American political environment. The harms from an excessive talent for political improvisation will materialize if (1) successful improvisation in a forgiving environment saps any incentive to improve defective institutions; (2)

---

[38] Harvey Leibenstein, *Allocative Efficiency Versus "X-Efficiency,"* 56 AM. ECON. REV. 392 (1966).

[39] 1 BRYCE, *supra* note, at 275.

[40] *Id.* at 263.

institutional improvements are necessary to survival or flourishing in a competitive environment and (3) those improvements cannot be costlessly introduced whenever the environment becomes competitive, either because (3A) there will simply be no time to do so, or because (3B) experimentation with improved institutions has long-run benefits but short-run costs, and is thus too risky under competitive conditions. Here too, the American democracy would be better were it not so good; a people less skilled at improvisation in "quiet times" would be forced to reconfigure their defective institutions before the military, political, and economic environment turned against them.

Endogenous effects of government by public opinion. Finally, government by opinion itself is a contributing cause of the phenomenon Bryce identifies. Government by opinion improves the quality of the American democracy; however, this good effect itself helps to ensure that the American democracy cannot become better still. Here is the full statement of Bryce's conjecture:

> [A] democratic system makes the people self-confident, and that self-confidence may easily pass into a jealousy of delegated power, an undervaluing of skill and knowledge, a belief that any citizen is good enough for any political work. This is perhaps more likely to happen with a people who have really reached a high level of political competence; and so one may say that *the American democracy is not better just because it is so good.* Were it less educated, less shrewd, less actively interested in public affairs, less independent in spirit, it might be more disposed, like the masses in Europe, to look up to the classes which have hitherto done the work of government.[41]

Although read in isolation, this passage might be interpreted to suggest that the citizens' "high level of political competence" is just an exogenous factor, elsewhere Bryce makes it clear that government by public opinion itself tends to increase that political competence.[42] Moreover, the context of the passage indicates that the "democratic system" to which it refers just means the American democratic system of government by public opinion, as opposed to representative democracy.

So read, this highly compressed passage contains a complex set of hypotheses, with causal arrows pointing in multiple directions. (1) Government by public opinion tends to increase political competence. (2) Government by public opinion also tends to increase popular self-confidence. (3) In the presence of increased political competence, popular self-confidence is

[41] *Id.* at 1255–56.
[42] *Id.* at 918–19.

more likely to "pass into" various populist pathologies, such as excessive or irrational distrust of political expertise. The net effect is that government by public opinion both produces one *direct* effect that brings the demos to a tolerably high level (claim (1)), yet also produces a second, *indirect* effect that prevents it from attaining a higher level still (claims (2) and (3)). And the two effects are not themselves mutually independent; rather, the indirect effect is more likely to operate when and because the direct effect operates (the initial clause of claim (3)). The knowledge, on the part of the citizenry, of their own high political competence tends to transmute into excessive self-confidence; the very mechanism that raises the quality of the American democracy prevents it from making further progress. At the heart of this complex hypothesis, then, is a psychological speculation about *political overconfidence bias*,[43] one that is in principle testable but that to my knowledge has not been studied as such. In other words, the validity of the hypothesis that underpins Bryce's normative evaluation of government by public opinion remains an open question.

PRECAUTIONS AND UNFORESEEN CONSEQUENCES

Bryce's deep critique of the American constitutional order contains two lessons, not one. The first is that the framers' large-scale precautions against populism and the government of mass public opinion turned out to be self-defeating. The second is that precautions against unforeseen consequences can themselves bring about other unforeseen consequences.

Only the first lesson is, strictly speaking, a perversity critique of the sort described in Chapter 2. On Bryce's view, the framers' precautions backfired on the very same margin they were intended to regulate; far from dampening the force of public opinion, they exacerbated it. The second lesson is somewhat different. In the longer run, and due to the operation of complex causal mechanisms, the framers' self-defeating precautions ended up producing a constitutional order that is constrained to work tolerably well, but only tolerably well – neither excellently nor abysmally. That was something of a fortuitous outcome, in the double sense that things could have gone worse, and that the outcome came about through political pathways

---

[43] For the general phenomenon of overconfidence bias, see Jayashree Mahajan, *The Overconfidence Effect in Marketing Management Predictions*, 29 J. MARKETING RES. 329 (1992); Stuart Oskamp, *Overconfidence in Case-Study Judgments*, *in* JUDGMENT UNDER UNCERTAINTY: HEURISTICS AND BIASES 287 (Daniel Kahneman et al. eds., 1982); and Paul W. Paese & Maryellen Kinnaly, *Peer Input and Revised Judgment: Exploring the Effects of (Un)biased Confidence*, 23 J. APP. SOC. PSYCH. 1989 (1993).

that the framers entirely failed to anticipate. Bryce's account, then, offers a mordant but sympathetic commentary on the limits of foreknowledge that afflict constitutional rulemakers: quite by chance, the framers' floundering enterprise struggled onto an unknown shore and found itself on decent, habitable terrain.

The sting in this account is that unforeseen consequences can stem from precautions themselves. A centerpiece of arguments for precautionary constitutionalism is that in the face of the limits of foreknowledge, and the uncertainty of our causal theories about politics, constitutional rules should be designed with a margin of safety against possible bad outcomes. Bryce's account illustrates that the conclusion need not follow from the premise, or rather that the conclusion is indeterminate. On precautionary premises, one should also build in a margin of safety against the unforeseen consequences that flow from the precautions themselves, requiring precautions against the precautions. As the argument for the mature position suggests, there is no escape from this conceptual tangle except to say that constitutional rulemakers should engage in optimal risk assessment, all things considered, and in light of all reasonably available information. Attempting to skew the constitutional rules to safeguard against the unforeseen may be precisely what brings the unforeseen about.

4

The Risks of Impartiality: On Judging in One's Own Cause

This chapter and the two that follow turn from the macro-level of the overall constitutional order to the micro-level of particular constitutional rules and principles. The same themes operate at both scales: in the large or in the small, precautionary constitutionalism focuses to excess on targeted political risks while ignoring countervailing risks, collateral harms, and unintended consequences. At either scale, a mature approach to constitutionalism strives for optimal rather than maximal precautions against salient political risks.

In this chapter, I study the political management of impartiality and its various antonyms, especially self-dealing and biased decision making. In constitutional theory, the appeal of impartiality commands widespread consensus; who could be in favor of official self-dealing or bias? Yet I will suggest that as a normative matter, impartiality is a good to be optimized, not maximized; and as a positive matter, U.S. constitutional law surprisingly often abandons the ideal of impartiality in favor of other goods.

The lens through which I will examine impartiality is the legal maxim *nemo iudex in sua causa*[1] – no man should be judge in his own case, or cause. The *nemo iudex* principle is widely thought to capture a bedrock principle

---

[1]   The principle is classically articulated in the Justinian *Codex*, which includes a provision titled *ne quis in sua causa judicet vel jus sibi dicat* or "no one shall be his own judge or decide his own case." Justinian *Codex* 3.5.1, FRED H. BLUME, ANNOTATED JUSTINIAN CODE (Timothy Kearley ed., 2d ed. 2008). The older *Codex Theodosianus* seemingly derives this principle from the rule that no man should be allowed to testify for himself. II.2.1. Similarly, by 1518 "the principle appears as a statement of the 'established' custom of England that peer of a jury 'be not of affinity to none of the parties.'" CHRISTOPHER SAINT GERMAIN, DOCTOR AND STUDENT, 23–24 (William Muchall ed., 1886), *cited in* Frederick Schauer, *English Natural Justice and American Due Process: An Analytical Comparison*, 18 WM. & MARY L. REV. 47, n.20 (1976).

of natural justice and constitutional democracy. The U.S. Supreme Court calls it "a mainstay of our system of government"[2] and regularly invokes it in diverse contexts,[3] most famously as a principle of natural law in *Calder v. Bull*[4] and, implicitly, to justify constitutional judicial review in *Marbury v. Madison*.[5]

I will argue that the *nemo iudex* principle is a misleading half-truth. Sometimes rulemakers in public law do and should design institutions with a view to the *nemo iudex* principle. In other cases, however, they do not and should not. In many settings, public law makes officials or institutions the judges of their own prerogatives, power, or legal authority. Decision-making institutions may determine their own membership, settle their own compensation, rule on the limits of their own jurisdiction, or adjudicate and punish violations of rules they themselves have created. Some examples:

- In many jurisdictions, legislatures determine the boundaries of the districts from which legislators are selected, or more generally structure the system by which they are elected.[6]
- In many jurisdictions, legislatures have broad authority to determine the qualifications of their own members and to expel members.[7]

---

[2] Gutierrez de Martinez v. Lamagno, 515 U.S. 417 (1995).

[3] *See, e.g.*, Nevada Comm'n on Ethics v. Carrigan, 131 S. Ct. 2343, 2348 (2011) (noting the principle that legislators should recuse themselves from voting on questions in which they have a personal interest because "the fundamental principles of the social compact [forbid] ... any man to be a judge in his own case") (quoting THOMAS JEFFERSON, A MANUAL OF PARLIAMENTARY PRACTICE FOR THE USE OF THE UNITED STATES SENATE 31 (1801)); Caperton v. A.T. Massey Coal Co., 556 U.S. 868, 870 (2009) ("[N]o man is allowed to be a judge in his own cause."); Tumey v. Ohio, 273 U.S. 510, 525 (1927) (invoking the principle of *nemo iudex* to hold that an individual's constitutional rights were violated when his case was heard before a judge who had a pecuniary interest in finding that individual guilty); Spencer v. Lapsley, 61 U.S. 264, 266 (1857) (noting that "[t]he act of Congress [at issue] proceeds upon an acknowledgment of the maxim, 'that a man should not be the judge in his own cause'").

[4] Calder v. Bull, 3 U.S. (3 Dall.) 386, 388 (1798) ("a law that makes a man a Judge in his own cause" is an act "contrary to the great first principles of the social compact" that "cannot be considered a rightful exercise of legislative authority").

[5] "To what purpose are powers limited, and to what purpose is that limitation committed to writing, if these limits may, at any time, be passed by those intended to be restrained?" Marbury v. Madison, 5 U.S. (1 Cranch) 137, 176 (1803).

[6] *See, e.g.*, Justin Levitt & Michael P. McDonald, *Taking the "Re" Out of Redistricting: State Constitutional Provisions on Redistricting Timing*, 95 GEO. L.J. 1247, 1255 n.38 (2007) (referring to Indiana, Michigan, Wisconsin, and California's constitutions, which vest the duty of apportionment in those states' legislatures).

[7] *See* H.W. DODDS, PROCEDURE IN STATE LEGISLATURES 3 (1918) ("The right to judge of the elections and qualifications of its own members is expressly conferred upon each by the constitutions of forty-six states.").

- In many jurisdictions, legislatures set their own salaries and compensation.[8]
- The president arguably has the power to pardon himself, and clearly has the power to pardon his friends, family, and advisers.[9]
- The vice president arguably has the power to preside at his own impeachment trial.[10]
- A ubiquitous feature of the administrative state is that agencies combine the functions of rulemaking, prosecution, and adjudication.[11]
- In America, federal judges and many state judiciaries rule on the constitutionality of legislative acts setting judicial salaries.[12]
- In many jurisdictions, judges have the final say over the limits of the judges' power, prerogatives, and jurisdiction.[13]
- A federal judge may rule on her own immunity from suit,[14] rule on motions asking that very judge to recuse herself for bias, and decide whether to hold litigants in contempt for violations of the judge's own commands. At the level of the Supreme Court, each Justice rules on motions asking that Justice to recuse, and the rulings are unreviewable.[15]

The list is heterogeneous on several dimensions, which I will explore at length later, but that very heterogeneity illustrates that the *nemo iudex* principle is qualified in many settings and on many different grounds.

I will offer two claims, one negative or destructive and one positive or constructive. The negative claim is that the *nemo iudex* principle cannot even be understood as a presumption to which public law sometimes makes exceptions. Rather it amounts to little more than a banal counsel

---

[8] *See, e.g.,* Ronald E. Weber, Presidential Address, *The Quality of State Legislative Representation: A Critical Assessment,* 61 J. POL. 609, 610 (1999).

[9] *See* discussion *infra,* at 103–105.

[10] *See* discussion *infra,* at 103 & n.325.

[11] *See* discussion *infra,* at 97–98.

[12] *See* Adrian Vermeule, *The Constitutional Law of Official Compensation,* 102 COLUM. L. REV. 501 (2002).

[13] *See, e.g.,* Paul D. Carrington, *Judicial Independence and Democratic Accountability in Highest State Courts,* 61 LAW & CONTEMP. PROBS., Summer 1998, at 79, 97 (noting that the "highest state courts in several states have a constitutional power to enact procedural rules for use in inferior courts," some state courts have held that "procedural matters are beyond the ken of legislatures and are [those courts' own] exclusive responsibility," and "[i]n some states, the power to enforce standards of judicial conduct is vested within the judicial branch").

[14] *See, e.g.,* Pierson v. Ray, 386 U.S. 547 (1967) (explaining that judges enjoy absolute immunity from suit for actions taken in the exercise of their judicial functions).

[15] *See* Louis J. Virelli III, *The (Un)constitutionality of Supreme Court Recusal Standards,* 2011 WIS. L. REV. 1181.

that impartiality is sometimes an important value in institutional design. Yet the value of impartiality constantly trades off against and competes with other values. Far from being a mainstay of our system of government, the most that can be said is that the *nemo iudex* principle sometimes holds, and sometimes doesn't.

More constructively, I will attempt to identify the main grounds on which, and the main conditions under which, rulemakers depart from, override, or qualify the *nemo iudex* principle. As we will see, in some cases there is no impartial official or institution in the picture, so that wherever decision-making authority is lodged, someone or other will have to be the judge in his own case. In other cases, even where it would be feasible to respect the *nemo iudex* principle, the costs of doing so will exceed the benefits. In general, this will be so when and because impartiality trades off against one of several competing considerations: the benefits of expertise, the value of institutional autonomy and independence, or the motivation and activity level of officials or institutions.

The upshot is that it is *never* a sufficient constitutional argument to point out that a proposed institution, or a proposed interpretation of ambiguous constitutional rules or practices, would violate the *nemo iudex* principle or would "put the fox in charge of the henhouse." One must go on to ask whether the conflict is avoidable or unavoidable, and if it is avoidable, whether it would be good or bad overall to avoid it. In a range of cases, violations of *nemo iudex* are either unavoidable or affirmatively desirable, on balance.

The largest aim is to illustrate my overall thesis about how constitutional and institutional designers do and should manage political risks. Among the various risks that rulemakers in public law must consider is the risk of self-dealing or self-serving bias on the part of decision-making officials or institutions. Yet there are many countervailing risks to consider, which implies that rulemakers will have to trade off those risks against one another; rather than selecting maximal precautions against official or institutional self-dealing, they will have to select optimal precautions. In the most pointed cases, the *nemo iudex* principle appears on both sides of the balance, so that preventing self-dealing by one decision maker will increase the risks of self-dealing by another decision maker. In such cases, the principle is in conflict with itself and an appeal to it will necessarily be question-begging. A mature analysis will consider risks of partiality and bias that may arise on all sides of the relevant institutional questions, and will also consider other political risks that a focus on promoting impartiality may create or exacerbate.

Nemo Iudex AND CLOSE RELATIVES

Although I will speak throughout of "the *nemo iudex* principle," this is actually a simplification for ease of exposition. In fact there are multiple subprinciples at work, and a congeries of Latin tags. These tags include *nemo debet esse iudex in propria causa* ("no man should be judge in his own cause") and *nemo potest esse simul actor et iudex* ("no man can be both litigant and judge at the same time"); the last version clarifies that the principle forbids simultaneous judging and litigation, in the very same case.

Core and periphery. If there is an inviolable core to these maxims – and I will later suggest that there isn't – the core is that no person should be literally permitted to judge his own cause, by sitting as a judge over litigation to which the person is a named party. There are, however, a variety of ways of extending *nemo iudex* outward from this situation. For one thing, the principle is often said to apply when judges sit to decide cases in which they have a more or less direct financial interest, even if the judge himself is not also one of the nominal litigants. A slight further extension involves cases in which the judge's relative or friends have a financial interest. Still further out are cases in which the judge's interest is that the case might expand the power or perquisites of the judicial branch as a whole, in which the judge holds only a fractional share, or of the government as a whole, in which the judge's fractional share is smaller still. Finally, the most aggressive extensions posit that not merely an interest in the litigation, but an appearance of an interest, such that the judges' impartiality "might reasonably be questioned,"[16] suffices to trigger the principle.

Although the principle and its relatives speak of judging, they have long since been extended to embrace other types of decision making, which the invoker of the principle implicitly analogizes to judging. When Madison invoked the principle in Federalist 10 to describe a majority legislative faction voting for legal rules that would favor the interests of that faction,[17] the usage was at least doubly and perhaps triply metaphorical. Not only

---

[16] *See* 28 U.S.C.A. § 455(a) (2006) ("Any justice, judge, or magistrate judge of the United States shall disqualify himself in any proceeding in which his impartiality might reasonably be questioned."); Liteky v. United States, 510 U.S. 540, 548 (1994) ("[q]uite simply and quite universally, recusal [is] required whenever 'impartiality might reasonably be questioned'").

[17] THE FEDERALIST No. 10, at 59 (James Madison) (Jacob E. Cooke ed., 1961) ("No man is allowed to be a judge in his own cause; because his interest would certainly bias his judgment, and, not improbably, corrupt his integrity.").

did the issue involve legislative rather than judicial voting, but the interests at issue were indirect rather than direct; and depending on whether Madison saw the interests of the faction as collective or distributed among the individuals who make up that faction, the cause that any given legislator was "judging" might be collective rather than individual.[18]

Where executive officials apply settled law to facts – a class of decisions that is hard to distinguish from judging, except by reference to the institutional attributes of the decision maker – the Court has also invoked *nemo iudex*. In *Gutierrez de Martinez v. Lamagno*,[19] the question was whether a court could review a certification by the Attorney General that a federal employee sued for a tort was acting within the scope of federal employment. In the circumstances of the case, the certification would have had the effect of immunizing the employee from litigation, and the Court saw this as implicating *nemo iudex*, on the ground that the Attorney General would be acting as judge in her own cause. Not only was this an extension of the maxim to executive decisions rather than judicial ones, but the Court's description of the Attorney General's decision as judging in her *own* cause was highly strained. At most, as the dissent pointed out, the Attorney General would be favoring the interests of other federal employees.[20]

Reformulations? One line of response to the many examples in which the constitutional system violates *nemo iudex*, as broadly understood by the Court and by commentators, is simply to reformulate the principle. Reformulations might address either (or both) of two margins, the weight of the principle and its scope. The former strategy would say that the principle does apply broadly, just with reduced force. The latter would attempt to preserve the strong force of the principle within some narrower domain.

Reformulation by reducing the weight of the principle is fully compatible with my account. Later, I will attempt to show that the principle identifies impartiality as an institutional good under certain conditions, that impartiality is merely one good among the many goods that institutional designers must take into account, and that in a wide range of cases rulemakers will have to trade off these goods against one another. So I

---

[18] "With equal, nay with greater reason, a body of men, are unfit to be both judges and parties, at the same time; yet, what are many of the most important acts of legislation, but so many judicial determinations, not indeed concerning the rights of single persons, but concerning the rights of large bodies of citizens; and what are the different classes of legislators, but advocates and parties to the causes which they determine?" *Id.*

[19] 515 U.S. 417 (1995).

[20] *Id.* at 448–49 (Souter, J., dissenting).

have no quarrel in principle with this approach. To be clear, however, this would indeed be a novel reformulation. The traditional conception holds that *nemo iudex* is an "inflexible"[21] principle that is fundamental to the legal system, rather than a mere reminder that impartial decision making is sometimes a good thing, in the right circumstances.

A different strategy would constrict the scope of the principle, in order to preserve its force within the new, narrower scope. The reformulation would say that *nemo iudex* as such applies only to cases in which judges are also named litigants, and presumably also to cases in which judges have a direct pecuniary interest in the outcome. Other institutional structures that create risks of partial or biased decision making might then be labeled (mere) "conflicts of interest" and deemed subject to institutional tradeoffs.

For several reasons, however, this approach fares poorly. The historical genesis of the principle is not at all consistent with the approach. Consider *Dr. Bonham's Case*, frequently cited for the sacrosanct status of *nemo iudex*, and according to some the foundation for something like constitutional judicial review.[22] The facts of the case involved an institutional conflict of interest, in which a chartered College of Physicians claimed legal authority to fine or imprison physicians practicing without a license. Coke's invocation of *nemo iudex* objected to this arrangement because it made the members of the college into "judges, ministers and parties" simultaneously,[23] but we will see that similar institutional conflicts of interest on the part of public and quasi-public agencies are a routine feature of the modern administrative state. If the reformulated principle condemns this sort of arrangement, it is too broad; if it does not, then it does not

---

[21] GEORGE FREDERICK WHARTON, LEGAL MAXIMS WITH OBSERVATIONS AND CASES 117 (New York, Baker, Voorhis & Co. 1878) ("The rule [of the *nemo iudex* maxim] is inflexible, and as well the king as the commoner is subjected to it").

[22] There is a running debate among legal historians on the question whether *Bonham's Case* counts as an example of judicial review of parliamentary legislation. For recent analyses, see PHILIP HAMBURGER, LAW AND JUDICIAL DUTY 622–30 (2008); and R.H. Helmholz, *Bonham's Case, Judicial Review, and the Law of Nature*, 1 J. LEGAL ANALYSIS 325 (2009).

[23] As to the College's power to levy fines, it appears that the College would receive a part of the fines, and in this sense had a pecuniary interest. But that was a corporate pecuniary interest, not a direct individual one; presumably the fines would go to the College's treasury, not into the pockets of the members who judged the case. (When federal judges levy fines, of course, the money likewise goes into the treasury of the organization that pays their salaries.) And in any event, the point would not apply to the College's power to imprison, which for Coke and the plaintiff was at least as objectionable as the power to fine.

even encompass *Dr. Bonham's Case* – the leading *nemo iudex* precedent at common law.

Furthermore, current constitutional law simply cannot be squared with the reformulation. On one hand, the Court invokes *nemo iudex* in situations that lie outside the scope of the narrowed reformulation, as in the attenuated circumstances of *Gutierrez de Martinez*.[24] On the other hand, constitutional law licenses violations of *nemo iudex* even in situations that should lie squarely within the core. When federal judges sit to decide cases concerning judicial salaries – cases brought by judge-plaintiffs to determine the salaries of the whole group of sitting judges, including the judges who will decide the case itself – there is no attenuated conflict of interest, but rather a direct violation. If the plaintiff-judges represent a class that includes the judge-judges, then the latter are litigants *eo nomine* and the violation of the *nemo iudex* maxim is quite literal. One cannot salvage *nemo iudex* by constricting its scope, trying to hive off the institutional violations while preserving a core domain for the principle, if at least some of the violations themselves lie within the core. Whatever the normative justifications for the reformulation – and I will argue in later sections that the normative arguments are complex and highly contingent – it fails the test of fit with current law.

All told, the *nemo iudex* principle is invoked promiscuously, in a range of different settings with different decision makers and different types of decisions. My suggestion, however, is that the principle is not consistently honored in any of these settings, whether inside or outside the situation of self-judging that lies at the putative core of *nemo iudex*. It is useful here to compare *nemo iudex* with any one of the many settled principles that indisputably pervade our morality and law – say, the principle that it is a legal and moral wrong to intentionally kill another person.[25] That principle is something like a presumption subject to exceptions, such as self-defense and defense of third parties. But those exceptions are plausibly deemed exceptional, relative to the large domain within which the principle unquestionably applies. By contrast, the list I gave earlier suggests that central structural features of the constitutional system are inconsistent with *nemo iudex*, not only in its broadest formulations but even in its narrower putative core. And as I will suggest later, constitutional rules and structures that are plausibly based on *nemo iudex* are for the most part afterthoughts – second-decimal adjustments or minor side-constraints.

---

[24] *See, e.g., Gutierrez de Martinez,* 515 U.S. 417.
[25] Thanks to John Goldberg for suggesting this comparison.

The upshot is that there are two ways of characterizing the actual scope and weight of *nemo iudex* in our constitutional and legal order. One might say *that nemo iudex* is a sham principle because it is more exception than rule, like a house that is mostly made of doors. Alternatively, one might say that *nemo iudex* is a genuine principle, just one that is both weak within the domain in which it applies, and that is also riddled with a large set of ill-defined exceptions – something like the moral principle against lying, which is frequently defeasible and actually defeated, and which is likewise riddled with a large set of ill-defined exceptions. Which of these two characterizations is best will turn, in part, on what counts as a "principle," a jurisprudential issue that I will leave to philosophers of law. For the purposes of constitutional theory, I need not choose between the two characterizations, because both are inconsistent with the traditional legal claim that *nemo iudex* is a mainstay or axiom of the American constitutional order. Whether described as a sham principle or as a weak and porous principle, *nemo iudex* amounts to far less than the received wisdom suggests.

In light of the numerous tradeoffs that I will detail later, *nemo iudex* is best understood merely as one competing consideration among many. *Nemo iudex* points to the value of impartial decision making, but there are many institutional goods besides impartiality, and in many settings rulemakers decide that those other goods are more important under the circumstances, or that none of the feasible institutional arrangements can produce impartiality. Or so I will proceed to argue.

THE COSTS OF AN IMPARTIAL DECISION MAKER

Where two parties are in conflict, appointing a third, impartial arbiter can be a costly exercise. If the state subsidizes the appointment, as when the state maintains a system of courts to which all parties may have nearly free access, those costs are subsidized and spread across all taxpayers. In some settings, however, the out-of-pocket costs of obtaining an impartial judgment may be decisive. Although this point is so obvious as to be nearly trivial, it illustrates that *nemo iudex* is subject to cost constraints.

In local tennis tournaments, for example, a common arrangement is that referees are present only for the last few rounds. In earlier rounds, the players themselves judge whether balls hit towards their side are in or out, in effect becoming judges in their own cause. The principal reason for this regime is that it is simply too expensive to staff local tournaments with a large complement of referees for all matches in the early rounds.

In theory, this structure also illustrates another idea: offsetting violations of *nemo iudex* may mimic impartiality.[26] In this example, because each player judges the shots hit to their own side, each is judge in her own cause, and thus both players are in a kind of repeat-play relationship for the duration of the match; the players thus have a tit-for-tat incentive to make fair calls. This mechanism is highly fragile, however. Self-serving bias is pervasive even if the players are seeking to cooperate, and crucial calls late in the match will no longer take place under an indefinite horizon of future cooperation. The result is defection and blatantly self-serving calls, which increase as the match progresses.

The constitutional system can draw on a cadre of state-subsidized impartial decision makers – the judges – so the cost constraint is ameliorated. However, it is still the case that the constraint bites to some degree. Statutes require federal judges to recuse themselves from a case when their impartiality "might reasonably be questioned,"[27] and if recusal occurs, a second judge is called in to preside. However, the first judge rules on the disqualification motion, and thus assesses her own bias, subject to deferential review.[28] One of the main justifications for this practice is the simple "inefficiency"[29] of calling in a second judge to decide a preliminary motion of this sort – although as we will see in Section III, there are other justifications as well. More generally, one of the reasons that officials cannot instantly obtain an impartial judicial opinion on the legal validity of their actions is that resource constraints create a queue for the use of the courts. The delay that is part and parcel of constitutional litigation arises, in part, simply because it is not feasible to create a cadre of judges of the size that would be necessary to eliminate the delay.

TRADEOFFS

I now turn to a more important set of cases in which the benefits of an impartial decision maker trade off against, and may be outweighed by, other goods or values. These tradeoffs are hardly susceptible of scientific analysis. In such cases, rulemakers engage in an impressionistic balancing, with ill-specified weights, under conditions of grave uncertainty. But the

---

[26] *Cf.* Jon Elster, *Mimicking Impartiality, in* JUSTICE AND DEMOCRACY: ESSAYS FOR BRIAN BARRY 112 (Keith Dowding, Robert E. Goodin & Carole Pateman eds., 2004).

[27] 28 U.S.C. § 455(a),.

[28] Susan B. Hoekema, *Questioning the Impartiality of Judges: Disqualifying Federal District Court Judges Under 28 U.S.C. § 455(a)*, 60 TEMP. L.Q. 697, 698 (1987).

[29] *Id.* at 713.

rulemakers cannot simply throw up their hands in the face of the conceptual and empirical difficulties; some rule or other must be chosen, and as we will see, rulemakers will sometimes have substantial reasons to conclude that *nemo iudex* should give way.

In terms of the categories laid out in Chapter 2, the tradeoffs I will now examine amount to jeopardy arguments: rulemakers compromise *nemo iudex* because doing so is necessary to address countervailing risks on other margins. Where the countervailing risk lies on the same margin – a risk that nemo iudex precautions will themselves create or exacerbate self-dealing or self-serving bias – the issue is one of perversity. I will take up such cases later in the chapter.

IMPARTIALITY AND EXPERTISE

In the theory of institutional design, a standard tradeoff involves a conflict between the values of impartiality and expertise. In some settings, the bias of decision makers can be reduced only by reducing the information they hold or their incentives to invest in acquiring new information. The rules for selecting petit juries exclude jurors with antecedent knowledge of the case in order to minimize bias, in contrast to the medieval English rules, under which jurors were selected from the locality. It has been argued that the impartiality produced by adversarial rules of litigation, which prohibit *ex parte* presentations and restrict the judges' ability to gather relevant information outside of court, have the effect of reducing the judges' information.[30] Conversely, selecting the most informed decision makers brings with it an increased risk of bias. In the administrative state, agencies are often staffed by actors with close ties to regulated groups. Although such actors are more likely to have an agenda, where the regulated domain is highly complex, actors of that sort will typically have indispensable specialized knowledge.[31]

Judicial bias and disqualification. Where the *nemo iudex* principle is qualified or violated, the actual or stated justification is sometimes that enforcing the principle would produce unacceptable costs by eliminating expertise or weeding out the best-informed decision makers. In the judicial

---

[30] Neil Komesar, *Stranger in A Strange Land: An Outsider's View of Antitrust and the Courts*, 41 LOY. U. CHI. L.J. 443, 446 (2010).

[31] *See* Saul Levmore, *Efficiency and Conspiracy: Conflicts of Interest, Anti-Nepotism Rules, and Separation Strategies*, 66 FORDHAM L. REV. 2099 (1998); Dorit Rubinstein Reiss, *The Benefits of Capture*, 47 WAKE FOREST L. REV. 569 (2012).

setting, judges rule on motions for disqualification, in effect ruling on their own bias rather than calling in a second judge. Although relevant statutes allow the inferior judges' rulings on their own bias to be reviewed by higher courts, the review is deferential (and decisions about recusal by Supreme Court Justices themselves are not reviewable at all).

One of the standard justifications for this set of rules is that the second judge lacks the first's information about the background circumstances of the case. The Court has held that the rules governing judicial bias and recusal contain an implied exception: bias in the pejorative sense arises only if the judge's preconceptions derive from an "extrajudicial source." Preconceptions that the judge has formed during preliminary stages of the proceeding, or related earlier proceedings, do not generally count as "bias" of the sort the law will find invidious. The justification for the exception is based in part on the value of the information held by the presiding judge, which would be lost if previous determinations in the case could create grounds for disqualification. As the Court put it in *Liteky v. United States*,[32]

> [t]he judge who presides at a trial may, upon completion of the evidence, be exceedingly ill disposed towards the defendant.... But the judge is not thereby recusable for bias or prejudice, since his knowledge and the opinion it produced were properly and necessarily acquired in the course of the proceedings, *and are indeed sometimes (as in a bench trial) necessary to completion of the judge's task*. As Judge Jerome Frank pithily put it: 'Impartiality is not gullibility. Disinterestedness does not mean child-like innocence.'[33]

By contrast, the rules for selecting petit jurors strictly maximize impartiality and thus in effect require child-like innocence.

Legislative districting. A similar tradeoff between impartiality and information can be observed in legislative settings. In most jurisdictions, legislatures determine the composition of the districts from which the legislators themselves are selected – an institutional conflict of interest that may produce incumbent-favoring gerrymanders, partisan gerrymanders, or collusive bipartisan gerrymanders. Many commentators thus call for independent and nonpartisan districting by expert commissions or courts.[34]

---

[32] 510 U.S. 540 (1994).

[33] *Id.* at 550–51 (quoting *In re* J.P. Linahan, Inc., 138 F.2d 650, 654 (2d Cir. 1943)) (emphasis added).

[34] *See, e.g.*, Jeffrey C. Kubin, *The Case for Redistricting Commissions*, 75 Tex. L. Rev. 837, 854 (1997) (arguing that "redistricting criteria can still play a role in limiting the gerrymanderer's options" because, "in order to satisfy potential state and federal court

One of the main defenses of the current regime, however, is that legislative redistricting is desirable because legislators possess crucial information about relevant constituencies and their distinctive problems – information that is perhaps held in a largely tacit or experiential form, and thus cannot be easily transmitted to nonlegislative redistricting bodies.[35] On this view, the basic tradeoff is that on the one hand, "incumbents' knowledge of their districts gives them almost unparalleled expertise as to the effect of a given set of lines and insiders are more likely to be sensitive to community concerns," while, on the other hand, "bipartisan or partisan gerrymanders sometimes intentionally disrupt or divide communities and often ignore policy goals en route to creating safe seats."[36] However, this tradeoff cashes out, and whatever the optimal design of redistricting institutions in a given political environment, it is fatally simplistic to condemn legislative redistricting on the ground that it puts the fox in charge of the henhouse.[37]

Administrative combination of functions. Perhaps the largest compromise of the *nemo iudex* principle to be found in public law is the combination of functions in administrative agencies – a routine feature of the massive administrative state. Although the variety of administrative institutions and procedures is bewildering, many agencies in some way or another combine the powers of rulemaking, investigation and prosecution, and adjudication. Such agencies, in other words, may decide cases that they themselves have investigated and decided to bring, under rules that they themselves have made. From a traditional perspective, this combination of functions makes the agencies both parties and judges – a violation of the core of the *nemo iudex* principle. Libertarian and originalist

review, gerrymanderers must conform their maps to the redistricting criteria contained within their commission's charge."); Laughlin McDonald, *The Looming 2010 Census: A Proposed Judicially Manageable Standard and Other Reform Options for Partisan Gerrymandering*, 46 HARV. J. ON LEGIS. 243, 266 (2009) (noting that options for redistricting reform include "limiting redistricting to once in a decade and putting redistricting in the hands of a non-partisan redistricting commission"); J. Gerald Hebert & Marina K. Jenkins, *The Need for State Redistricting Reform to Rein in Partisan Gerrymandering*, 29 YALE L. & POL'Y REV. 543, 558 (2011) (arguing that "[s]tate-level redistricting reform, particularly in the form of independent redistricting commissions, is absolutely necessary in order to fulfill the promise of government for the people, by the people").

35 Nathaniel Persily, *In Defense of Foxes Guarding Henhouses: The Case for Judicial Acquiescence to Incumbent-Protecting Gerrymanders*, 116 HARV. L. REV. 649, 671 (2002).

36 *Id.* at 678–79.

37 *Id.*

critics of the administrative state thus routinely complain that agencies act as judges in their own cause.[38]

As discussed in Chapter 2, however, both Congress and the Supreme Court have rejected such claims. The Administrative Procedure Act requires that separate personnel perform the functions of investigation and prosecution, on the one hand, and adjudication, on the other, at lower levels of the administrative agency.[39] However, the statute exempts the agency or its members – that is, the top-level agency heads or commissioners – from this separation requirement;[40] many agency heads thus hear and decide cases that they themselves have directed subordinates to investigate and prosecute, and in which the agency itself is one of the named parties. The Supreme Court has consistently upheld this arrangement against due process challenges complaining that the combination of prosecutorial and adjudicative functions compromises the impartiality of agencies.[41] And the main ground for the Court's decisions has been that the combination of functions is necessary to secure expert administrative decision making in a complex society.

As we have seen, *Withrow v. Larkin*[42] rejected "[t]he contention that the combination of investigative and adjudicative functions necessarily creates an unconstitutional risk of bias in administrative adjudication."[43] A rule barring combination of administrative functions "would bring down too many procedures designed, and working well, for a governmental structure of great and growing complexity."[44] Here the court echoed one of the original New Deal defenses of the combination of functions, which held that the development of administrative expertise would be hamstrung if agencies could not shape their own regulatory agendas by bringing cases that the agency itself would adjudicate.[45] Given basic tradeoffs between impartiality and informed expertise in the administrative state, consistent implementation of *nemo iudex* would promote impartiality at too great a price.

---

[38] *See, e.g.,* Ilya Shapiro & Caitlyn W. McCarthy, *Are Federal Agencies the Sole Judges of Their Own Authority?,* 34 REG. 4, 5 (2011) (libertarian critique); Gary Lawson, *The Rise and Rise of the Administrative State,* 107 HARV. L. REV. 1231, 1248 (1994) (originalist critique).

[39] 5 U.S.C. § 554(d)(2) (2006).

[40] *Id.* § 554(d)(2)(C).

[41] See Marcello v. Bonds, 349 U.S. 302 (1955); FTC v. Cement Inst., 333 U.S. 683 (1948).

[42] 421 U.S. 35 (1975).

[43] *Id.* at 47.

[44] *Id.* at 49–50 (quoting Richardson v. Perales, 402 U.S. 389 (1971)).

[45] JAMES M. LANDIS, THE ADMINISTRATIVE PROCESS (1938).

IMPARTIALITY AND INDEPENDENCE

In other settings, rulemakers qualify or violate the *nemo iudex* principle in order to ensure the independence or autonomy of institutions. In these settings, a given institution is made judge in its own cause because allocating decision-making authority to a different institution creates a risk that the second institution will leverage its authority to control the first, in ways that will be undesirable from a larger systemic perspective. Where this is so, giving the first institution the authority to act as judge in its own cause may create a risk of self-dealing, but the rulemaker may believe this to be an acceptable risk – an unavoidable precondition for, and byproduct of, a system of institutional independence that is desirable overall.

Legislative salaries. The network of constitutional rules governing legislative salaries illustrate these tradeoffs. The enacted Constitution authorized the Congress, acting by law, to pay its members a salary out of the national treasury. This outcome emerged only after extensive debates among the delegates at the Philadelphia convention, debates centering on three related questions. First, should the legislators be paid at all? Second, if they were to be paid, should they be paid by the states from which they were selected – as was the practice under the Articles of Confederation – or instead by legislative appropriations from the national treasury? Third, should the amount of compensation be fixed by the convention or left to the discretion of future legislators themselves?

For present purposes, the second and third questions are the most critical. Madison argued at the convention that legislators should not be allowed to compensate themselves, because of the risk of self-dealing: "Mr. Madison thought the members of the [legislature] too much interested to ascertain their own compensation. It [would] be indecent to put their hands into the public purse for the sake of their own pockets."[46] On the other hand, Madison, like many other delegates, also argued that "it would be improper to leave the members of the [National] legislature to be provided for by the State [Legislatures]: because it would create an improper dependence."[47] As Hamilton put it in one of his rare interventions, "[t]hose who pay are the masters of those who are paid,"[48] and he "pressed the distinction between State [Governments and] the people. The former [would]

---

[46] 1 THE RECORDS OF THE FEDERAL CONVENTION OF 1787, at 373–74 (Max Farrand ed., 1911).
[47] *Id.* at 215–16.
[48] *Id.* at 373.

be the rivals of the [General Government]. The State legislatures ought not therefore to be the pay masters of the latter."[49]

In the face of this dilemma, Madison argued for a constitutionally fixed standard of compensation, perhaps indexed to the price of wheat or some other commodity to allow increase over time. Most of the other delegates, however, thought that a fixed compensation was undesirable or unworkable, either because its visibility would instigate opposition to the proposed constitution,[50] or because any fixed standard would be insufficiently sensitive to changing circumstances.[51] As between the solutions that allowed for variable compensation – payment by the states or self-payment by federal legislators – the convention opted for the latter solution, several members arguing that the risk of self-dealing was low, perhaps because the great visibility of legislative salaries would trigger popular oversight. Indeed, Roger Sherman "was not afraid that the Legislature would make their own wages too high; but too low."[52] Throughout the debate, delegates took account of Gerry's observation that "there are difficulties on both sides,"[53] and offered judgments about how best to balance the competing risks – a far cry from simple invocation of *nemo iudex*.

A different solution would be to let a different branch of the national government, such as the president, set the salaries for federal legislators. Towards the close of the debate, the convention agreed to a motion to provide that payment from the national treasury should be "ascertained by law," that is, by statute as opposed to an internal legislative rule. Although the shape of the executive branch was still fluid and contested when this amendment was carried, the eventual consequence was that the president would have the power to veto a bill setting legislative salaries. Here too, however, legislators would still play a role in setting their own compensation; no one raised the possibility of a pure regime in which, for example, the president acting alone would set the legislature's salary. Despite its apparent compatibility with *nemo iudex*, the obvious concern about

---

[49] *Id.* at 374.

[50] Ghorum argued that the fixed compensation could not be made "as liberal as it ought to be without exciting an enmity [against] the whole plan." *Id.* at 372. Franklin objected on the ground that the convention itself could be accused of self-dealing: "He wished the Convention to stand fair with the people. There were in it a number of young men who would probably be of the Senate. If lucrative appointments should be recommended we might be chargeable with having carved out places for ourselves." *Id.* at 427.

[51] Wilson "was [against] *fixing* the compensation, as circumstances would change and call for a change of the amount." *Id.* at 373.

[52] 2 THE RECORDS OF THE FEDERAL CONVENTION OF 1787, *supra* note, at 291.

[53] *Id.*

such a regime would be that the president could leverage his power over compensation to compromise legislative autonomy. In light of the notorious practices by which British monarchs of the eighteenth century had corrupted Members of Parliament, the convention adopted several provisions intended to check executive vote buying,[54] and presidential control over legislators' compensation would have been inconsistent with those efforts.

Judicial salaries and the rule of necessity. The value of institutional independence is also said to underpin the Supreme Court's invocation of the "rule of necessity" in cases where federal judges bring lawsuits complaining that their salaries have been unconstitutionally diminished. Article III's Compensation Clause provides that the judges "shall at stated times receive for their services a compensation which shall not be diminished during their continuance in office."[55] In some cases, judges bring suits that will determine the compensation of all federal judges as such, so that every federal judge has a direct financial interest in the outcome.[56] The implication is that any judge who decides the case is sitting in her own cause, a core violation of *nemo iudex*. The Court, however, allows such suits to proceed under the common-law rule of necessity, which holds that if all judges would be disqualified, none are.[57]

It is hardly obvious that the rule of necessity is really necessary. If the case cannot proceed without a *nemo iudex* violation, perhaps it should not proceed at all. The Court sometimes cites an "absolute duty of judges to hear and decide cases within their jurisdiction,"[58] a phantom duty that is routinely violated by federal judges under a myriad of prudential doctrines that license abstention from the exercise of jurisdiction.[59] Alternatively, the Court sometimes points to the need for judge-litigants to obtain a forum for litigating their individual constitutional rights,[60] but this rationale is no

---

[54] The Ineligibility and Emoluments Clauses state that "No Senator or Representative shall, during the Time for which he was elected, be appointed to any civil Office under the Authority of the United States, which shall have been created, or the Emoluments whereof shall have been encreased during such time; and no Person holding any Office under the United States, shall be a Member of either House during his Continuance in Office." U.S. CONST. art. I, § 6, cl. 2.
[55] *Id.* art. III, § 1.
[56] *See, e.g.*, United States v. Will, 449 U.S. 200 (1980).
[57] Charles Gardner Geyh, *Roscoe Pound and the Future of the Good Government Movement*, 8 S. TEX. L. REV. 871, 885 (2007).
[58] *Will*, 449 U.S. at 215.
[59] RICHARD H. FALLON, JR. ET AL., HART AND WECHSLER'S THE FEDERAL COURTS AND THE FEDERAL SYSTEM 150 (6th ed. 2009).
[60] *Will*, 449 U.S. at 201.

more successful. If the rule of necessity even applies, then what is at stake is really an attempt by judge-litigants to obtain a forum that is necessarily biased in their favor, and it is unclear why it is better that they should enjoy such a forum than that their constitutional claims should be remitted to whatever protection the political process will afford.

If there is a plausible rationale for the rule of necessity, it is that suits for compensation by judge-litigants produce a positive externality by helping to protect the independence of the judges from political retaliation – one of the main aims of the Article III rules. As the Court puts it, "the Compensation Clause is designed to benefit, not the judges as individuals, but the public interest in a competent and independent judiciary."[61] Judges say, in other words, that the risk of biased adjudication in the judges' own favor is an unavoidable byproduct of a regime that minimizes the risks of political interference with judicial independence. On this happy view, the judges' interests align with those of the overall system; what is good for judicial salaries is good for the nation.[62] Whatever the ultimate merits of that claim, the tradeoff between impartiality and independence is clear.

Qualifications and expulsion of legislators. A final example involves the authority of each chamber of Congress, under Article I, to "judge" the "elections, returns and qualifications" of its members and to expel members.[63] Although there is a norm that legislators do not vote on their own personal qualifications or expulsion, this regime nonetheless violates the extended sense of *nemo iudex* that Madison invoked in Federalist 10; in the aggregate, each house as a group determines its own composition. The standard defense of this arrangement, offered by Justice Joseph Story in his *Commentaries on the Constitution*, holds that

> [t]he only possible question on such a subject is, as to the body, in which such a power shall be lodged. If lodged in any other, than the legislative body

---

[61] *Id.* at 217 (citing Evans v. Gore, 253 U.S. 245, 253 (2001)).

[62] Expanding the lens beyond the U.S. federal court system to include state courts and the courts of other nations, some judiciaries have asserted powers to determine their own budgets or their own membership. Courts in several U.S. states have ordered legislatures to appropriate judicially specified amounts to fund the court system, asserting that the power to do so is inherent in or necessary for judicial independence. The leading case is *Commonwealth ex rel. Carroll v. Tate*, 274 A.2d 193 (Pa. 1971); for further discussion and citations, see Adrian Vermeule, *The Judicial Power in the State (and Federal) Courts*, 2000 SUP. CT. REV. 357. In India, the Supreme Court has held that judicial independence requires the government to appoint the most senior judge of the Court to the position of Chief Justice, despite the absence of any textual provision to that effect in the Constitution. *See In re* Appointment of Judges Case, Special Reference No. 1 of 1998 (1998) 7 S.C.C. 739 (India).

[63] U.S. CONST. art. I, § 5, cl. 1

itself, its independence, its purity, and even its existence and action may be destroyed, or put into imminent danger.[64]

Story's argument refers in explicit terms to the political risk that committing the power to judge qualifications elsewhere would compromise the independence of the chamber. Implicitly, Story trades this off against the risk of institutional self-dealing that is created by cameral self-judging of qualifications, and finds the former risk more serious. As we will see in Section IV, however, the Philadelphia Convention also adopted substitute protections against the latter risk.

IMPARTIALITY AND INSTITUTIONAL "ENERGY"

At least since Machiavelli's analysis of glory-seeking as a spur to executive action,[65] constitutional actors and analysts have discussed the effects of constitutional rules on institutional "energy."[66] Although the nature of institutional energy is obscure, and different discussions seem to use the term to mean different things, a straightforward interpretation is that institutions and officials that at least partly control their own agendas may choose varying levels of activity or outputs, and that constitutional rules may shape and constrain such choices. The more institutional activity is desirable, the more costly are any rules that give institutional actors an incentive to do nothing rather than something.

For present purposes, the important point is that in certain environments, impartiality may trade off against institutional activity. Where constitutional rules assign decision-making authority to self-interested or biased actors, the benefit may be that those actors will have greater motivation or incentive to act, for the very reason that they have a stake in doing so. A fallacy lurking behind the stock arguments for the *nemo iudex* principle is that biased action (somehow defined) is necessarily socially undesirable action. On the contrary, self-interested or biased motivation may be the spur to undertake action that happens to be socially desirable from some external perspective. Where this occurs, constitutional actors are led, as if by an invisible hand, to promote social welfare as a byproduct of promoting their own interests.

---

[64] JOSEPH STORY, COMMENTARIES ON THE CONSTITUTION OF THE UNITED STATES 295–96 (Boston, Hilliard, Gray & Co. 1833).

[65] *See* Adrian Vermeule, *The Glorious Commander-in-Chief*, *in* THE LIMITS OF CONSTITUTIONAL DEMOCRACY 157 (Jeffrey K. Tulis & Stephen Macedo eds., 2010).

[66] THE FEDERALIST NO. 70, at 391 (Alexander Hamilton) (Charles Kessler & Clinton Rossiter ed., 1999).

Presidential self-pardons. An example involves the debate over presidential self-pardons. To date this debate is strictly hypothetical; no president has ever issued a pardon for himself. Yet the structure of the debate helps to illuminate the scope and limits of *nemo iudex*. For critics of the possibility of presidential self-pardons,[67] *nemo iudex* is a deep principle of the constitutional structure, which should be read into specific provisions where possible. The critics accordingly claim that the facially unqualified language of Article II's Pardon Clause – "The President ... shall have power to grant reprieves and pardons for offenses against the United States, except in cases of impeachment"[68] – should be read as containing an implied prohibition against presidential self-pardons. On this view, the Constitution's specific provisions evidence a general "structural distaste" for "self-dealing" and "self-judging."[69] The asserted examples of this structural distaste include the constitutional prohibitions on legislators accepting offices whose emoluments they have voted on, the Twenty-Seventh Amendment's ban on salary raises without an intervening election, and a putative prohibition on the vice president presiding over the Senate during his own impeachment trial – although the last example is an entirely implicit prohibition that rests on nothing more solid than the same "structural distaste" for self-judging, the same assertion of *nemo iudex*, that underlies the main argument against presidential self-pardons.[70]

One of the main responses to this critique invokes (although in different terms) the risk that a structural prohibition on presidential self-pardons may rule out self-pardons that would be desirable from a social point of view. On this view, the Philadelphia convention, which touched on the issue only en passant, rejected Edmund Randolph's "view that [presidential] self-dealing may be a problem" and instead opted for "a stronger presidency with the risk of occasional abuse."[71] The problem with simplistic invocation of *nemo iudex* in this setting is that "even a presidential self-pardon may not be solely an act of self-dealing.... Richard Nixon could have thereby spared Gerald Ford the odious task

---

[67] Brian C. Kalt, *Pardon Me?: The Constitutional Case Against Presidential Self-Pardons*, 106 YALE L.J. 779 (1996).

[68] U.S. CONST. art. II, § 2, cl. 1.

[69] Kalt, *supra* note, at 794–95.

[70] On the question whether the vice president may preside at his own impeachment, *compare* Michael Stokes Paulsen, *Someone Should Have Told Spiro Agnew*, 14 CONST. COMMENT. 245 (1997) (yes), *with* Joel K. Goldstein, *Can the Vice President Preside at His Own Impeachment Trial? A Critique of Bare Textualism*, 44 ST. LOUIS U. L. J. 849 (2000) (no).

[71] Robert Nida & Rebecca L. Spiro, *The President As His Own Judge and Jury: A Legal Analysis of the Presidential Self-Pardon Power*, 52 OKLA. L. REV. 197, 218 (1999).

of issuing a pardon for his predecessor. Although self-dealing may be a factor, the country may actually be a significant beneficiary of the self-pardon concept."[72] A structural constraint on presidential self-pardons may result in too few pardons, sacrificing social welfare on the altar of impartiality.

In this example, the critique of presidential self-pardons illustrates a methodological mistake about constitutional law. Some of the Constitution's provisions may rest on the logic of *nemo iudex*, as in the examples given earlier – although it is striking that these examples are mostly marginal or second-decimal rules. With respect to the issue of legislative salaries, for example, the main feature of the constitutional design is that legislators vote on their own salaries, whereas the asserted examples of *nemo iudex* safeguards, involving emoluments and the Twenty-Seventh Amendment's delay rule, just tweak the rules around the edges to soften the core violation. Even insofar as the examples are valid, however, they cannot be generalized into a constitutional principle against, or a "structural distaste" for, self-dealing or self-judging. In some contexts, constitutional rulemakers follow *nemo iudex*, in others they do not, depending on context-specific judgments about the direction and magnitude of competing political risks, and about relevant tradeoffs. Just as it is treacherous in the extreme to generalize principles of "federalism" from the Constitution's many, highly specific and calibrated provisions for assigning powers and duties between states and Union,[73] so too any generalization of a structural *nemo iudex* principle would have to deliberately overlook central features of the constitutional design.

Presidential pardons for treason. At Philadelphia, the main thread of debate over the pardon power involved the question whether the power should cover the offense of treason. Randolph moved that it should not, holding that "the prerogative of pardon in these cases was too great a trust" either because "[t]he President himself may be guilty" – the self-pardoning issue – or because "[t]he Traytors may be his own instruments."[74] Madison noted that lodging the power to pardon treason in the legislature would create problems of its own, but said that the power was "peculiarly

---

[72] *Id.* at 219.

[73] John F. Manning, *Federalism and the Generality Problem in Constitutional Interpretation*, 122 HARV. L. REV. 2003, 2004 (2009) (arguing that "the specific means chosen to implement our form of concurrent sovereignty in fact define the concept of federalism and that, contrary to the Court's recent cases, there is no freestanding federalism").

[74] 2 THE RECORDS OF THE FEDERAL CONVENTION OF 1787, *supra* note, at 626 (quoting Madison (Sept. 15)).

improper for the President,"[75] presumably because of Randolph's concerns over direct self-dealing or indirect cronyism. The convention, however, voted down Randolph's motion and thereby included treason within the scope of the president's pardon power.

Later commentators such as Hamilton and Story justified that decision by appealing to institutional energy and activity levels. The "principal argument," in Hamilton's view, was that

> [i]n seasons of insurrection or rebellion, there are often critical moments, when a well timed offer of pardon to the insurgents or rebels may restore the tranquility of the commonwealth; and which, if suffered to pass unimproved, it may never be possible afterwards to recall. The dilatory process of convening the Legislature, or one of its branches, for the purpose of obtaining its sanction to the measure, would frequently be the occasion of letting slip the golden opportunity. The loss of a week, a day, an hour, may sometimes be fatal.[76]

The implicit structure of this argument differs from the argument for presidential self-pardons. In the latter case presidential self-interest is itself the spur that motivates a socially desirable level of activity, whereas here the presidency is assumed, for exogenous reasons, to be more active and decisive than the legislature. Yet the two arguments have a common feature: even if presidential power to pardon for treason creates risks of direct self-dealing or indirect cronyism, those risks are an unavoidable and acceptable byproduct of the institutional allocation of pardoning power that produces optimal levels of activity.

Legislative qualifications. In some cases, the tradeoff between impartiality on the one hand and energy or motivation on the other is closely tied to the issue of institutional autonomy or independence, discussed in Section II. Story's argument that each chamber of the bicameral Congress should have the authority to judge the qualifications of its members tied together independence and motivation by observing, in effect, that only institutional self-interest would provide the necessary motivation for institutional self-defense, and that institutional self-defense is necessary to the maintenance of an ongoing system of independent institutions that check and balance one another. In Story's words,

> [n]o other body, but itself, can have the same motives to preserve and perpetuate these attributes; no other body can be so perpetually watchful to guard

[75] *Id.*
[76] THE FEDERALIST No. 74, at 500, 500–01 (Alexander Hamilton) (James E. Cooke ed., 1961); *see also* STORY, *supra* note, § 1494.

its own rights and privileges from infringement, to purify and vindicate its own character, and to preserve the rights, and sustain the free choice of its constituents.[77]

Legislation, partiality, and the system of checks and balances. Similar reasoning implies that Madison's famous *nemo iudex* argument in Federalist 10 must be understood in conjunction with his argument for checks and balances in Federalist 51. In the former, Madison argued that

> [n]o man is allowed to be judge in his own cause, because his interest would certainly bias his judgment, and, not improbably, corrupt his integrity. With equal, nay with greater reason, a body of men are unfit to be both judges and parties at the same time....[78]

Accordingly, Madison argued, legislative majorities would make biased and partisan decisions.

Whatever the merits of this reasoning taken in isolation, its point was nearly the opposite of later commentators who cite Madison as a proponent of the *nemo iudex* principle, in some cases to justify judicial review.[79] Madison's point was not that legislative partiality could be directly eliminated; indeed Madison seems to have thought that any attempt to make legislatures act impartially would prove futile. Rather, the effects of legislative partiality should be offset by structural devices of checks and balances. In the language of Madison's Federalist 51, such devices would make "ambition ... counteract ambition,"[80] harnessing the motivational energy of partial, biased, or self-interested officials to promote the power and independence of the institutions in which those officials served.

Federalist 51 thus offers an invisible-hand argument for competition among self-serving individuals and institutions, an argument ultimately derived from the Scottish Enlightenment theorists, David Hume, Adam

---

[77] STORY, *supra* note, at 295.

[78] THE FEDERALIST No. 10, at 59 (James Madison) (James E. Cooke ed., 1961).

[79] "*Marbury v. Madison* holds that it is 'emphatically the province and duty of the judicial department to say what the law is.' The Court does not permit the executive to interpret ambiguous constitutional provisions as it sees fit. Courts construe the document independently, not with deference to executive interpretations of unclear provisions. Why is the executive not permitted to construe constitutional ambiguities as it sees fit? The simplest answer is that foxes are not permitted to guard henhouses, or, in other words, those who are limited by law cannot decide on the scope of the limitation." Cass R. Sunstein, *Beyond Marbury: The Executive's Power to Say What the Law Is*, 115 YALE L.J. 2580, 2584 (2006) (footnote omitted).

[80] THE FEDERALIST No. 51, at 322 (James Madison) (Clinton Rossiter ed., 1961).

Ferguson, and Adam Smith, who influenced Madison.[81] Read in tandem, the point of Federalist 10 and 51 is that the cure for biased decision making on the part of legislatures is not legislative impartiality, but rather equally biased decision making by competing institutions. And the key argument for such a system of offsetting biases, according to Federalist 51, is that only the motivational energy supplied by "ambition" will suffice to protect institutions from mutual encroachment, thus ensuring the ongoing maintenance of a system in which separated powers check and balance one another.

Elsewhere, I have claimed that the Madisonian argument for checks and balances fails.[82] (The previous chapter added that, as a precaution, the system of checks and balances is actually self-defeating, on Bryce's argument). It specifies no mechanism for ensuring that institutions will pursue "their" interests, as opposed to the interests of the individuals or political parties who happen to staff them at any given time,[83] and equally fails to ensure that competition among institutions will produce impartial lawmaking, liberty, efficiency, a stable system of interactions among autonomous institutions, or any other social or political good. Whatever the substantive merits of Madison's argument, however, its structure is important. It illustrates that multiplying, rather than attempting to reduce, violations of *nemo iudex* may be necessary to produce systematically valuable institutional energy and motivation – here the spurs of ambition, self-interest, and institutional interest, which Madison assumed would work in harness to maintain the system of mutually checking institutions.

UNAVOIDABLE VIOLATIONS

Perhaps the starkest response to an invocation of *nemo iudex* is some version of "you're another" or *tu quoque*. On this response, the alternative decision maker is said to be equally partial or biased. In the strongest versions of this argument, the claim is that for structural reasons there can be *no* impartial decision maker in the relevant domain, so that any allocation of decision-making authority must necessarily violate *nemo iudex*. In terms of the categories laid out in Chapter 2, the claim is one of perversity;

---

[81] Roy Branson, *James Madison and the Scottish Enlightenment*, 40 J. HIST. IDEAS 235 (Apr.–Jun. 1979).

[82] ADRIAN VERMEULE, THE SYSTEM OF THE CONSTITUTION (2011).

[83] *See* Daryl J. Levinson, *Empire-Building Government in Constitutional Law*, 118 HARV. L. REV. 915, 927 (2005); Daryl J. Levinson & Richard H. Pildes, *Separation of Parties, Not Powers*, 119 HARV. L. REV. 2311, 2324 (2006).

the same risk of self-dealing or self-serving bias lies on all sides of the possible allocation of decision-making authority.

Federal judicial review of state court decisions. Here too, Joseph Story provides an early example of this response – not as a commentator, but as a Supreme Court Justice. In *Martin v. Hunter's Lessee*,[84] the main issue was whether the Court could review and, if necessary, overturn state court decisions on matters of federal law. In the many-faceted debate that resulted, one of the main issues was a background fear on the part of state officials and Antifederalists that federal courts would be biased in favor of extending the scope of federal laws and federal constitutional power, including the power of the federal judges themselves. Federal judges deciding federal questions, in other words, would be acting as the arbiters of their own power. As against this concern, Story argued, among other things, that there was no impartial decision maker anywhere in the picture:

> From the very nature of things, the absolute right of decision, in the last resort, must rest somewhere – wherever it may be vested it is susceptible of abuse. In all questions of jurisdiction the inferior, or appellate court, must pronounce the final judgment; and common sense, as well as legal reasoning, has conferred it on the latter.[85]

Although Story was too much of a political veteran to be explicit here, given the sensitivity of state-federal relations in his day, his point was that if the federal courts are not the final judges of their own jurisdiction, the state courts will be the final judges of *their* own jurisdiction. As the latter regime would also violate *nemo iudex*, the choice between the two regimes must be made on other grounds.[86]

Judicial review in general. Later commentators have transposed Story's argument into an objection against judicial review of individual rights claims, and indeed generalized from it an objection to judicial review generally. The background is a long and disreputable tradition in which *nemo iudex* is invoked, in the most facile manner imaginable, to justify judicial review. After all, the reasoning runs, if there is no independent body charged with deciding whether legislatures have stayed within the constitutional boundaries of their powers, then the only judge of that question

---

[84] 14 U.S. (1 Wheat.) 304 (1816).

[85] *Id.* at 345.

[86] *Cf.* Virelli, *supra* note, at 1228 (arguing that "the absence of a constitutionally recognized third-party arbiter" militates against statutory standards of recusal for Supreme Court Justices).

is the legislature itself; and this would violate *nemo iudex* (citing Madison in Federalist) or "put the fox in charge of the henhouse."[87] As against this sort of claim, Jeremy Waldron argues quite rightly that no institutional arrangement can avoid the *nemo iudex* problem:

> Those who invoke the maxim *nemo iudex in sua causa* in this context say that it requires that a final decision about rights should not be left in the hands of the people. Rather, it should be passed on to an independent and impartial institution such as a court. It is hard to see the force of this argument. Almost any conceivable decision-rule will eventually involve someone deciding in his own case. Unless we envisage a literally endless chain of appeals, there will always be some person or institution whose decision is final. And of that person or institution, we can always say that because it has the last word, its members are ipso facto ruling on the acceptability of their own view.[88]

The issue is somewhat more complicated than Waldron allows, but his basic point is correct: judicial review allows the Court to rule on the limits of its own power, and thus puts the fox in charge of the henhouse just as much as does a system with no judicial review at all. The complication is that there is a third way between legislative and judicial supremacy in constitutional matters. The third way is a departmentalist system in which both Congress and the Court can decide constitutional questions as they see fit, with neither having the authority to bind the judgment of the other. But in that sort of system, both Congress and the Court still do rule – so far as their rulings go – on the limits of their own power. The departmentalist system, in other words, puts several foxes in charge of several henhouses. That may or may not be a better system, all things considered, than either the system of legislative supremacy or the system of judicial supremacy, depending on whether the foxes somehow check one another. But it is not a system that avoids violating the *nemo iudex* principle; on the contrary, it multiplies the violations.

Legislative districting (redux). The unavoidability arguments offered by Story and Waldron rebut *nemo iudex* on conceptual grounds: in the relevant settings, there is no possible allocation of decision-making authority that avoids making some official or institution judge in its own cause. In other settings, the unavoidability argument is not conceptual, but institutional.

[87] David Currie, *The Constitution in the Supreme Court: The Powers of the Federal Courts, 1801–1835*, 49 U. CHI. L. REV. 646, 657 (1982).
[88] Jeremy Waldron, *The Core of the Case Against Judicial Review*, 115 YALE L.J. 1346, 1400–01 (2006) (emphasis added).

Although it may be possible, in the abstract, to allocate decision-making authority to an impartial institution, the incentives of the relevant political actors ensure that no such institution will actually come into being.

An example involves legislative districting. As we have seen, the current system – in which legislators themselves determine the shape and composition of their own districts – represents a large-scale violation of *nemo iudex*. Accordingly, a popular position holds that districting should be entrusted to independent and impartial expert commissions or bodies, who will supposedly enjoy the freedom to draw districts based on objective, welfare-maximizing criteria. Against this argument, proponents of legislative districting offer many rebuttals, one of which is that independent and impartial districting is infeasible because it is not incentive-compatible. As the districting commission must itself be created by the political system it is set up to regulate, the political actors who create it will predictably rig its powers, procedures, and composition to achieve the same ends that they pursue in a system of legislative districting. On this view,

> [i]t is almost impossible to design institutions to be authentically nonpartisan and politically disinterested.... Whoever draws the lines must get authority from somewhere – the person will either be appointed or elected. Elected officials, as former Florida Secretary of State Katherine Harris demonstrated, are almost certainly conflicted. And appointed officials will be beholden to those appointing them or at least selected because their intentions are well-known.[89]

Alternatively, political actors may simply undo the independence of the districting commission if it produces politically unacceptable results. In Arizona in 2011, the Republican governor and state senate fired the chair of an independent districting commission, claiming that she displayed a bias in favor of Democrats.[90] This was a rare case of an observable confrontation, but the threat of such action will implicitly constrain "independent" commissions by virtue of the law of anticipated reactions. Sometimes the underlying commitment problem can be overcome by law or norms, but it is an open question how often, and for how long, true independence can be sustained.

"Independent" agencies and courts. Similar political mechanisms underpin two other examples, which are sufficiently familiar in the public-law

---

[89] Persily, *supra* note, at 674.
[90] *See* Marc Lacey, Arizona Governor and Senate Oust Redistricitng Leader, N.Y. Times (Nov. 2, 2011), http://www.nytimes.com/2011/11/02/us/chairwoman-of-arizona-redistricting-commission-ousted.html.

literature that I will mention them only briefly. The first involves the "independent agencies" – agencies whose members can be discharged only for cause, and who typically serve staggered terms. Although such structures theoretically insulate the independent agencies from presidential control, evidence suggests that by the end of their first term, presidents typically control policymaking at "independent" agencies, in part by appointing members whose political preferences are predictable.[91]

Second and more famously, a large body of political science evidence shows that the Supreme Court itself follows the election returns, albeit with a lag, largely because appointments to the Court are made by the same political system that the Constitution is supposed to regulate. Although genuinely countermajoritarian rulings are possible in the short run,[92] in the long run constitutional law is highly elastic, and changes as changing public opinion affects the selection of Justices by the president and the Senate. At least in this long-run sense, a genuinely independent and politically impartial Court is not an incentive-compatible arrangement.

Combination of functions (redux). Finally, James Landis's argument for the combination of prosecutorial and adjudicative functions in administrative agencies relied, in part, on the claim that separating functions by lodging adjudicative power in courts alone would merely risk a different form of bias. On this argument, although the combination of administrative functions risks biased decision making by agencies that decide the cases they themselves have initiated, judicial determination of agency prosecutions risks running aground on the ideological biases of the judges, whose opinions will on average have been formed in an earlier era. As Landis put it,

> [j]udicial interpretation of the statutory standards laid down by the Congress plainly gave the judges power to mold the statute to their own conceptions; and that molding had too frequently set at naught the public and political effort which had so hopefully expended itself in the passage of the statute. Judicial interpretation suffered not only from inexpertness but more from the slowness of that process to attune itself to the demands of the day.[93]

---

[91] Neal Devins & David E. Lewis, *Not-So Independent Agencies: Party Polarization and the Limits of Institutional Design*, 88 B.U. L. Rev. 459, 468 (2008).

[92] Richard H. Pildes, *Is the Supreme Court A "Majoritarian" Institution?*, 2010 Sup. Ct. Rev. 103, 116.

[93] Landis, *supra* note, at 97.

Although, as discussed earlier, the political appointment mechanism ensures that in the long run independent judges will follow the election returns, it does not follow that they are legally impartial at any given time. Rather, the risk is that, given the lag-time inherent in the appointment mechanism, the judges will impose the views of "the day before yesterday"[94] on the administrative agencies. Landis argues in effect that the insulation of the judiciary from current politics itself creates scope for the operation of ideological biases, as opposed to impartial legality; hence there is no impartial institution in the picture, and the combination of functions in agencies cannot be rejected simply on the ground that it creates a risk of biased decision making. Rather, one must compare the biases of all relevant institutional alternatives.[95]

THE CALCULUS OF POLITICAL RISKS: RULES OF THUMB

If *nemo iudex* is a misleading half-truth, what follows? At a minimum, "facile invocation"[96] of *nemo iudex* should, one hopes, come to be widely seen as an embarrassing slip – the intellectual equivalent of burping at a dinner party. By facile invocation, I mean the assumption that reciting *nemo iudex* is a *sufficient* argument for some institutional arrangement or other. On the contrary, *nemo iudex* is never sufficient. *Nemo iudex* problems may afflict all possible arrangements, so that some fox or other must necessarily be placed in charge of some henhouse or other, and other considerations will have to be called into service to determine institutional arrangements. Alternatively, the value of impartial decision making that underpins *nemo iudex* may be overbalanced by other values, such as expertise, institutional independence, and institutional energy. Clearing the intellectual ground in this way is at least a step forward.

The constructive claim is more difficult. In general, the theory of public law should attempt to make progress toward specifying the conditions under which rulemakers should entrust officials or institutions with authority to act as judges in their own cause. The difficulty is that although

---

[94] *Id.* (quoting Albert Venn Dicey, Law and Opinion in England 369 (2d ed. 1926)).

[95] *Cf.* Komesar, *supra* note (arguing that while "antitrust administrative agencies are highly imperfect decision-makers," such an "insight[] do[es] not make the case for augmenting the decision-making of these imperfect administrative agencies with court-based judicial review or private damage actions" because these other options must be carefully analyzed themselves).

[96] Waldron, *supra* note, at 1401.

the competing political risks and the main tradeoffs can be stated in the abstract, it is not possible to say in the abstract how the balance should be struck. In particular contexts, with respect to different institutional problems, the calculus of political risks will come out differently; the questions are inherently local, and are afflicted by severe empirical uncertainty. Nonetheless, it may be possible to suggest some pragmatic rules of thumb for coping with the tradeoffs and identifying, in a rough-and-ready way, conditions under which *nemo iudex* should be either discarded or honored, and how if at all it should be implemented. I will discuss three such rules of thumb: *marginalism*, *optimizing*, and the availability of *substitute protections* against self-dealing by officials or institutions.

Marginalism. Rulemakers will rarely face an all-out choice between impartiality, as such, and some competing value, as such. Rather they will have to adopt rules and institutions in a political context in which some other rules and institutions are already settled. This is true even at constitutional conventions. Framers do not usually consider all institutions as up for grabs all at once, but instead accept some extant institutions for political reasons, and also consider institutional choices piecemeal, reaching agreement on some issues – for example, the composition of the legislature – before considering others – for example, the powers of the courts.

The extant institutions will often build in some protections against official self-dealing or biased decision making. Where that is so, the problem facing rulemakers is marginalist. The question is not whether impartiality as such is desirable. Instead, the question is whether, given some extant set of institutional checks or precautions against official self-dealing, it is desirable to add *further* precautions. If each additional precaution produces diminishing marginal benefits and increasing costs to the other values discussed earlier, precautions should be added just up to the point at which the benefit equals the cost, so that the net benefit is zero. Needless to say, in the rough and tumble of rule-design for real polities, the location of that point will usually be unclear, and rulemakers will have to proceed by informed guesswork.

The Philadelphia debate over congressional salaries turned in part on this theme. Given the structure of the new federal legislature, a decisive fraction of the participants believed that political checks would sufficiently deter self-dealing by federal legislators empowered to set their own salaries. Indeed, as we have seen, Roger Sherman worried that the federal legislators would be subject to so much public pressure that they would set their salaries too low, rather than too high[97] – bending over backwards to demonstrate their lack of self-interest. In modern terms, given the robust political checks already in place, the convention seems to have believed that extra precautions would have slight marginal benefits, and indeed might even have net costs. Whether or not their assessment was correct, the structure of the analysis illustrates that a marginalist approach can cut daunting problems down to size and make design choices more tractable, even under conditions of grave uncertainty.

Optimizing. As a corollary of the marginalist approach, rulemakers will ordinarily do best by optimizing across all relevant values in a given domain, rather than by maximizing any one of them. Where impartiality trades off against information, institutional autonomy, or institutional activity, it will rarely be the best strategy to simply choose one value whole-sale and pursue it to the maximum possible extent, giving no weight to the competing values. Rather, on the assumption that pursuit of any one value has diminishing marginal benefits (or conversely that violation of any one value produces increasing marginal costs as the violation becomes increasingly severe),[98] it will usually be best to have some of each, rather than all of one and none of the other(s). This is not a conceptual or analytic claim, but a seat-of-the-pants empirical judgment about the shape of the marginal cost and benefit curves that institutional designers usually face.

For whatever reasons, many of the institutions of the U.S. constitutional order are structured as optimizing compromises of this kind. We have seen, for example, that the structure of congressional authority over salaries pursues the "some of both" strategy. The core feature that legislators set their own salaries tends to promote institutional autonomy, but rules like the Twenty-Seventh Amendment and the Emoluments Clause temper that feature with collateral protections for impartiality. I believe there is no deep evolutionary logic to such outcomes, which result for the most part from the unpredictable interplay of political forces combined with a large dose of path-dependence. Yet even modern rulemakers who have better theoretical tools and, perhaps, more freedom of action could do worse than to try to reproduce the optimizing effect of such arrangements.

The availability of substitute protections. In the example of congressional salaries, political checks against self-dealing already provided substitute

---

[97] 2 THE RECORDS OF THE FEDERAL CONVENTION OF 1787, *supra* note, at 291.

[98] *See* Yair Listokin, *Taxation and Marriage: A Reappraisal* (Yale L. & Econ. Working Paper No. 451, 2012), *available at* http://papers.ssrn.com/sol3/papers.cfm?abstract_id=2070171.

protections. In other examples, rulemakers can promote values that trade off against *nemo iudex* while simultaneously adjusting some other margin of institutional design to safeguard against the risks of self-dealing. Where there is a choice of alternative means by which to promote impartiality or suppress self-dealing, the *nemo iudex* approach – barring the decision maker from making decisions in which he has an interest – need not be the best solution, all things considered. As Landis argued in defense of the combination of functions in agencies, "the fact that there is this fusion of prosecution and adjudication in a single administrative agency does not imply the absence of all checks. It implies simply the absence of the traditional check."[99]

I will illustrate the theme of substitute protections with two examples from the original Constitution. In the debate at the Philadelphia convention over presidential pardons for treason, Wilson dismissed concerns about presidential self-dealing by arguing that "[p]ardon is necessary in cases of treason, and is best placed in the hands of the Executive. If he be himself a party to the guilt he can be impeached and prosecuted."[100] Tracking this argument in part, the convention specifically excluded cases of impeachment from the scope of the pardon power.[101] In modern terms, the expected harm of presidential self-dealing through abuse of the pardon power is a function both of the risk that self-dealing will occur and of the magnitude of the harm if it does occur. Wilson's argument points out that the magnitude of the harm is limited; although the president might use the pardon power to immunize himself from criminal punishment, no amount of self-pardoning will keep him in office if a sufficient majority desires to remove him.

Another illustration involves the authority of the Houses of Congress to "judge" the qualifications of their members and to expel members. As we have seen, Story's argument for entrusting that authority to the respective chambers was that placing the authority anywhere else would create an unacceptable threat to institutional autonomy. The Philadelphia convention, however, was concerned about the risk that cameral authority over qualifications would be abused by majority legislative factions to expel or otherwise oppress members of minority legislative factions – the same type of group self-dealing by legislative majorities that Madison classed as a violation of *nemo iudex* in Federalist 10. At the convention, "Mr. Madison

---

[99] LANDIS, *supra* note, at 98.
[100] *Id.* (emphasis added).
[101] *See* U.S. CONST. art. II, §2.

observed that the right of expulsion was too important to be exercised by a bare majority of a quorum: and *in emergencies of faction might be dangerously abused.* He moved that [expulsion would require a two-thirds vote of the chamber]."[102] Morris objected that a supermajority requirement "may produce abuses on the side of the minority. A few men, from factious motives, may keep in a member who ought to be expelled."[103] But the convention unanimously approved Madison's amendment, one state divided.[104]

In both of these examples, the risk of self-dealing was addressed not by shifting decision-making authority to another official or institution, but by adjusting a different margin of institutional design – either the availability of impeachment for corrupt presidential pardons (an adjustment to the *sanction* for a biased decision) or the voting rule for legislative expulsions (an adjustment to the *threshold* necessary for a biased decision). The point generalizes. *Nemo iudex* arguments often assume, implicitly, that identifying a problem – the risk of self-dealing – necessarily implies a particular solution – transferring decision-making authority away from the biased decision maker. But in some institutional settings, other types of precautions or remedies are also available, and the assumption no longer holds.

Where other precautions or remedies are indeed available, the rulemaker faces a choice and should adopt the solution that produces greatest net benefits, not necessarily the solution that strictly minimizes the risk of self-dealing. As compared to a regime in which another institution decides on expulsion, Madison's supermajority solution may not be the one that strictly minimizes the risk of factional self-dealing in the legislative chamber. Given the benefits of institutional autonomy identified by Story, however, the combination of cameral expulsion authority with a supermajority voting rule has a plausible claim to represent an optimal set of precautions – or at least a better set of precautions than any feasible competitor.

IMPARTIALITY AND THE MATURE POSITION

Billed as one of the law's great maxims, *nemo iudex* is in fact a shifty partial truth, useful at some times and in some settings, useless or positively

[102] JAMES MADISON, NOTES OF DEBATES IN THE FEDERAL CONVENTION OF 1787, at 431 (Ohio University Press, bicentennial ed. 1987) (emphasis added).
[103] JAMES MADISON, JOURNAL OF THE FEDERAL CONVENTION 500 (E.H. Scott ed., The Lawbook Exchange, Ltd., 2003) (1840).
[104] *Id.*

misleading in others. Perhaps many grand legal principles have this characteristic, when closely inspected. But it requires no close inspection to see
that *nemo iudex* is massively contradicted by central features of our constitutional order. In a constitutional system where legislators shape their own
elections and compensate themselves, judges decide cases about their own
salaries, and administrators rule on the validity of the cases they themselves
have brought, under rules they themselves have written – in a system like
that, the real puzzle is how *nemo iudex* acquired and maintains its grip on
the legal mind. A mature, well-rounded analysis should see the impartiality
of decision makers as one institutional good among others, to be pursued,
or not, as a larger calculus of institutional optimization suggests.

5

The Risks of Deliberation: Second Opinions

A standing anxiety of constitutional rulemaking, especially in the liberal tradition, is that lawmakers within the constitutional system will make hasty or ill-considered decisions under the influence of passion or prejudice. Accordingly, constitutional rulemakers often institute precautions against such decisions; *second-opinion mechanisms* are a leading example of such precautions. Many institutional structures, rules, and practices have been justified as mechanisms for requiring or permitting decision makers to obtain second opinions. Examples include judicial review of statutes or of agency action, bicameralism, the separation of powers, and certain elements of the law of legislative procedure. These deliberative procedural mechanisms have many attractions, especially from the standpoint of liberal theorists: they are in some sense value-neutral, and thus promise to improve the quality of decision making without dictating substantive outcomes *a priori*.

Yet additional layers of deliberation and procedure are never costless or risk-free, and second opinions are hardly costless either. Such mechanisms increase the direct costs and opportunity costs of the lawmaking system and, under certain conditions, can actually have perverse results, encouraging rather than suppressing ill-considered decisions. In this chapter, I will attempt a mature consideration of both sides of the ledger. I will thus illustrate both the conditions under which second-opinion mechanisms increase the expected quality of decisions and the overall utility of the constitutional system, and also the conditions under which such mechanisms create countervailing risks or perverse effects, and thus create costs in excess of their benefits.

SECOND-OPINION MECHANISMS: EXAMPLES

I will begin by lumping together a range of examples and arguments, whose common theme is that institutional arrangements are said to be justified as second-opinion mechanisms. These examples are somewhat heterogeneous, and the reader will be impatient for distinctions, so I will then turn from lumping to splitting, offering a taxonomy that will clarify the similarities and differences among second-opinion mechanisms.

To be clear, here and throughout I analyze lawmaking institutions only insofar as they are justified on second-opinion grounds. In many cases, there are also entirely different justifications for the relevant institution; I do not claim that the second-opinion rationale is the exclusive justification, or the most important one. Indeed, in several cases I do not even believe the second-opinion justification succeeds. The idea is not to figure out the best justifications for the relevant institutions, but to identify and assess second-opinion arguments in a range of institutional settings.

Bicameralism. A stock defense of bicameralism is that a second legislative chamber can supply a second, superior opinion. In one version, the idea is simply that "[a] second chamber, regardless of its level of expertise and wisdom, constitutes ... a quality-control mechanism" that both encourages lawmakers to proceed more carefully in the first instance, and also helps to "discover mistakes after they have been committed."[1] In a stronger version, however, the second or "upper" chamber is said to be epistemically superior, by virtue of its design and composition, to the first or "lower" chamber. In polities in which the lower chamber is constituted in a populist fashion, with short terms and population-based representation, elites tend to argue that the upper chamber offers a calmer and more detached perspective. Publius argued that the U.S. Senate, whose members were to be indirectly elected for long terms, would amount to a "temperate and respectable body of citizens" who could "defen[d] ... the people against their own temporary errors and delusions."[2] Here the implied charge is that members of the lower House will either be drunk with popular emotion or, by virtue of the electoral connection, will be constrained by self-interest to behave as if they are.[3] Making explicit the association between electoral representation and drunkenness, Sir John A. Macdonald, Canada's first prime minister, famously described Canada's appointed Senate as an institution of "sober second thought."[4]

[1] GEORGE TSEBELIS & JEANNETTE MONEY, BICAMERALISM 40 (1997).
[2] THE FEDERALIST No. 63, at 382 (James Madison) (Clinton Rossiter ed., 1961).
[3] For relevant mechanisms, see Jon Elster, *The Night of August 4, 1789: A Study of Social Interaction in Collective Decision-Making*, 45 REVUE EUROPÉENNE DES SCIENCES SOCIALES 71 (2007).
[4] PARLIAMENTARY DEBATES ON THE SUBJECT OF THE CONFEDERATION OF THE BRITISH NORTH AMERICAN PROVINCES 35 (Quebec, Hunter, Rose & Co. 1865).

Separation of powers. An analogous but more general argument is that the separation of legislative, executive and judicial powers functions as a "'second opinion' structure ... [based on] the principle, embodied in the Constitution, that independent affirmation by more than one branch of government is appropriate when proposed actions seriously affect fundamental rights or change the nature of society itself."[5] In the context of war powers, a standard view is that "authorization [of war-making] by the entire Congress was foreseeably calculated ... to slow the process down, to insure that there would be a pause, a 'sober second thought,' before the nation was plunged into anything as momentous as war."[6]

Advice and consent. When the president nominates certain classes of federal officials, Senate confirmation is required. Charles Black argued that presidents do and should consider the "policy orientations" of nominees, and that the Senate can and should do so as well: "The Constitution certainly permits, if it does not compel, the taking of a second opinion on this crucial question, from a body just as responsible to the electorate, and just as close to the electorate, as is the President. Is it not wisdom to take that second opinion in all fullness of scope?"[7]

Constitutional amendment. In the United States, "[t]he [Article V] process of garnering significant support at both the federal and state levels imposes significant transaction costs and time delays, which allow ample time for sober second thoughts."[8]

Two-enactment requirements and three-reading rules. Some constitutions require constitutional amendments, or certain types of legislation, to be enacted at two successive legislative sessions in order to take effect (perhaps with an intervening election).[9] Among the possible rationales for such requirements, one is that the lapse in time allows for sober second thought.[10] Unlike the similar justification for bicameralism, this is a strictly

---

[5] Joel Yellin, *High Technology and the Courts: Nuclear Power and the Need for Institutional Reform*, 94 HARV. L. REV. 489, 497 (1981).

[6] William Van Alstyne, *Congress, the President, and the Power to Declare War: A Requiem for Vietnam*, 121 U. PA. L. REV. 1, 20 (1972).

[7] Charles Black, *A Note on Senatorial Consideration of Supreme Court Nominees*, 79 YALE L.J. 657, 660 (1969).

[8] Doni Gewirtzman, *Our Founding Feelings: Emotion, Commitment, and Imagination in Constitutional Culture*, 43 U. RICH. L. REV. 623, 646–47 (2009).

[9] See, for example, Article 138 of the Italian Constitution, Art. 138 Costituzione [Cost.] (It.), and section 88 of Denmark's Constitutional Act, Grundloven [Constitutional Act] § 88 (Den.).

[10] *See* JON ELSTER, ULYSSES UNBOUND: STUDIES IN RATIONALITY, PRECOMMITMENT, AND CONSTRAINTS (2000).

intertemporal argument that might apply even within a unicameral legislative body. Moreover, individual legislative chambers, whether in a unicameral or bicameral legislature, sometimes have "two-reading rules" or "three-reading rules" that purport to institutionalize sobriety.[11] However, when such a rule is not constitutional but is instead created by the chamber itself, the rule is not genuinely entrenched and can be waived by (super) majority vote when passions run high.[12]

Sunset clauses. "Sunset clauses" in legislation have been justified in similar terms.[13] They differ from two-enactment requirements in the nature of the default position: under sunset clauses, the interim status quo is that the legislation goes into effect when initially enacted and is then subject to reapproval, whereas under two-enactment requirements, the legislation does not go into effect unless approved in the second session. Despite this difference, the sunset clause pushes the question onto the legislative agenda a second time and thus encourages the legislature to take a second look at the policy questions.

Judicial review of statutes. Many theorists have attempted to justify judicial review on grounds similar to the justification for upper chambers in a bicameral legislature. As Alexander Bickel argued, quoting Harlan Fiske Stone, judicial review is a mechanism for ensuring a "sober second thought" in the lawmaking process.[14] Whereas the argument for upper chambers pictures the lower and more populist legislative chamber as supplying the unsober first thought, the Stone/Bickel justification for judicial

---

[11] In some chambers, procedures differ somewhat on different readings, in which case the chamber does not issue successive opinions on the same question, strictly speaking.

[12] Adrian Vermeule, *The Constitutional Law of Congressional Procedure*, 71 U. CHI. L. REV. 361, 431–34 (2004). For a two-reading rule entrenched by the constitution, see 1958 Const. art. 45 (Fr.); for a three-reading rule created by the legislative chamber, see H.R. Rule XVI, cl. 8, 112th Cong. (2011). For Bentham's analysis and defense of three-reading rules, see THE COLLECTED WORKS OF JEREMY BENTHAM: POLITICAL TACTICS 131 (Michael James et al. eds., 1999); for an argument that Bentham overlooked the commitment problems that such rules create, see Vermeule, *supra*, at 433.

[13] Jacob E. Gersen, *Temporary Legislation*, 74 U. CHI. L. REV. 247, 266–73 (2007); Kent Roach, *The Role and Capacities of Courts and Legislatures in Reviewing Canada's Anti-Terrorism Law*, 24 WINDSOR REV. LEGAL & SOC. ISSUES 5, 6 (2008).

[14] ALEXANDER M. BICKEL, THE LEAST DANGEROUS BRANCH: THE SUPREME COURT AT THE BAR OF POLITICS 26 (2nd ed. 1986) (quoting Harlan F. Stone, *The Common Law in the United States*, 50 HARV. L. REV. 4, 25 (1936)). Other theorists made the same claim before Bickel. *See, e.g.*, Albert M. Sacks, *The Supreme Court, 1953 Term – Foreword*, 68 HARV. L. REV. 96 (1954). Yet other theorists have renewed the claim since Bickel. *See, e.g.*, Keith E. Whittington, *Herbert Wechsler's Complaint and the Revival of Grand Constitutional Theory*, 34 U. RICH. L. REV 509 (2001). Yet Bickel's version is the best known, and I will use it as a synecdoche for the intellectual tradition.

review pictures the "political branches" as a whole – House, Senate, and president – as supplying the unsober first thought. In a variant, judicial review has also been said to supply simply a "second opinion"[15] – a justification that casts no implicit aspersions on the sobriety of the first opinion.

"The passive virtues." Whereas Bickel justified judicial review as a mechanism of sober second thought *by the judges*, he also advocated legal techniques that would in effect require *the legislators themselves* to reconsider an issue.[16] By construing statutes narrowly to avoid constitutional questions, by invalidating statutes on procedural rather than substantive grounds, and through other exercises of "the passive virtues,"[17] Bickel thought that courts could encourage or force legislatures to squarely face and deliberate on constitutional objections to their enactments. In some cases this deliberation may occur before the enactment of a statute, but in other cases the legislature may reconsider the statute after a remand from the judges on constitutional or quasi-constitutional grounds, and the reconsideration yields something like a second legislative opinion. These ideas can cut in the opposite direction as well; it has been argued, somewhat mischievously, that "[t]he reenactment of a statute already held unconstitutional can be justified as providing the courts with an opportunity for sober second thought."[18]

Judicial review of agency action. In a twist, judicial review of agency action is not usually defended as a mechanism for ensuring sober second thought, perhaps because agencies are not usually seen as populist bodies that might become politically intemperate. Rather, judicial review of agency action is defended as a cure for the pathologies of expertise: "the wisdom of obtaining a 'second opinion' from nonexperts – which is at the heart of judicial review of agency action – acts as a hedge against the tunnel vision that can easily limit an expert agency's perspective."[19] The picture is

[15] Thomas M. Franck, *On Proportionality of Countermeasures in International Law*, 102 Am. J. Int'l L. 715, 717 (2008).

[16] Alexander M. Bickel, *The Supreme Court, 1960 Term – Foreword: The Passive Virtues*, 75 Harv. L. Rev. 40, 77–78 (1961); *see also* Dan T. Coenen, *A Constitution of Collaboration: Protecting Fundamental Values with Second-Look Rules of Interbranch Dialogue*, 42 Wm. & Mary L. Rev. 1575, 1704–08 (2001).

[17] Bickel, *supra* note, at 40.

[18] Robert F. Nagel, *Disagreement and Interpretation*, 56 Law & Contemp. Probs. 11, 13 (1993).

[19] John S. Applegate, *A Beginning And Not An End In Itself: The Role of Risk Assessment in Environmental Decision-Making*, 63 U. Cin. L. Rev. 1643, 1652 (1995).

not that the agency is drunk while the judges are sober, but rather that the agency is myopic while the judges are broadminded.

Precedent and multiple opinions. In the currently prevailing version of *stare decisis*, a single decision by the high court of a jurisdiction suffices to create binding precedent. However, in an older approach, a single decision was not enough. Only a string of two or more judicial opinions would be taken to establish a binding legal rule.[20] These might be opinions from different courts, or from the same court at different times.

The "two-court" rule. As a rule of prudential administration, the Supreme Court says that it will typically accept factual findings concurred in by two lower courts (district court and appeals court).[21] However, the Court has departed from this rule when the findings at issue require "broadly social judgments" with constitutional implications.[22]

Federal habeas corpus. In substance, although not in terms, it has been argued that broad rights to habeas corpus review of state-court decisions in federal court are desirable because federal habeas review supplies a second opinion, by a high-quality tribunal.[23] When Justice Holmes argued for federal habeas review of sham trials in which southern juries were terrorized by racially inflamed mobs, the implicit argument was that federal review supplies a sober second thought.[24]

OIRA review. Under a series of executive orders from presidents of different parties, the Office of Information and Regulatory Affairs (OIRA) has authority to review agency regulations, in particular [an agency's] use of (or failure to use) cost-benefit analysis. President Obama recently justified OIRA review on the ground, among others, that it offers "a dispassionate and analytical 'second opinion' on agency actions."[25]

Government lawyering. The Office of Legal Counsel (OLC) supplies formal written opinions to the president on matters of law. Within OLC, there is an unwritten norm – the "two-deputy rule" – that the head of the office obtains a first draft opinion from one deputy, and then

---

[20] Todd Zywicki & Anthony B. Sanders, *Posner, Hayek, and the Economic Analysis of Law*, 93 Iowa L. Rev. 559, 579 (2008).

[21] United States v. Appalachian Elec. Power Co., 311 U.S. 377, 403 (1940).

[22] Baumgartner v. United States, 322 U.S. 665, 671 (1944).

[23] *See* Gary Peller, *In Defense of Habeas Corpus Relitigation*, 16 Harv. C.R.-C.L. L. Rev. 579, 602–90 (1982); Robert M. Cover, *The Uses of Jurisdictional Redundancy: Interest, Ideology and Innovation*, 22 Wm. & Mary L. Rev. 639, 648 (1981).

[24] *See, e.g.*, Moore v. Dempsey, 261 U.S. 86, 91 (1923) (Holmes, J.) (granting federal habeas corpus and suggesting that "counsel, jury and judge were swept to the fatal end by an irresistible wave of public passion").

[25] Memorandum of January 30, 2009: Regulatory Review, 74 Fed. Reg. 21 (Feb. 3, 2009).

obtains a cold review of the draft from a second deputy with no previous involvement.[26]

DISTINCTIONS, ASSUMPTIONS, AND A DEFINITION

Given the heterogeneity of this list, some conceptual distinctions will help to map the terrain, clarify assumptions, and define the class of second-opinion mechanisms that I will analyze.

Judgment aggregation vs. preference aggregation. The very idea of a "second opinion" implies that opinion-givers are expressing judgments rather than preferences about the question at hand. The arguments canvassed earlier appeal, even if implicitly, to the idea that additional opinions might produce better answers; they suppose that there is a fact of the matter, about which opinions are offered. My hope is to explicate, evaluate, and improve those arguments, taking them on their own terms. So I will accept their premises and assume that the opinion-givers have common preferences, values, or goals, and the collective problem is to make the best possible use of the dispersed bits of information or expertise that each of them possesses.

The plausibility of this assumption varies with the nature of the institution and the decision. Where members of a decision-making group or institution have common aims but imperfect information, decision making is an exercise in the pooling or aggregation of diverse factual, causal, or instrumental judgments. Administrative agencies, expert advisory bodies, and courts often engage in this sort of epistemic voting. Legislatures often amount to a forum for bargaining among political parties with different aims, but there are always substantial domains in which the major parties have common aims. Second-opinion arguments rest on an epistemic assumption that is not always plausible, but is sometimes indispensable.

On this conception, all second-opinion arguments are epistemic. This is simply a stipulation. If we like, we can define second "opinions" more broadly to include nonepistemic questions about whether adding decision makers or vetogates to the lawmaking process improves preference aggregation, as opposed to judgment aggregation. Although that broader definition strikes me as linguistically odd, it might make sense for some purposes, but not for my purposes here. In any event, the converse does not hold; an

---

[26] *See* Walter E. Dellinger et al., Principles to Guide the Office of Legal Counsel (Dec. 21, 2004), *available at* http://www.acslaw.org/files/2004%20programs_OLC%20principles_white%20paper.pdf.

epistemic argument need not rest on the benefits of second opinions. One might, for example, argue in favor of paramount and exclusive judicial authority to interpret the Constitution, on the ground that a division of epistemic labor between legislatures who specialize in policy questions and judges who specialize in legal questions would produce the best array of decisions overall. Whatever the (de)merits of this argument, it is epistemic but does not cite the benefits of second opinions. To the contrary, it argues for a single opinion on constitutionality.

Again, I make no suggestion that judgment aggregation is the exclusive rationale for the institutional arrangements I consider, or even the most important rationale. Bicameralism, for example, is often best analyzed in a model of preference aggregation and bargaining between different social, economic, geographic, or political groups or interests, who compromise by designing a legislature with two chambers, each of which is dominated by one group. But insofar as institutional arrangements are (said to be) justified as second-opinion mechanisms, I will consider the conditions under which such a justification might be valid, whatever other rationales there might be for the relevant institution.

Aggregation and counting: how many opinions? It is apparent that many second-opinion arguments implicitly count institutions as single opinion-givers. The House is counted as giving one opinion, the Senate another, and so on. This implicitly aggregates the opinions of many individuals into one. But why should this be so? If a legislative chamber has hundreds of members, and a court has a handful, should they each be counted as giving one opinion? If so, should each opinion be given the same weight? (As we will see, statistical principles of aggregation suggest that the number of individuals in a group can strongly affect the quality of the group's collective judgments.) Perhaps all or most second-opinion arguments are fundamentally spurious, because they equate unlikes, and because they rest on implausible aggregation rules.

In what follows, I will generally bracket and set aside this external critique of second-opinion arguments. My aim is to evaluate the internal logic of such arguments. So I will accept the implicitly aggregative premises of the arguments and then ask whether the arguments succeed, even if institutions can be treated as single opinion-givers. In any event, I believe that it can sometimes make sense to aggregate in that way, at least for certain purposes. Almost all multimember institutions use formal or informal voting rules or practices of consensus designed to ensure that the institution "speaks with one voice." Moreover, as we will see, cascades and other processes of opinion-formation within groups of individuals can radically reduce the epistemic independence of voting members, especially when hot emotions are engaged, and this can cause multimember institutions to behave as though possessed of a single mind. None of this implies that it always makes sense to treat institutions as single-opinion givers, let alone to give all institutional opinions equal weight. It is just to say that a blanket dismissal of second-opinion arguments on such grounds is equally implausible.

Simultaneous vs. sequential opinions. Multiple opinions might be rendered either simultaneously or sequentially. In medical and legal contexts, patients and clients usually obtain a second opinion only after obtaining a first, but they might instead obtain multiple opinions simultaneously from several doctors or lawyers. Where two chambers must both approve a bill in order for it to become law, nothing prevents both chambers from voting simultaneously on the same text. That said, the institutional dynamics of sequential opinion-giving are importantly different from simultaneous opinion-giving; sequential opinion-giving gives rise to both a distinctive benefit and distinctive risk. The benefit is that second or subsequent opinion-givers may learn from the first opinion, while the distinctive risk is that the second or subsequent opinion-giver will copy the first or otherwise render an opinion that lacks sufficient independence to add value to the decision-making process (the risk of information cascades, discussed later). I will focus, for the most part, on the sequential case, as second-opinion mechanisms in real-world legal systems usually take this form.

Whole vs. partial opinions. The second opinion might consider all the issues considered in the first, or only a subset of those issues. When a patient obtains the opinion of both a general practitioner and a specialist, the second opinion is partial. Somewhat analogously, judicial review considers only a subset of the questions posed by the legislative or agency action under review. I will consider both types of second opinions, as the context warrants.

Ex ante vs. ex post opinions. In many cases, a second opinion is obtained before the relevant decision is taken, at least if the decision is costly to reverse. In an extended sense, however, "second opinions" or "second thoughts" sometimes refer to *reconsideration* after a decision has been taken. In this sense, petitions for judicial rehearing and legislative motions to reconsider might be understood to fall within the ambit of second opinions. Under the doctrine of *stare decisis*, courts typically adhere to the rule or rationale of previous decisions, yet a court might reconsider and overrule a precedent, citing the need for a "sober second thought" or the desirability of following even wisdom that comes too late.[27]

The difference between reconsideration of a binding decision, on the one hand, and second opinions, on the other, may be illustrated by contrasting the usual doctrine of *stare decisis* with an older version of common-law precedent, mentioned earlier. Under modern *stare decisis*, the court issues a binding decision in the first case but may reconsider it later. The older approach, by contrast, held that multiple judicial opinions were required in order to establish binding law in the first place. "The key distinction is that under a principle of stare decisis, a single case authored by an author-itative court standing alone is binding in all subsequent cases; whereas precedent, as traditionally applied, arose only through a pattern of several cases decided in agreement with one another...."[28]

The same opinion-giver vs. different opinion-givers. Some second-opinion mechanisms require two opinions from different individuals or institutions. This is the typical case in private-law settings, where a patient or client obtains a first opinion from one professional and then obtains a second opinion from a third party. By contrast, other second-opinion mechanisms obtain two different opinions in succession from the same opinion-giver, either under different procedures or after a lapse of time. Two-enactment rules or two-reading rules, for example, can be justified as an attempt to obtain a sober second thought from the same legislative body that produced the first decision.

Individual vs. collective decision makers. The decision maker who obtains two or more opinions before acting may either be an individual, such as a patient or client, or else a collective body, such as a multimem-ber agency or court. In the former case, the individual may obtain two or more opinions from experts, but may also obtain two or more opinions from *herself* before taking action. Standard maxims of practical decision making urge this course, as in the advice to "think twice" before making serious decisions. Formalizing and testing this sort of pragmatic advice, a small but growing literature examines the possibility that an individual decision maker may sample an internal probability distribution in order to generate two or more estimates of an uncertain quantity.[29] This procedure

---

[27] Henslee v. Union Planters Nat'l Bank, 335 U.S. 595, 600 (1949) (Frankfurter, J., dissent-ing) ("Wisdom too often never comes, and so one ought not to reject it merely because it comes late.").

[28] Zywicki & Sanders, *supra* note, at 579.

[29] *See, e.g.,* Edward Vul & Harold Pashler, *Measuring the Crowd Within: Probabilistic Representations within Individuals,* 19 Pscyhol. Sci. 645 (2008); Stefan M. Herzog &

has been shown to produce better quantitative estimates, somewhat akin to averaging multiple estimates within a group; the individual thus draws on a sort of internal "wisdom of crowds."[30] The accuracy benefit is especially large if the self-sampling individual allows substantial time to elapse between the estimates.[31]

Mandatory vs. optional second opinions. In many cases second opinions are optional, but in some cases they are mandatory. Where patients fund their own medical care, a second opinion is strictly optional, yet under some health-insurance plans, a second opinion is mandatory for certain procedures.[32] Likewise, under the Oregon Death with Dignity Act, patients could obtain a prescription for drugs necessary for self-euthanasia, but only if two doctors agreed that the patient was terminal.[33] Under the constitutional requirement of advise and consent, Senate approval is indispensable to presidential appointment of certain classes of officers, whereas, under bicameralism, both chambers must agree before the law is changed.

Advisory vs. binding opinions. Even if the second opinion is mandatory, it may be advisory or instead binding. In the binding case, the usual default rule is that the proposed action cannot be taken unless both opinion-givers approve it; later I will illustrate both that case and some alternative default rules. In the advisory case, law makes it mandatory to obtain a second opinion, but does not require the decision maker to follow either opinion, and in particular does not require that the two (or more) opinion-givers agree. Statutes often require administrative agencies to consult with other agencies or officials, or with advisory committees, thus obtaining a second opinion before taking action. However, these statutes do not usually give the party consulted a veto over the decision or require the decision-making agency to follow the consulted party's opinion (although the decision-making agency may have to give reasons, on the record, for refusing to do so).[34]

Ralph Hertwig, *The Wisdom of Many in One Mind: Improving Individual Judgments with Dialectical Bootstrapping*, 20 PSYCHOL. SCI. 231 (2009).

[30] *See* Vul & Pashler, *supra* note ; Herzog & Hertwig, *supra* note. For the wisdom of crowds in group settings, see JAMES SUROWIECKI, THE WISDOM OF CROWDS: WHY THE MANY ARE SMARTER THAN THE FEW AND HOW COLLECTIVE WISDOM SHAPES BUSINESS, ECONOMIES, SOCIETIES, AND NATIONS (2004).

[31] Vul and Pashler conjecture that this is due to the gradual erosion of an anchoring effect, which compromises the independence of guesses made in close succession. *See* Vul & Pashler, *supra* note.

[32] Sir Richard Bayliss, *Second Opinions*, 296 BRIT. MED. J. 808, 808 (1988).

[33] OR. REV. STAT. § 127.800(8) (West 2003).

[34] For examples, see Adrian Vermeule, *The Parliament of the Experts*, 58 DUKE L.J. 2231, 2233–35 (2009).

Second-opinion mechanisms: a definition. Given these distinctions, I am now in a position to define the class of mechanisms that I will analyze. I will generally define a second-opinion mechanism as an institutional arrangement that either permits or requires two successive opinions on some issue of fact, causation, policy, or law from some decision-making body or bodies. On the dimensions given earlier, this definition focuses on (1) judgment aggregation through (2) sequential opinions issued (3) before the legal status quo changes. On other dimensions, my analysis will be catholic; I will consider cases involving (4) whole or partial opinions issued (5) by the same and different opinion-givers, (6) by individual or collective decision makers, (7) in mandatory or optional opinions, and (8) in advisory or binding opinions. Obviously one might delimit the subject matter differently. The basic motivation for the choices embodied in the definition is strictly pragmatic; I believe it accounts for the main cases of interest to constitutional and institutional designers, and captures the common usage of "second opinions." However, the proof of that claim must be in the pudding, and in any event, I will consider other cases for purposes of comparison and contrast as the analysis proceeds.

BENEFITS, COSTS, AND COMPARATIVE STATICS

From the standpoint of actors within the institutional system, when and why might it be desirable to obtain a second (or third or Nth) opinion before taking action? From the standpoint of an institutional designer, when and why might it be desirable to create institutional arrangements that permit or require second (or third or Nth) opinions before in-system decision makers take action? I will attempt to lay out the main benefits and costs of second-opinion mechanisms, and then develop some comparative statics – the conditions under which second-opinion mechanisms are most or least successful.

BENEFITS

Cooling-off and the "sober second thought." Second-opinion justifications often point to the benefits of *cooling off*: the first opinion is assumed to be emotion-laden or otherwise overheated, while the second opinion is more temperate. At their core, second opinions represent an additional filter that selects out bad decisions – a precaution against the risk of hasty or ill-considered decision making.

Sometimes the sober second thought is literally that:

> Wrongfully condemned by king Philip [of Macedon] when he was in liquor, [a woman] cried out that she appealed the judgment. When he asked to whom she appealed, "to Philip," she said, "but to Philip sober." She dissipated the fumes of wine as he yawned, and by her ready courage forced the drunkard to come to his senses and, after a more careful examination of the case, to render a juster verdict.[35]

Yet sobriety can also be contrasted, metaphorically, with political passion and intemperance. When upper legislative chambers are said to provide a sober second thought, the implicit image is aristocratic: lower chambers are awash with politically intemperate popular representatives, while the senators or lords can hold their political liquor. Similarly, in a famous (and apocryphal) anecdote about bicameralism, upper chambers are said to lower the political temperature:

> When Jefferson returned from France he was breakfasting with Washington, and asked him why he agreed to a Senate. "Why," said Washington, "did you just now pour that coffee into your saucer before drinking it?" "To cool it," said Jefferson; "my throat is not made of brass." "Even so," said Washington, "we pour our legislation into the Senatorial saucer to cool it."[36]

Epistemic diversity. A distinct, but related, justification for second-opinion mechanisms points to the value of *epistemic diversity*.[37] Unlike the cooling-off justification, this does not require an assumption that the second opinion is superior to the first. The picture is just that the two opinions are delivered from different angles, and that the difference is itself epistemically valuable, because it can help the decision maker triangulate on the truth. This idea can rest on either of two related mechanisms: statistical aggregation or perspectival aggregation.

Statistical aggregation is typically illustrated by the problem of estimating a fixed but unknown quantity. In tasks of this sort, a decision

---

[35] VALERIUS MAXIMUS, FACTA ET DICTA MEMORABILIA (MEMORABLE DOINGS AND SAYINGS) 27 (Shackleton Bailey trans., 2000).
[36] Thomas Wentworth Higginson, *The Birth of a Nation,* 68 HARPER'S NEW MONTHLY MAG. 238, 242 (1884). For the apocryphal character of the anecdote, see RESPECTFULLY QUOTED 60 (Suzy Platt ed., 1992).
[37] *See generally* SCOTT E. PAGE, THE DIFFERENCE: HOW THE POWER OF DIVERSITY CREATES BETTER GROUPS, FIRMS, SCHOOLS, AND SOCIETIES (2007) (arguing that collective wisdom often transcends that of the sum of its parts).

procedure that averages multiple estimates produces clear epistemic benefits. The average error of two estimates will tend to be lower than the error of a single estimate, because random error washes out. Across individuals, averaging can even wash out systematic biases, so long as different individuals have different systematic biases that are uncorrelated with one another.[38]

Tasks involving quantitative estimation are simplistic; of course most epistemic tasks that the legal system must undertake are far more complex. But the estimation task merely illustrates that where there is a right answer, somehow defined, the average of multiple independent estimates will tend to converge on the truth, for purely statistical reasons. The larger the number of independent estimates, the more likely it becomes that idiosyncratic estimates will be washed out. Some will err on the high side, some on the low side, and the average of the group of estimates will converge on the truth as the number of estimates increases. This statistical point underlies the Condorcet Jury Theorem, which holds, in its simplest form, that where a group votes on a binary choice, where each voter is even slightly more likely to be right than wrong, and where the voters' errors are uncorrelated (the votes are "independent"), then a majority of the group will be more likely to be correct than the individual voter, and the chance that the majority is correct converges on certainty as the size of the group increases.[39]

Another mechanism involves perspectival aggregation, illustrated by Aristotle's idea of "the Wisdom of the Multitude"[40]:

> For the many, of whom each individual is not a good man, when they meet together may be better than the few good, if regarded not individually but collectively, just as a feast to which many contribute is better than a dinner provided out of a single purse. For each individual among the many has a share of excellence and practical wisdom, and when they meet together, just as they become in a manner one man, who has many feet, and hands, and senses, so too with regard to their character and thought. Hence the many are better judges than a single man of music and poetry; for some

[38] Vul & Pashler, *supra* note ; Herzog & Hertwig, *supra* note ; Richard P. Larrick & Jack B. Soll, *Intuitions About Combining Opinions: Misappreciation of the Averaging Principle*, 52 MGMT. SCI. 111, 112 (2006).
[39] For an introduction to the vast literature on the Theorem, and for legal applications, see ADRIAN VERMEULE, LAW AND THE LIMITS OF REASON (2009).
[40] JEREMY WALDRON, THE DIGNITY OF LEGISLATION 92 (1999).

understand one part, and some another, and among them they understand the whole.[41]

In conventional cases, the doctor or lawyer who offers a second opinion may supply a new perspective that helps the patient or client to obtain a well-rounded picture of the problem, akin to the story of the blind men and the elephant. The extreme case of perspectivalism is supplied by Herodotus, who recounted of the Persians that

> [i]t is also their general practice to deliberate upon affairs of weight when they are drunk; and then on the morrow, when they are sober, the decision to which they came the night before is put before them by the master of the house in which it is made; and if it is then approved of, they act on it; if not, they set it aside. *Sometimes, however, they are sober at their first deliberation, but in this case they always reconsider the matter under the influence of wine.*[42]

Herodotus's Persians affirmatively value the drunkard's perspective, to the extent of making it a practice to get drunk for the very purpose of making decisions.

The mechanisms underpinning the diversity rationale are intrinsically fragile and sensitive to the detailed conditions of decision making. The main issue is the degree to which the opinions are correlated, or instead independent; the greater the correlation, the less the benefit of additional opinions, because the less likely it is that random errors or systematic biases will wash out.

One problem is that *common expertise implies common blind spots.* Consulting two doctors or twelve will not guarantee epistemic diversity if standardized medical training and "best practices" incorporate a uniform but erroneous belief. The greater the correlation of views across experts, due to common training or a common base of information, the more quickly the marginal benefits from consulting the next expert diminish. One review of laboratory experiments on quantitative estimates finds that typically, three to six opinions exhaust the accuracy benefit that can be obtained from additional opinions.[43] Importantly, that number does not

---

[41] *Id.* (quoting ARISTOTLE, THE POLITICS, bk. III, ch. 11, at 66 (Stephen Everson ed., Cambridge University Press 1988) (c. 350 B.C.)).

[42] 1 THE HISTORY OF HERODOTUS 211 (George Rawlinson trans., New York, D. Appleton & Co., 1889) (c. 440 B.C.) (emphasis added).

[43] Ilan Yaniv, *The Benefit of Additional Opinions*, 13 CURRENT DIRECTIONS IN PSYCHOL. SCI. 75, 75 (2004).

take into account the direct costs and opportunity costs of obtaining further opinions, so the optimal number of opinions will typically be fewer; I return to this point later.

Another problem involves *information cascades*,[44] in which the failure of independence results not from common training but from rational copying of others' judgments where information is costly. (By contrast, *reputational cascades*[45] arise when voters are concerned that expressing a certain judgment will incur social opprobrium.) An information cascade arises when a second or subsequent opinion-giver rationally ignores her private information and free-rides on opinions given earlier in the sequence, producing a series of highly correlated but unreliable opinions. This problem can be forestalled either by disclosing to the second opinion-giver all of the underlying information possessed by the first, or else by keeping the second opinion-giver ignorant of the existence or content of the first opinion.[46] By contrast, the independence-compromising effect of common professional training and best-practice standards obtains even if the second opinion-giver is unaware of the first.

Legitimacy and certainty. Finally, a second opinion may provide extra *legitimacy* to the decision or raise the decision maker's *certainty* that it is correct – at least so long as the second opinion coincides with the first. The relationship between the two notions is that legitimacy can be construed in epistemic terms, as public certainty or confidence that a governmental decision is correct; so legitimacy in this sense is really just a special case, albeit an important case, of certainty.[47] As it is tolerably obvious to say that, in general, a second confirming opinion will increase certainty, I will focus on some examples of legitimation and on its special problems.

Charles Black and Alexander Bickel famously argued that when judges uphold a statute after judicial review, they confer on it additional political legitimacy over and above the legitimacy it obtains from being enacted by

---

[44] *See* Abhijit V. Banerjee, *A Simple Model of Herd Behavior*, 107 Q.J. ECON. 797 (1992); Sushil Bikhchandani et al., *A Theory of Fads, Fashion, Custom, and Cultural Change as Informational Cascades*, 100 J. POL. ECON. 992 (1992); Ivo Welch, *Sequential Scales, Learning, and Cascades*, 47 J. FIN. 695 (1992).

[45] *See* Timur Kuran, *Ethnic Norms and Their Transformation Through Reputational Cascades*, 27 J. LEGAL STUD. 623 (1998); Timur Kuran & Cass Sunstein, *Availability Cascades and Risk Regulation*, 51 STAN. L. REV. 683 (1999).

[46] Jon Elster, *Concluding Reflections on Collective Wisdom* (2010) (unpublished manuscript).

[47] For an exploration of various senses of legitimacy, see generally Richard H. Fallon, Jr., *Legitimacy and the Constitution*, 118 HARV. L. REV. 1787 (2005).

Congress.[48] The conception of legitimacy that underpins this argument is unclear,[49] but can be interpreted epistemically. Where citizens cannot directly observe the state of the world, yet know that different branches of government, controlled by officials with uncorrelated or opposing biases, have agreed on a common policy, citizens can more confidently infer that the policy is correct.

Another example involves the series of executive orders that have given OIRA broad power to require executive agencies to employ cost-benefit analysis. Although President Reagan's initial order was controversial, subsequent Democratic and Republican presidents have left its basic framework in place, although with minor adjustments that shift over time. It has accordingly been argued that bipartisan approval of cost-benefit analysis now makes it a legitimate and established feature of the administrative state.[50] One interpretation is that the public now has greater reason to be confident that cost-benefit analysis is a beneficial tool of administration overall, despite its real costs.

So construed, legitimacy is hardly an unproblematic notion. For one thing, legitimacy may simply supervene on, or be parasitic on, other rationales for second opinions; perhaps a second-opinion mechanism has legitimating effect only insofar as it produces other benefits. Yet legitimacy may nonetheless amount to an independent benefit, just as a sentence enhancement is parasitic on an underlying sentence, yet increases its effects. Another problem is that legitimacy in the sense of increased certainty is a double-edged sword: a disagreement between the two opinion-givers may make the final decision less legitimate than it would have been if only one or the other opinion-giver had been consulted. If the House approves a bill and the Senate votes it down, the result may be more public discontent than if the bill had simply been rejected by a unicameral legislature. Although a high court composed of a left-party bloc and a right-party bloc will provide extra legitimacy to decisions on which the two blocs agree, disagreement between the blocs will exacerbate political tensions, perhaps even to a higher level than would occur were the Court dominated by a single viewpoint.

---

[48] BICKEL, *supra* note, at 29–33 (citing CHARLES BLACK, THE PEOPLE AND THE COURT: JUDICIAL REVIEW IN A DEMOCRACY 34 (1960)).

[49] Bickel defines legitimacy as "the stability of a good government over time" and says that it is "the fruit of consent to specific actions or to the authority to act." *Id.* at 172

[50] *See generally* CASS R. SUNSTEIN, THE COST-BENEFIT STATE (2002) (exploring how federal regulations are increasingly evaluated using cost-benefit analysis).

RISKS AND COSTS: FUTILITY, JEOPARDY, AND PERVERSITY

So much for the main benefits of second opinions. As always, however, precautions can create their own countervailing problems. I will focus on futility problems, which arise because adding opinions produces no marginal benefit to decision making; jeopardy problems, in which second-opinion mechanisms prove too costly on other margins; and perversity problems, in which second-opinion mechanisms may themselves create an increased risk of hasty or ill-considered decisions.

Correlation of errors: futility problems. As the correlation of errors across opinion-givers increases, the benefit of obtaining additional opinions decreases. In cases where the question is how many expert opinions to obtain, the marginal benefit diminishes because of the inherent correlation of opinions among experts in the same field.[51] As previously referenced, a review of relevant psychology experiments finds that in typical cases of estimation, "as few as three to six judgments might suffice to achieve most of what can be gained from averaging a larger number of opinions."[52] This speaks only to the issue of accuracy; if the direct costs and opportunity costs of obtaining additional opinions are also factored in, the optimal number of opinions will almost always be fewer. At the limit, it might be that even one additional opinion brings no marginal benefit on net, or even produces net costs. Even if net marginal costs are avoided, it is still true that if the correlation of errors is very high, second or nth opinions may simply be futile.

Direct costs and opportunity costs: jeopardy problems. The process of obtaining a second opinion has both direct costs and opportunity costs. In private settings, the direct cost is that the patient or client (or an insurance company or government agency acting as an insurance company) must pay out of pocket for the time spent by the second doctor or second lawyer in formulating her opinion. Direct costs are sometimes important in public settings as well. A system in which two juries sat in succession, to ensure a second opinion on every case that goes to trial, would simply be too expensive.

Samuel Johnson illustrated the opportunity costs of deliberation in the following way:

> [T]ake the case of a man who is ill. I call two physicians; they differ in opinion. I am not to lie down and die between them: I must do something.[53]

---

[51] Yaniv, *supra* note, at 75.

[52] *Id.* at 76.

[53] JAMES BOSWELL, THE JOURNAL OF A TOUR TO THE HEBRIDES WITH SAMUEL JOHNSON, L.L.D. 29 (London, Routledge, Warne & Routledge, 1860).

Whatever the best course of treatment may be, doing nothing is clearly worst of all. Johnson's "lie down and die between them" gestures at Buridan's Ass, who failed to understand opportunity costs and starved to death between two equally tempting haystacks.

If opportunity costs are sufficiently high, even a second opinion might be undesirable, let alone a third. In medicine, if time is of the essence, obtaining a second opinion might amount to a fatal blunder. The opportunity cost is that the patient or client must postpone a decision until the second opinion is obtained, and in the meantime the disease may be making headway. Likewise, the reason why there is only one captain of the ship, and the main argument for a "unitary executive,"[54] is that in emergencies there is no time for second opinions or for decision making by committee.

In many public settings, opportunity costs loom larger than direct costs. The direct costs of obtaining a second opinion from, for example, a panel of judges reviewing agency action is small; there are legal fees, and the litigant must pay a modest filing fee, but access to the system is at least formally open to all and parties do not directly pay judges or other officials for their time. Rather public opinion-providers in effect use a system of nonprice rationing through waiting time. The main cost of obtaining judicial review of agency action is not litigation cost, but delay – it can take months or years to obtain a final judicial ruling. As I will suggest later, the opportunity costs of second opinions are a major consideration in many public-law applications.

In terms of the framework developed in Chapter 2, the direct and opportunity costs of second opinions represent a jeopardy problem. To the extent that precautions against ill-considered decisions neglect such costs, they may result in institutional arrangements whose costs simply exceed their benefits. Ill-considered decisions are merely one bad among others, and deliberation merely one good among others.

Epistemic moral hazard: perversity problems. When the opinion of a first expert will be reviewed by a second expert, and the first expert anticipates that review, what, if anything, will be the effect on the first expert's opinion? If the decision of one institution is to be reviewed by another, and the members of the first institution know this, will their decisions be

---

[54] See Alexander Hamilton's argument in THE FEDERALIST No. 70, at 421–28 (Alexander Hamilton) (Charles Kessler & Clinton Rossiter ed., 1999). I use the phrase "unitary executive" in one of its many senses; in another, more technical legal sense, it refers to the question whether all officials exercising executive power must be removable at will by the president. *Compare* Myers v. United States, 272 U.S. 52 (1926), (yes) *with* Humphrey's Executor v. United States, 295 U.S. 602 (1935) (no).

better or worse? In such cases several different effects are possible. Studies of mandatory second opinions in medical decision making have sometimes suggested that the main benefit of the mandatory second opinion is a *sentinel effect*: the first doctor, anticipating review by a second, is more diligent than she would otherwise be.[55] However, anticipation of review might also induce an epistemic variety of *moral hazard*: the second opinion might induce the first doctor to make a sloppy or hasty diagnosis, anticipating that the second doctor will catch any errors.

Epistemic moral hazard creates a perversity problem. Assuming that the second opinion-giver is an imperfect detector of the errors of the first, the moral-hazard effect can mean that a system of mandatory second opinions might actually create more errors than it prevents. The general point is that anticipation of review may induce the first opinion-giver to invest too little in acquiring information, or may discourage her from using expertise she already possesses.[56]

The causal mechanisms in these examples generalize to other contexts. As to bicameralism, for example, Joseph Story argued that a second chamber would create a sentinel effect by "operat[ing] indirectly as a preventive" against bad legislation.[57] By contrast, a stock argument for unicameralism invokes moral hazard: "[T]he presence of a second house encourages and enables legislative carelessness – as when one house hastily accepts the actions of the other house on faith, without independent evaluation, or passes ill-conceived legislation, relying on the other house to correct or reject it."[58] In general, the law of anticipated reactions suggests that the behavior of first opinion-givers will be different in a system with second opinions than where no second opinions are obtained, but the nature of the difference is unclear and highly contingent. The most that can be said in the abstract is that as the chance of sentinel effects increases, the benefits of second-opinion mechanisms increase, while as the risk of moral hazard increases, the costs of second-opinion mechanisms increase. And in some contexts, the good and bad effects may occur simultaneously.

[55] Suzanne Grisez Martin et al., *Impact of a Mandatory Second-Opinion Program on Medicaid Surgery Rates*, 20 MED. CARE 21, 31 (1982).
[56] *See* Matthew C. Stephenson, *Information Acquisition and Institutional Design*, 124 HARV. L. REV. 1422, 1438–46 (2011).
[57] JOSEPH STORY, COMMENTARIES ON THE CONSTITUTION OF THE UNITED STATES § 556, at 414 (5th ed. 1905).
[58] TOM TODD, MINN. HOUSE OF REPRESENTATIVES RESEARCH DEP'T, UNICAMERAL OR BICAMERAL STATE LEGISLATURES: THE POLICY DEBATE (Aug. 1999), *available at* http://www.house.leg.state.mn.us/hrd/pubs/uni-bicam.pdf.

Optimizing the costs and benefits. As we have seen, the benefits of second opinions diminish at the margin, while the main costs of second opinions are the direct costs of obtaining a second opinion, the opportunity costs of delayed decision making, and the moral-hazard risk that the prospect of a second opinion will reduce the quality of the first opinion. These costs imply an optimization problem, as illustrated by the words of the Master:

> Chi Wen Tzu [an official] thought three times before he acted. Hearing of this, Confucius said, "Twice is enough."[59]

Each successive reconsideration of a given problem has diminishing marginal benefits and increasing marginal costs; Confucius may be suggesting that in practice two thoughts or opinions are typically optimal.[60] Whether or not that is so, the designer of second-opinion mechanisms must generally trade off the marginal benefit of consulting another opinion-giver, which diminishes due to the partial correlation of biases, against the marginal direct costs, opportunity costs, and moral-hazard risks of obtaining additional opinions.

SECOND OPINIONS: PRECAUTIONARY AND OPTIMIZING APPROACHES

Second opinions are a procedural mechanism that promise to improve the quality of decision making. Such mechanisms are widely observed in constitutional rulemaking, as a precaution against the risks of insufficient deliberation and of decision making that is distorted by passion and prejudice. The problem is that marginal increments of deliberation and procedure are never costless or risk-free; liberal theories of constitutional rulemaking, which tend to valorize value-neutral procedure, are chronically insensitive to the downside costs of further procedure.

I have argued that second-opinion mechanisms can be futile, if there is a high correlation of errors across opinion-givers; can create jeopardy problems, if the direct costs and opportunity costs of additional opinion outweigh their benefits; and can even create perverse harms by reducing

---

[59] CONFUCIUS, LUN YU 5:19 (William Cheung ed., 1985), *available at* http://www.confucius.org/lunyu/lange.htm.

[60] In a different yet compatible gloss, Confucius is suggesting that repeated deliberation amounts to vacillation rather than prudence. *See* E. BRUCE BROOKS & A. TAKEO BROOKS, THE ORIGINAL ANALECTS: SAYINGS OF CONFUCIUS AND HIS SUCCESSORS 26 (1998).

the quality of decisions, if the anticipation of a second opinion causes the first opinion to be inferior ("epistemic moral hazard"). The mature approach to second opinions, and to additional or marginal layers of decision-making procedure generally, is to optimize across all of these risks, without any systematic precautionary bias that assumes more procedure is necessarily better than less.

6

The Risks of Expertise: Political Administration and Expert Groupthink

For a final case study in the management of political risks, I turn to the administrative state. Here the relevant law is only partly constitutional in the strict sense. The eighteenth-century origins of America's written constitution implies that constitutional text is often silent on crucial questions about the administrative state, which is largely a creation of the late nineteenth and twentieth centuries. Even where the written constitution does speak to the relevant issues, its pronouncements are obscure, even Delphic, and must be elicited through controversial methods of interpretation. Thus the law structuring and governing the administrative state stems in large part from quasi-constitutional framework statutes, especially the Administrative Procedure Act of 1946 (APA).

Here too, however, political risk management is central to the enterprise, and the contrast between precautionary and mature regulation of political risks is central to the analysis. In the face of countervailing political risks and competing political forces, the administrative state struggles to find a *modus vivendi*, let alone an optimum. At the level of theory, law, democracy, and expertise all have their claims. At the level of concrete politics, competing institutions and interest groups buffet the administrative agencies. Within a field of perpetual conflict structured by congressional statutes and the oversight of congressional committees, on the one hand, and presidential policies and White House oversight, on the other, agencies make decisions of law, policy, and scientific fact or causation. The third leg of this triad is critical; given the complexity of the issues that agencies decide, facts and causation are routinely difficult and contested, and agencies are either permitted or required to base their decisions on the views of expert, panels or experts on the agency's own internal staff.

This interaction – among background political institutions, agencies, experts, and complex issues at the frontiers of science and policy – creates two political risks of special interest here. These are political risks in the second-order sense we have used throughout; they arise from the allocation of decision-making power to political appointees in the agencies or political actors in the presidential bureaucracy, on the one hand, or to experts, on the other.

The first such risk is the *politicization of expertise* – the strategic use of scientific and technocratic arguments by interest groups, politicians, and political appointees to agencies, in the service of ulterior aims. The "science charade"[1] can but need not take the form of bogus causal and factual arguments; where a scientific consensus has not yet gelled, politically motivated selection among plausible arguments often suffices. In many cases,[2] expert consensus is used as an implicit benchmark for determining that science has been politicized, yet that benchmark is itself undertheorized.

Public law's standard reaction to the risk of politicization takes one of two forms: either to insulate the agency from politics by making its head(s) independent – not subject to being fired by the president or Congress – or else to require agencies to consider the recommendations of independent expert panels. In the most important cases, agencies are obligated by statute to give great weight to expert views. When revising National Ambient Air Quality Standards, the Environmental Protection Agency (EPA) must consider the report of its permanent Clean Air Scientific Advisory Committee and explain any departure from the committee's "findings" and "recommendations."[3] Likewise, Congress established an Advisory Commission on Childhood Vaccines within the Department of Health and Human Services. If the Secretary of that department receives a recommendation from the Commission, the Secretary must either conduct a rulemaking in accordance with the recommendation or publish, in the Federal Register, a "statement of reasons" for refusing to do so.[4]

One way of understanding these measures is as a set of institutional precautions against politics. Insulation of independent agencies, and a

---

[1] *See* Wendy E. Wagner, *The Science Charade in Toxic Risk Regulation*, 95 COLUM. L. REV. 1613, 1617 (1995).

[2] Shapiro offers two examples of "science denial" and "politicization" by the Bush administration. Sidney A. Shapiro, *OMB and the Politicization of Risk Assessment*, 37 ENVTL. L. 1083, 1086–87 (2007). The first is that the administration "refus[ed] to acknowledge or act on the overwhelming scientific evidence of global climate change...." *Id.* at 1086. In the second, "[t]he Food and Drug Administration ... refused to approve the emergency contraceptive Plan B, despite the fact that two scientific advisory committees had overwhelmingly found that the drug was safe and effective." *Id.* at 1086–87.

[3] 42 U.S.C. § 7607(d)(3) (2006).

[4] *Id.* § 300aa-14(c)(2).

mandatory role for experts, is intended to safeguard agency decision making against the interference of interest groups, the White House, and other political actors. But the solution itself creates a second, countervailing risk: the risk of pathological decision making by experts. Expert panels are groups, and in many cases such panels perform superbly, not only because their members are experts, but because they benefit from various mechanisms of collective wisdom[5] – the "wisdom of (expert) crowds." Yet by the same token, groups of experts can suffer both from the pathologies intrinsic to all group decision making – the "folly of (expert) crowds" – as well as pathologies distinctive to professional expertise. Groups of experts may suffer from overconfidence, technocratic myopia, false consensus, and insufficient motivation, to name only a few of the relevant problems.

The upshot is that administrative law must accommodate, trade off, and if possible optimize these competing risks. In this chapter, I will explain the distinctive strengths and weaknesses of decision making by politically influenced agencies, on the one hand, and groups of experts, on the other, and I will offer explore arguments and principles that attempt to accommodate the competing political risks – principles that attempt to implement a mature, rather than precautionary, perspective on all relevant harms. As throughout, my enterprise is not to get the right first-order rules on the merits, but to get the structure of the analysis right. Whether or not the principles I discuss strike the right balance, the larger point is that here, as in earlier chapters, precautions against one sort of risk (like politicization) must take account of countervailing risks, including risks created by the precautions themselves. As to all relevant risks that may arise in the administrative state, optimal rather than maximal precautions are the touchstone of good administrative design.

AGENCIES AND EXPERTS: SOME PRINCIPLES

Must an agency follow expert consensus, or even the view of a majority of experts, on questions of fact and causation? As I mentioned, some regulatory statutes, notably the Clean Air Act, establish an expert panel and require the agency to submit its proposed rules to the panel. Although the agency is not obligated by statute to do what the panel says, the agency must give an adequate reason if it rejects the findings or recommendations

---

[5] *See generally* COLLECTIVE WISDOM: PRINCIPLES AND MECHANISMS (Jon Elster & Hélène Landemore eds., 2012) (analyzing the advantages and potential downsides of collective decision making).

of a panel majority.[6] Sometimes, courts unthinkingly construe a requirement of reason-giving as merely requiring a first-order reason – a reasoned
statement of the agency's substantive views about the factual or causal or
predictive questions at issue.

In light of the countervailing risks of politicized science and expert
pathologies, however, this approach may be mistaken. I will suggest that
a mature consideration of the tradeoffs implies the following approach:
courts should require the agency to follow expert consensus unless the
agency gives a valid second-order reason to the contrary. The agency, in
other words, would be required to offer a valid second-order reason to
think that the expert panel's factual findings are epistemically suspect, relative to that of the agency. Absent such a second-order reason, the views of
the expert panel as to factual matters should trump the agency's own first-
order judgment, which represents nothing more than another expert vote
and as such is defeated by the expert consensus or (super)majority view to
the contrary, where that exists.

Nothing in this analysis implies that agencies must defer to a panel's
view about how alternative policies should be evaluated, given the facts.
As to that question, the agency's judgment controls, insofar as the law
permits. The consequence is that the agency will have an incentive to be
clear when its decisions are based on evaluative differences with the panel,
thus making the agency's normative commitments transparent to outside
monitors – Congress, courts, and the public.

Interestingly, although the voting rules for expert panels are usually left
unclear, a simple majority of experts rather than a supermajority is usually assumed to be controlling, not in the sense that it can bind the agency
without more, but in the sense that a majority is entitled to state the view
of "the panel" as such. As we will see, there is sound epistemic reason for
this assumption. Under a broad range of conditions, the views of a simple
majority of experts are more likely to be correct than the views of any other
subgroup; requiring a supermajority of experts on the panel to agree in
order to force the agency to respond with reasons would in effect privilege
the views of a lesser subgroup, with bad epistemic consequences.

WHY RESPECT EXPERT PANELS?

In order to understand the conditions under which agencies must defer to
the conclusions of experts, we have to start with a simpler question. Let us

---

[6]   42 U.S.C. § 7607(d)(3).

assume that agencies are never politicized – that agencies simply wish to make welfare-maximizing decisions, but that the costs of information and the complexity of policy issues make agencies unsure what to do. Under conditions of this sort, why should agencies pay any attention at all to the *conclusions* offered by groups of experts? The experts' reasons might, of course, be independently convincing to the agency, or not. But does the bare fact that a group of experts, or the majority of a group, has concluded one way or another have any intrinsic weight, apart from reasons? Why should agencies count expert noses in that way?

There is an affirmative basis for counting expert noses, one rooted in the theory of decision making under risk and uncertainty. Optimal decision making requires optimal information gathering. The agency's problem is to find facts correctly, but it cannot invest unlimited resources in doing so. By counting the noses of experts, under certain conditions, the agency will be able to maximize the overall quality of its decisions, taking into account both the accuracy of its decisions and the costs of decision making.

What are those conditions? In particular, why should a vote of experts be thought more epistemically reliable than the agency's own views? The answer lies in the rational-choice theory of committee decision making. For present purposes, this body of theory can be divided into two branches, involving respectively the *aggregation of information* that expert panel members possess and the *acquisition of information* by those members.

I will begin with the aggregation question, best approached through the lens of the Condorcet Jury Theorem, which was introduced in Chapter 5. Roughly, assume a group of sincere voters – voters trying to get the right answer – whose competence is, on average,[7] at least slightly better than random. With two choices,[8] this means that the voters are slightly more likely to be correct than incorrect. In order to bracket the issue of information acquisition, we will assume for the moment that the voters' level of competence is exogenous; it is just there.

The Jury Theorem then shows that a majority vote of this group is increasingly likely to be correct as the size of the group increases, as the average competence of its members increases, or as its cognitive diversity increases, where diversity means that the biases of the group's members

---

[7] *See* Bernard Grofman, Guillermo Owen & Scott L. Feld, *Thirteen Theorems in Search of the Truth*, 15 THEORY & DECISION 261, 273–74 (1983).

[8] The Theorem can be extended to more than two choices, but as nothing in my discussion depends on this wrinkle, I will assume the two-option case. Note that at least some multiple-option cases can be reduced to two-option cases through successive pairwise comparison.

are negatively correlated.[9] Where the voters are themselves experts, the second two conditions – competence and diversity – tend to work at cross-purposes. Experts tend to have high individual competence, but as we have seen in the previous chapter, experts may also have highly correlated biases, perhaps because of common professional training or because they copy each other's opinions.

For now, the key point is just that majority voting most effectively aggregates the information dispersed among the panel of experts. Nose-counting of the assembled experts is just a means by which the agency can in effect aggregate expert views, even if the agency itself lacks first-order competence. The agency's nose-counting is itself a rational second-order epistemic strategy.

The Jury Theorem can be extended to qualified majority ("supermajority") rules, but only with restrictions.[10] It has been shown that qualified majority rules maximize the probability of making a correct decision, but only if the status quo is stipulated to prevail in the event that no alternative garners the requisite supermajority.[11] This is a suspect condition in the administrative state, where the regulatory status quo – which may just be the default common-law baseline – has no necessary priority, either in theory[12] or under the terms of the APA.[13]

If the status quo preference is abandoned, then a weaker result holds: "for sufficiently large [decision-making groups] ... if the average competence of the voters is greater than the fraction of the votes needed for passage ... a group decision is more likely to be correct than the decision of a single randomly chosen individual."[14] This condition is stringent; if the decision-making group uses a two-thirds majority rule, for example, then average competence must be at least 0.67. Absent these conditions, the

---

[9] Lu Hong & Scott E. Page, *Some Microfoundations of Collective Wisdom*, in COLLECTIVE WISDOM: PRINCIPLES AND MECHANISMS (Jon Elster & Helene Landemore eds., Cambridge University Press 2012).

[10] This paragraph is adapted from Adrian Vermeule, *Many-Minds Arguments in Legal Theory*, 1 J. LEGAL ANALYSIS 1 (2009).

[11] Ruth C. Ben-Yashar & Shmuel I. Nitzan, *The Optimal Decision Rule for Fixed-Size Committees in Dichotomous Choice Situations: The General Result*, 38 INT'L ECON. REV. 175, 179–83 (1997).

[12] Cass R. Sunstein, *Reviewing Agency Inaction After Heckler v. Chaney*, 52 U. CHI. L. REV. 653, 656–57 (1985).

[13] APA provisions treat agency action and inaction equivalently. 5 U.S.C. §§ 551(13), 706(1) (2006). In practice, however, reviewing courts are more reluctant to force agency action than to block it. *See, e.g.*, Heckler v. Chaney, 470 U.S. 821, 831 (1985).

[14] Mark Fey, *A Note on the Condorcet Jury Theorem with Supermajority Voting Rules*, 20 SOC. CHOICE & WELFARE 27, 31 (2003).

background logic of the Jury Theorem is that majority voting is epistemically preferred. Any lesser subgroup of decision makers is less likely to be correct, given the Theorem's other conditions; and majority voting alone gives no privilege to the status quo, in line with the administrative state's general assumption that failure to regulate where regulation is justified is just as dangerous as regulation where regulation is unjustified.

I turn now to the problem of acquiring information. The standard treatment of the Jury Theorem assumes that information is exogenous. If this assumption is relaxed, it is apparent that there is a tradeoff between the number of experts and the epistemic quality of their views. If information is exogenous, then the more experts, the more likely it is that the group decision will be accurate, so long as each is at least slightly better than random and holding all else constant. However, where experts must decide how much information to acquire – how much epistemic effort to invest in the panel's activities – increasing numbers makes each expert less likely to be the decisive vote, which reduces the effort each will expend. Increasing panel size need not increase the aggregate information panelists hold, because less information will be acquired.[15] In short, with endogenous information, experts will have an incentive to engage in epistemic free riding.[16]

This problem has at least three consequences. First, it creates an optimization problem: institutional designers setting up committees must trade off the quantity of panelists against the quality of their contributions and votes.[17] However, in most of the real-world cases I will discuss, Congress has set or capped the number of panel members, or the agency has done so before the agency action giving rise to the litigation, or the number is extrinsically determined in some other way; I will thus bracket this set of issues. Second, the danger of epistemic free-riding within the panel may give agencies good second-order reasons to reject the panel's recommendations, under conditions where the problem is especially likely to be serious. I return to these problems later.

Finally, the problem of endogenous information provides further reason to think that majority rule is the best voting rule for expert panels

[15] For this reason, polling the members of the National Academy of Sciences about a relevant problem might well yield less information than voting within a small panel of experts focused on the same problem. Thanks to Stuart Benjamin for raising this issue.

[16] Christian List & Philip Pettit, *An Epistemic Free-Riding Problem?*, in KARL POPPER: CRITICAL APPRAISALS 128, 138–40 (Philip Catton & Graham Macdonald eds., 2004).

[17] Drora Karotkin & Jacob Paroush, *Optimum Committee Size: Quality-Versus-Quantity Dilemma*, 20 SOC. CHOICE & WELFARE 429, 433 (2003).

and the best nose-counting rule for agencies attempting to take advantage of expert opinion, at least where experts face highly complex regulatory problems. It has been shown that as the quality of information decreases, so that each voter will get a very imperfect idea of the truth even after investing effort, the optimal voting rule will fall, from unanimity down toward simple majority.[18] The basic intuition is that the larger the supermajority needed to make a decision, such as making a finding for the agency to use, the less each panelist will invest in acquiring information, because the imperfection of the information acquired makes it less likely that any individual panelist will be decisive. (Imagine you sit on a twelve-member panel that requires a unanimous vote to act. Your vote only matters if all eleven others vote identically. If the facts are highly unclear, what are the chances that everyone else will vote the same way?) If the panel faces an extremely blurry informational environment, as it does in most of the hard regulatory problems for which Congress or the agency has thought an expert panel necessary, then a voting rule approaching simple majority is likely to be best.

A similar point holds if the concern is not that experts will fail to invest in acquiring information, but rather that experts will manipulate or distort the information they already possess in order to produce preferred outcomes. In one illuminating model of a deliberative expert committee,[19] majority rule induces the members to reveal their private information with less distortion than under unanimity. The reason is that if a unanimous vote is necessary to depart from the status quo, then members biased in favor of change have strong incentives to overclaim or otherwise manipulate their information. By contrast, majority rule minimizes the net incentives for distortion by panel members with different biases for and against change.

PROBLEMS WITH EXPERT GROUPS

So far we have seen some virtues of decision making by expert groups, and I have argued that agencies who are uncertain what view to take of

---

[18] Nicola Persico, *Committee Design with Endogenous Information*, 71 REV. ECON. STUD. 165, 167 (2004).

[19] David Austen-Smith & Timothy J. Feddersen, *Deliberation and Voting Rules*, in SOCIAL CHOICE AND STRATEGIC DECISIONS 269 (David Austen-Smith & John Duggan eds., 2005); *see also* David Austen-Smith & Timothy J. Feddersen, *Deliberation, Preference Uncertainty, and Voting Rules*, 100 AM. POL. SCI. REV. 209, 210 (2006).

first-order factual or causal problems often have excellent reason to count noses – in other words, to follow a second-order epistemic strategy of deference to what (a majority of) the expert panel thinks. That said, expert panels suffer from both pathologies incident to group decision making generally, and pathologies distinctive to experts. A mature consideration of the costs and benefits of expert decision making in the administrative state must take all of these costs into account. I will first detail the countervailing risks, and then consider some mature principles that attempt to incorporate awareness of those risks as well.

Judgment falsification and groupthink. A major problem is false consensus, herding, or groupthink within groups of experts. In a Jury Theorem framework, the concern is that a group of experts in a given field will have highly correlated biases, because of common professional training, because they copy each other's opinions, or even because the expert panel fakes an appearance of consensus for public consumption; in the last case, experts will not be voting sincerely, which undermines the operation of the Theorem. I will touch on each of these hazards in turn.

Common professional training is a built-in hazard of expert panels drawn from a scientific field or subfield. Copying may occur because of an "information cascade," in which individual experts rationally use the views of other experts as the basis for forming their own views, thus reducing the number of independent opinions expressed by the group overall. Here there is a kind of epistemic free-riding[20] or "cognitive loafing,"[21] as some within the group benefit from the information provided by others' views without contributing information themselves. Copying may also occur because of a "reputational cascade,"[22] in which experts follow the views of senior scientists or powerful figures in the field, for fear of being stamped as incompetent or odd.

As to the falsification of expert judgments, case studies have shown that expert panels sometimes gin up a consensus that does not actually exist.[23] The panel may do this in order to maximize its members' joint influence on agencies and other decision makers, or out of paternalistic concern that the agency or public will become confused if the panel ventilates its disputes,

---

[20] *See* List & Pettit, *supra* note, at 138–40.
[21] Mark Seidenfeld, *Cognitive Loafing, Social Conformity, and Judicial Review of Agency Rulemaking*, 87 CORNELL L. REV. 486, 486 (2002).
[22] Timur Kuran & Cass R. Sunstein, *Availability Cascades and Risk Regulation*, 51 STAN. L. REV. 683, 685–89, 727–28 (1999).
[23] John Beatty, *Masking Disagreement Among Experts*, 3 EPISTEME 52, 55 (2006).

or because the panel's members have a professional interest in preserving a public reputation for expertise.[24] When this occurs, some on the panel are falsifying their judgments, and the panel as a whole conceals information – about the presence and magnitude of expert disagreement – that is useful for decision makers.

The conditions for expert groupthink. Whether such concerns are serious depends on the composition, structure, and decision-making process of the expert panel. What factors make groupthink or judgment falsification more or less likely? I will use "groupthink," itself an ill-defined notion, as shorthand for the various forms of epistemic free-riding, informational and reputational cascades, and falsification of judgments I have mentioned. Although the problems are somewhat different, it turns out that the institutional determinants of the various types of groupthink overlap a great deal.

First, groupthink is less likely as the diversity of panel membership increases.[25] Many panels are chosen uniformly from specialists in relevant scientific subfields. In other cases, statutes require that expert panels contain professionals from different fields, or even nonprofessionals, and these can be understood as means for diversifying the panel's training, assumptions and intellectual outlook. In Jury Theorem terms, this approach trades off reduced average competence, because diversification requires that some specialists in the subfield must be bumped off a panel of fixed size, for reduced correlation of biases across the group. Depending on the precise composition, the benefits of reduced correlation can more than compensate for the loss, in which case some degree of diversification will be epistemically optimal.[26] I will return to these issues shortly.

Another major cause of groupthink is sequential, rather than simultaneous, expression of views among the panel experts. If experts express their judgments in ignorance of other experts' judgments, herding and cascades are ruled out, although false consensus arising from experts' concern for reputation is still possible.[27] Ideally, experts should vote simultaneously

---

[24]   *Id.* at 53–54. *See generally* Bauke Visser & Otto H. Swank, *On Committees of Experts*, 122 Q.J. ECON. 337 (2007) (showing conditions under which a panel of experts concerned for their individual reputations will generate false consensus).

[25]   CASS R. SUNSTEIN, WHY SOCIETIES NEED DISSENT 141–44 (2003).

[26]   Krishna K. Ladha, *The Condorcet Jury Theorem, Free Speech, and Correlated Votes*, 36 AM. J. POL. SCI. 617, 629 (1992).

[27]   For a model in which expert panels, voting simultaneously, nonetheless generate false consensus, see Visser & Swank, *supra* note. The basic mechanism in the model is that experts believe that the audience believes that competent experts will all have the same view of the facts, in which case disagreement among the panel implies that some of its

rather than sequentially, in order to prevent informational and reputational cascades. In real-world conditions, however, simultaneity is difficult to achieve; deliberation prior to voting will give experts a sense of where other experts stand. These tensions are on display in a recent set of guidelines issued by the Food and Drug Administration for its many expert advisory committees.[28] On the one hand, the guidelines expressly recommend simultaneous voting, citing the academic literature on the risks of information cascades.[29] On the other hand, the guidelines recommend extensive deliberation before voting, and recommend against the use of secret ballots,[30] which can help block reputational cascades by preventing panel members from knowing how others voted.

The structure of experts' compensation is also important. If experts receive no compensation or merely nominal compensation, as is the case with many scientific panels, then the incentives for epistemic free-riding or cognitive loafing are at a maximum, increasing the risks of herding within the panel. Even if experts are rewarded for their own performance, information cascades are still a risk, because in an information cascade it is individually rational to follow the views of a sufficient number of others, even if one's private information is to the contrary. Both theory[31] and experiments[32] suggest that the best way to prevent information cascades from forming is to reward individuals on the basis of the accuracy of a majority vote within the group, rather than for individual accuracy. Under this reward structure, the individual's incentive is to reveal her private information to the group, maximizing the chance that (a majority of) the group as a whole will make the correct decision.

All this said, however, the groupthink concern does not show that nose-counting is necessarily an impermissible epistemic strategy for agencies. What it shows is that agencies and reviewing courts will sometimes have valid second-order, epistemic reasons for discounting the views of an

members are less competent. On further assumptions, this causes the minority to go along with the majority even if the minority disagrees. This mechanism is unaffected by the simultaneity of voting.

[28] U.S. Dep't. of Health & Human Servs., Food & Drug Admin., Guidance for FDA Advisory Committee Members and FDA Staff: Voting Procedures for Advisory Committee Meetings (2008), *available at* http://www.fda.gov/oc/advisory/GuidancePolicyRegs/ACVotingFINALGuidance080408.pdf.

[29] *Id.* at 5 n.1.

[30] *Id.* at 4.

[31] Vladislav Kargin, *Prevention of Herding by Experts*, 78 Econ. Letters 401, 402 (2003).

[32] Angela A. Hung, & Charles R. Plott, *Information Cascades: Replication and an Extension to Majority Rule and Conformity-Rewarding Institutions*, 91 Am. Econ. Rev. 1508, 1509 (2001).

expert consensus or an expert majority. I will turn to such cases later. In other cases, however, such concerns are not implicated; or, if they are implicated, the agency may still rationally decide that nose-counting is a better epistemic strategy than the available alternatives. Where either of these conditions is met, there is nothing wrong with nose-counting of experts by agencies.

I conclude that a factual finding based on nose-counting of experts should count as an adequately reasoned decision, absent special reason for second-order concern about strategic behavior, judgment falsification, or expert groupthink. Where those conditions do not obtain, nose-counting is a valid basis for decision within the terms of the APA.[33] Nothing in the Act, in the conceptual framework of administrative law, or in the theory of rational decision making requires this exclusion of second-order reasons. Nose-counting of experts is a ubiquitous second-order strategy for lay decision makers; although it is not the only such strategy, there is often no alternative. To force lay decision makers, in such cases, to arbitrate an expert disagreement by coughing up a first-order "reason" for which they lack any epistemic foundation is itself a guarantee of unreasoned decision making.

OPTIMAL PRECAUTIONS: WHEN CAN AGENCIES REJECT EXPERT VIEWS?

So far we have discussed cases in which agencies are entirely nonpolitical; wishing only to maximize welfare, they decide that it is a good epistemic strategy to defer to the consensus or majority view of a group of experts. We are now in position to discuss the more difficult questions. When should law allow agencies to refuse to defer? Suppose that agencies wish to depart from the majority or supermajority view of an expert panel, as to matters of fact, causation, or prediction. Should they be allowed to do so? Under what conditions, and based on what reasons?

Here the main worry is that under the pressure of politics, agencies will reject expert views as to issues of fact or causation for illegitimate reasons, or on scientifically untenable grounds. A perspective that emphasizes the need for precautions against politics will urge that agencies should

---

[33] *Cf.* Fed. Power Comm'n v. Florida Power & Light Co., 404 U.S. 453, 464–65 (1972) ("[W]ell-reasoned expert testimony – based on what is known and uncontradicted by empirical evidence – may in and of itself be 'substantial evidence' when first-hand evidence on the question … is unavailable.").

never or almost never be allowed to reject the factual or causal conclusions of expert panels. A perspective that emphasizes the risks of pathological decision making among expert groups will grant agencies substantial freedom to reject expert conclusions. I will offer a set of principles intended to accommodate both concerns – a set of optimal precautions that takes both risks into account.

An example: fine particulate matter. I will start with an example, not to take a substantive position on the merits of the controversy, but to make concrete the analytic structure of the issues. During the George W. Bush administration, in 2006, EPA decided to reject the recommendations of its Clean Air Scientific Advisory Committee (CASAC) about the revision of the National Ambient Air Quality Standards (NAAQS) for fine particulate matter.[34] CASAC, following a 20–2 vote of its subpanel on particulate matter, recommended an annual standard between twelve and fourteen micrograms per cubic meter, but EPA rejected the recommendation and maintained the extant annual standard of fifteen micrograms. This was the first time that EPA had ever directly rejected a CASAC recommendation in the NAAQS revision process.

A section of the Clean Air Act obligates the Administrator to explain why his proposed rules "differ[] ... from ... [CASAC's] findings [or] recommendations."[35] The Administrator explained the rejection on several grounds: (1) the agency's choice was based on its own view of "the most directly relevant body of scientific studies";[36] (2) CASAC saw less scientific uncertainty than the Administrator thought was actually present;[37] and (3) the CASAC recommendation was not unanimous, because two of twenty-two members of the particulate matter panel dissented.[38] Compressing these grounds somewhat, we may understand the Administrator as giving two types of reasons for departing from CASAC's findings and recommendation: (1) first-order scientific reasons based on the agency's own expertise – in this case its expert assessment of the best available science, and of

---

[34] The 2006 NAAQS regulations that resulted were successfully challenged, so far as relevant here, in the D.C. Circuit by a coalition of State Attorneys General and health and environmental groups. *See* Am. Farm Bureau Fed'n & Nat'l Pork Producers' Council v. EPA, 559 F.3d 512 (D.C. Cir. 2009) (overturning the EPA's decision as to the annual standard for fine particulate matter on the ground that EPA failed to adequately explain its decision).

[35] 42 U.S.C. § 7607(d)(3) (2006).

[36] National Ambient Air Quality Standards for Particulate Matter, 71 Fed. Reg. 61,144, 61,174 (Oct. 17, 2006) (codified at 40 C.F.R. § 50.6 (2008)).

[37] *Id.*

[38] *Id.* at 61,174 n.44.

the level of scientific uncertainty; and (2) the second-order reason, offered to diminish the epistemic force of the panel's conclusions, that the panel was not unanimous, implying that reasonable experts could disagree.

I believe that the second type of reason was, in principle, the right type for the agency to offer – whether or not, on the facts, it was sufficient to justify rejecting the panel's factual findings. In order to prevail, the Administrator would either have to give a valid second-order reason for rejecting the panel's factual findings, or else show that the agency's regulatory priorities or evaluation of alternative policies were in themselves an adequate basis for disagreement. In the latter case, the Administrator would have had to make transparent his normative differences with the panel, making it easier for Congress, the courts, and the public to monitor the agency's commitments and behavior. As it turned out, the D.C. Circuit later overturned the Administrator's decision as to the annual standard for fine particulate matter, finding that the Administrator had "failed adequately to explain its reason for not accepting the CASAC's recommendations."[39]

EXPERT DISAGREEMENT AND FIRST-ORDER REASONS

I suggest that the Administrator's first-order view of the scientific merits should have no special weight as against a panel's factual findings. The Administrator is an expert, at least in the sense that her view is typically informed by the expertise of the scientists on her staff (although as we will see, this is not always true, and was not true in the particulate matter rulemaking). But the members of the scientific panel are of course expert as well. The administrator's view should thus be understood to count as just another vote, among others. If the expert panel is tied, it follows that the agency's vote is decisive and the agency can choose either view. If, however, a decisive majority of experts favors a certain view, then the administrator's contrary view is simply another vote for the dissenting side, and as such is defeated.[40]

This approach is entirely consistent with believing – if anyone does believe this – that the Administrator is the single most competent expert in the picture. A main point of the Jury Theorem is that a group of somewhat

---

[39] *Am. Farm Bureau Fed'n & Nat'l Pork Producers' Council*, 559 F.3d at 521.

[40] This approach creates a discontinuity: where the expert panel is tied the administrator necessarily prevails, but not otherwise, so the switch of a small number of votes on the panel can in theory be dispositive for the outcome. This is, however, a standard property of majority rule – under May's Theorem, it is one of the conditions that majority rule can alone satisfy jointly – and it is a routine property of majority voting in legislatures.

less expert voters, so long as their competence is better than random, can be markedly superior to a single expert of higher competence. Indeed, under identifiable conditions, the accuracy of the group's median or mean member will necessarily exceed that of its single most competent member.[41]

The agency can, of course, hear what the panel has to say, review its methods and conclusions, and then form its own judgments. This does not show that the agency's conclusions can incorporate all of the panel's expertise, and add to it the agency's own. To see this, we can imagine that the Administrator is placed on the panel; some statutory panels, set up to advise a given agency, do include the heads of other agencies or government officials. In such circumstances, the Administrator could likewise consider the information available to other panel members, but the Administrator would merely have one vote among others, and a contrary majority view of experts would trump his view. I suggest that the same logic holds when statues require the Administrator to consider the panel's factual findings and to give a reason for departing from them. In such cases, the agency's own first-order view of the facts should not suffice to trump the panel's aggregate expertise.

FACTS, CAUSATION, AND VALUES

The best epistemic practice is thus to treat the agency's first-order reasons as just another vote that is outweighed by a contrary body of expert votes, as to factual and causal matters. The only type of "reason" that suffices is a reason to think that, epistemically, the agency is better positioned than a (super)majority of the panel to get the facts right. Although such a showing is not impossible – shortly, I will canvass some valid second-order reasons that agencies might be able to offer and substantiate, in particular cases – it will usually be difficult.

Nothing in this argument, however, suggests that agencies must defer to the panel's evaluation of possible policies, given certain facts. As we have seen, courts allow agencies to set regulatory priorities and allocate resources, even in the face of panel recommendations to the contrary.[42] The logic of that restriction is that agencies may evaluate possible policies in light of their own preferences, rather than the panel's, insofar as the law

[41] SCOTT E. PAGE, *The Difference: How the Power of Diversity Creates Better Groups, Firms, Schools, and Societies* 158 (2007).
[42] *See* Int'l Union, UAW v. Chao, 361 F.3d 249 (3d Cir. 2004) (agency allowed to reject advisory committee recommendation on the ground that the agency had rationally set other priorities).

permits. A statutory duty to give reasons for rejecting a panel's "findings" and "recommendations,"[43] then, is best understood as two very different duties with different consequences. As to findings, agencies must adopt the factual bases of a panel's conclusions, absent some valid second-order reason for rejecting them. By contrast, the agency need not adopt the panel's overall recommendations for policies, if agencies have a standard first-order reason for evaluating competing policies differently or for setting different regulatory priorities. Yet even in such cases, the agency will be forced to openly state its evaluative differences with the panel or its different regulatory priorities, thereby reducing the costs of monitoring to reviewing courts and democratic bodies.

EX ANTE INCENTIVES

In principle, it is possible that members of expert panels might invest less in acquiring information when, and because, agencies defer to them on factual questions. If the agency must accept the panel's work, the panel might do it less carefully. Yet the opposite effect seems at least equally possible: expert panels who know they will receive no deference have little incentive to get things right, whereas expert panels may invest more time in acquiring information precisely when, and because, they know that the agency is presumptively obliged to accept their findings. Requiring agency deference to panel findings, in other words, eliminates a kind of epistemic moral hazard that can arise when the panel is aware that the agency is likely to ignore its work; this is the moral-hazard risk of multiple opinions, discussed in Chapter 5. In light of this point, the ex ante incentives of the framework suggested here are ambiguous and unclear; at a minimum, there is no ground for concern that the framework will systematically undermine expert panels' incentives to acquire information.

SECOND-ORDER REASONS

On the approach I have suggested, the key issue involves *comparative epistemic competence*: whether the agency or expert is best positioned to determine relevant facts, where reviewing courts who lack direct knowledge themselves should place their epistemic bets, and, more generally,

---

[43] The Clean Air Act obliges the Administrator to explain any differences between the policies he adopts and CASAC's "findings" or "recommendations." *See* 42 U.S.C. § 7607(d) (3) (2006).

how fact-finding authority should be allocated between agencies and their expert advisors. Agencies are not always obliged to find facts in accordance with the expert panel's view. Rather, agencies should be allowed to reject panel findings if they have the right sort of second-order reason and substantiate it.

In general, valid second-order reasons will give reviewing courts confidence that the best epistemic bet is to rely on the agency's first-order views rather than those of the expert panel. Agencies should be able to reject panel findings only if they can give concrete reason to think that the epistemic quality of the expert panel's conclusions are low, relative to the agency's own views. Some illustrations of the possible second-order reasons agencies might give are as follows.

Track records. In some cases, agencies will have information about the accuracy of an expert panel's past factual estimates, or the causal theories it advanced, or its past predictions. Where this is so, agencies might be able to show that the panel has often erred. However, this is likely to be a rare case, and courts should be wary of this sort of second-order claim, for several reasons.

Mere inaccuracy does not show that a past panel's conclusions were epistemically flawed, or that the agency's own first-order views are likely to be systematically superior. Because factual determinations, causal theories and predictions of any complexity will inevitably have a stochastic element – an element of irreducible randomness, arising from the costs of information or built into the nature of things – it is perfectly possible that the panel's conclusions are systematically superior to the agency's, from an ex ante perspective, even if the panel's conclusions have sometimes turned out to be wrong. Furthermore, panels whose members serve for long periods may develop endogenous expertise[44] through experience and institutional learning over time. In such cases, the panel's initial findings and predictions may be flawed, but their quality will systematically improve over time. From the standpoint of the reviewing court, the best epistemic bet overall may still be to trust the conclusions of the expert panel over the agency's views.

These points imply that a high rate of turnover among panel members may make it difficult to gauge the track record of the panel. Indeed, as turnover increases, "the panel" becomes an increasingly ill-defined entity.

---

[44] *See* Matthew C. Stephenson, *Bureaucratic Decision Costs and Endogenous Agency Expertise*, 23 J.L. ECON. & ORG. 469, 472 (2007); Matthew C. Stephenson, *Information Acquisition and Institutional Design*, 124 HARV. L. REV. 1422 (2011).

Reviewing courts could plausibly, and without much difficulty, discount the validity of an agency's appeal to the panel's track record by the rate at which panel membership has changed over time. Such a practice would reduce, at the margin, agency incentives to manipulate the composition of expert panels by substituting new members whose viewpoints will predictably track the agency's own.[45] By doing so, the agency would also be undercutting its own ability to appeal to the panel's track record as a basis for departing from its views.

Comparative qualifications. In some cases, agencies will have valid reason to reject nose-counting – to decline to follow a (super)majority view of the panel – because the agency validly weights votes by the qualifications of the voters. In the black-lung cases, we have seen, it is perfectly rational for the agency adjudicator to believe the diagnoses of two doctors with special qualifications in detecting pneumoconiosis over the diagnoses of three general practitioners. Counting weighted votes is an epistemic improvement, so long as the weights track competence and – a crucial qualification – so long as the discounted voters bring no cognitive diversity to the group. If the latter condition does not hold, because the discounted voters bring new perspectives or have views that, by training or profession, are likely to be uncorrelated with the views of highly competent experts, then the logic of the Jury Theorem suggests that the group's overall epistemic performance will be better than the views of even its most expert members.[46]

Bias. In other cases, agencies might be able to point to systematic bias among members of the panel in order to impeach the epistemic warrant for their conclusions. If statutes create a panel composed, for example, largely of experts drawn from a certain discipline, profession, or industry, and if the panel's recommendations track apparent disciplinary or professional biases or industry interests, there is valid ground for concern. Agencies will have better second-order reason to depart from panel recommendations when the panel's composition is narrowly defined or drawn predominantly from industry.

Here there are two relevant interpretations of the vague term "bias": motivational and epistemic. In the former sense bias means that the expert

---

[45] In the 1980s, the EPA was accused of manipulating the membership of its Science Advisory Board in this way. A Reagan administration "hit list" was discovered containing the names of advisors whose views were no longer sympathetic to that of the administration. Most of the scientists on the list were, indeed, "retired" by the Reagan EPA. Nicholas A. Ashford, *Advisory Committees in OSHA and EPA: Their Use in Regulatory Decisionmaking,* 9 SCI. TECH. & HUM. VALUES 72, 72 n.1, 77 n.16 (1984).

[46] Ladha, *supra* note, at 617.

is not even trying to reach the right answer, as opposed to the answer that benefits his firm or career; in the latter sense, bias means that the expert has blind spots arising precisely from his specialized training or knowledge. In Jury Theorem terms, bias may thus be understood either as a simple violation of the condition of sincere voting, at the level of individuals, or else as a concern that about the positive correlation of errors across the group. If members of a scientific subdiscipline, profession, or industry have highly correlated perspectives, it is less likely that errors will wash out at the group level.

In many cases, however, the underlying statutes require a mix of professions, disciplines, and perspectives, specifying with particularity how the panel should be composed. Under the Clean Air Act, for example, CASAC comprises "at least one member of the National Academy of Sciences, one physician, and one person representing State air pollution control agencies."[47] Likewise, the Advisory Commission on Childhood Vaccines is comprised of health experts, members of the general public (two of whom have children who have suffered vaccine-related injury or death), lawyers, and officials from relevant agencies. Even more pointedly, the National Institutes of Health (NIH) Revitalization Act of 1993[48] authorizes the Secretary of Health and Human Services to appoint an Ethics Advisory Board.[49] If such a board is appointed, it must have between fourteen and twenty members, among which must be at least one attorney, one ethicist, one practicing physician, one theologian, while no fewer than one-third but no more than one-half of the members must be "scientists with substantial accomplishments in biomedical or behavioral research."[50] Most generally, the Federal Advisory Committee Act indirectly requires that committees have a "balanced composition."[51]

Requirements of this sort trade off some scientific competence, at the margin, for greater representation of affected interests and reduced correlation of errors at the group level. Individual epistemic competence of the panel members is just one good, which should be optimized, not maximized; balanced panels of this sort can create overall gains by sacrificing some expertise for a reduced chance that the biases of any one affected interest will dominate. In the case of the NIH Revitalization Act

---

[47] 42 U.S.C. § 7409(d)(2)(A) (2006).
[48] National Institutes of Health Revitalization Act of 1993, Pub. L. No. 103–43, 107 Stat. 126 (codified as amended in scattered sections of 42 U.S.C.).
[49] 42 U.S.C. § 289a-1 (Supp. 2008).
[50] *Id.* § 289a-1(b)(5)(C).
[51] 5 U.S.C. app. 2 §§ 1–16 (2007 & Supp. 2008).

of 1993, the lower bound on biomedical scientists (at least one-third of the panel) promotes expertise, the upper bound (no more than one-half of the panel) promotes epistemic diversity by restricting the representation of a particular scientific subfield. Similarly, a diversity of affected interests minimizes the chance that panel members will deliberately falsify an appearance of consensus in order to maximize their influence. Because diverse interests will predictably have cross-cutting agendas, the chances that the panel can agree on a single position are reduced; more likely is open disagreement, providing more information to agencies and reviewing courts.

The cost of epistemic diversity is a slightly increased chance that some members of a panel will believe something truly bizarre – that lead is good for you, or that last week's cold weather shows that climate change is not occurring.[52] Under the approach I am suggesting, the agency would be barred from simply rejecting these conclusions on the first-order ground that the agency knows them to be false. Yet in order for such bizarre views to make any difference, they must (1) obtain the agreement of a majority of panel members, expert as well as nonexpert, (2) under circumstances in which the agency has no valid second-order reason to reject the panel's conclusions. The wackier the error, the less likely it is that those additional two conditions will hold, so this is another self-limiting problem.

The consequences for administrative law are straightforward. Where requirements of epistemic diversity are in place, courts should be reluctant to accept an agency's appeal to systematic disciplinary, professional, or industry-based bias. Where an expert panel is drawn solely from a narrow professional subcategory or subdiscipline, or staffed largely by representatives from a particular industry or segment of industry, an agency appeal to bias should be taken more seriously.

Groupthink and judgment falsification. In general, agencies should be allowed to depart from the views of experts when there is good reason to think that herding or groupthink has occurred. In such cases the agency has a valid second-order reason for discounting an expert majority view, or consensus; if the problem is serious, the agency's first-order view may be the only independently formed first-order view in the field. Here there is a good deal of overlap with the vague idea of "bias," interpreted in its epistemic rather than motivational sense. Even if the goal of all panel members is

[52] Thanks to Lisa Heinzerling for these examples.

to get the answer right, copying of others' views, while individually rational, can make the group decision uninformed.

Although various forms of groupthink are a real concern, there are two relevant cautions. First, the mere fact that some experts on a panel follow the views of other experts does not amount to groupthink, or necessarily reduce the overall epistemic competence of the group. If panel members defer to a highly competent opinion leader, group epistemic competence can increase overall. Equivalently, herding or information cascades cannot be inferred from the bare fact that some members of the panel copy the views of others. If the copying members have *meta-expertise* – if they are quite adept at figuring out who among them are the best experts – then copying can actually improve the group's overall performance.[53] The copiers "may be poor meteorologists, but good judges of meteorologists."[54]

Second, the risk of groupthink is sensitive to the composition and structure of the panel and the decision-making processes it uses. Accordingly, agencies will have valid second-order reasons to discount the consensus of expert panels when they can point to features of the panel's composition, structure, or decision-making process that raise red flags. Where an expert panel is all drawn from the same subfield, where experts vote or express judgments in sequence and with knowledge of each others' views, and where experts are uncompensated or where their compensation is a function of individual rather than group performance, and where a panel's views are completely unanimous on an issue the agency has independent reason to think is at least difficult, then the risk of harmful groupthink is at an apogee and reviewing courts should take the agency's second-order concerns most seriously.

The unanimity dilemma. Special problems arise where an expert panel is unanimous or reports "consensus" without a formal vote. In such cases, both agencies and reviewing courts are in something of an epistemic dilemma. Unanimity can arise either because all experts on the panel, whatever their biases, are receiving a strong and uniform signal from reality about an issue of fact or causation. It can also be a sign of herding, or cascades, or judgment falsification. Unanimity is epistemically ambiguous. By contrast, the most powerful expert consensus is one that is a supermajority, but not unanimous. The open dissent shows that the supermajority's

---

[53] David Coady, *When Experts Disagree*, 3 EPISTEME 68, 71 (2006).
[54] *Id.* at 72.

view has been epistemically tested by vigorous disagreement, yet has still prevailed.

Unanimity, then, is both potentially powerful and potentially suspect. Under what conditions is it most likely to be one or the other? Where reviewing courts have a prior belief that the issue is an easy one, or that the facts lean strongly in one direction, unanimity is best taken as a warning that an agency's contrary view would lack any basis in fact. In most regulatory issues that reach the stage of final agency action, however, and for which an expert panel has been appointed, it is unlikely in the extreme that the issue is antecedently known to be an easy one, or that the facts overwhelmingly favor one view. In such circumstances unanimity is likely to be suspect, while disagreement within the panel should actually increase the agency's, and the reviewing court's, epistemic confidence in the conclusions of the panel majority or supermajority.

One somewhat counterintuitive implication is that agencies should not generally be allowed to impeach the conclusions of a panel majority by claiming that disagreement within the panel shows that the minority view is "reasonable." It may be so, but the question is where agencies and reviewing courts should place their epistemic bets: with the minority or with the majority. The logic of expert aggregation suggests that placing epistemic bets on panel majorities is the better course, on average. And if panels collectively desire to maximize the chance the agency will adopt their recommendations, a legal rule that allows agencies to impeach panel conclusions by pointing to reasonable dissent will give panels incentives to falsify an appearance of consensus, thus suppressing useful information.

In the 2006 controversy over fine particulate matter, the Administrator pointed out that the CASAC subcommittee was not unanimous, as a basis for differing from its recommendations. This argument is analytically misguided. The questions at issue were hardly simple, whatever their correct resolution. CASAC's decision, endorsed by a large but nonunanimous supermajority, actually offered firmer grounds for epistemic confidence than a unanimous one, by showing that relevant arguments had been ventilated; using nonunanimity as a basis for rejecting the panel's views gives CASAC members a heightened incentive to create a false appearance of consensus in the future. In any event, the reviewing court paid no heed to the Administrator's observation.[55]

---

[55] *See* Am. Farm Bureau Fed'n & Nat'l Pork Producers' Council v. EPA, 559 F.3d 512, 517–18 (D.C. Cir. 2009) (ignoring the Administrator's attempt to impeach CASAC's recommendation).

POLITICIZATION AND EXPERT PATHOLOGIES:
A MATURE POSITION

I have attempted to indicate some second-order principles for allocating decision-making competence between agencies and expert panels. The former are influenced by politics, both for good and for ill, while the latter display the virtues and vices both of groups generally and of expert groups in particular. These traits and conditions give rise to two (clusters of) distinctive risks, which trade off against one another: the risks of politicized distortion of factual and causal judgments (the "science charade") on the one hand, and the pathologies of expert groupthink on the other.

The principles I have suggested attempt to optimize these risks. In the usual case, agencies have good second-order reasons to count expert noses and to defer to the views of a majority or supermajority of an expert panel. Law should not force agencies to cough up their own, independent first-order judgment on complex issues of scientific fact and causation. The harder issues arise where agencies wish to depart from the views of an expert panel. In such cases, the risk of politicization is real, and agencies should be allowed to reject expert views only where the agency can offer a valid second-order reason to believe that the expert panel has suffered from some form of groupthink or false consensus. Expert views should presumptively prevail, unless there is reason to believe that the agency is in a comparatively better epistemic position than the expert panel – a possible but unlikely case.

Other plausible principles could doubtless be recommended to accommodate the competing concerns. Whatever the merits, the analysis is intended to illustrate that a mature analysis will take into account all relevant second-order risks. Rather than pursuing one-sided precautions against politicized agency decision making, or against expert pathologies, the administrative state should relate the two risks and trade them off within a larger framework – an optimal set of principles for agency decision making.

Conclusion

Constitutional Rulemaking Without a Style

At the end of Chapter 1, I attempted to put precautionary constitutionalism in its best light. On the precautionary approach, constitutional rules should build in redundant and robust safeguards against the risks that officials will predictably abuse their power and discretion, and that institutions will predictably attempt to expand their power. Safeguards are necessary because once abuses occur it may be too late to do anything about it; in the extreme, abuses will immunize themselves from correction. Above all, constitutional rulemakers should attempt to limit the downside risks of politics, ensuring that worst-case scenarios do not come to pass. Eschewing attempts to make a constitution that does good or promotes justice, they should limit themselves to preventing abuses and to limiting the possibility that officials will exploit their positions in ways that reduce the welfare or compromise the liberty of the whole polity.

This is a venerable vision of the proper aims and goals of constitutional law. It has been advocated by a series of impressive minds in many contexts, ranging from the founding era to modern legal and political theory, especially liberal constitutional theory. It is highly plausible on its face; in many settings in law and elsewhere, limiting the downside risks of choices is a sensible strategy, and aiming for too much can produce serious blunders. If the precautionary approach to constitutionalism is systematically mistaken, it is not trivially mistaken, nor is it fallacious in any simple way.

Yet as I have also tried to show, an equally venerable and impressive line of critics – both constitutional actors and constitutional analysts, including figures like Story who played both roles – have criticized precautionary constitutionalism root and branch. Three main lines of criticism stand out: arguments based on futility, jeopardy, and perversity. In some cases constitutional precautions will fail the test of incentive-incompatibility, failing to stick when the risks they seek to prevent materialize, perhaps because those very risks have materialized. In some cases precautions, although sensible in themselves, will prove too costly on other margins, and thus fail a kind of rough calculus of costs and benefits (which is not necessarily the same thing as cost-benefit analysis in the technical sense; the distinction is discussed in Chapter 2). Here an important case involves the availability of ex post correction. Precautions may overlook the possibility of ex post remedies, in which case ex ante precautions will impose unnecessary costs. Finally, in the most dramatic cases, precautions will actually exacerbate the very risks they target, so that the same risk appears on both sides of the ledger; where this is so, precautions may prove self-defeating.

The overall theme of the critiques is that precautionary constitution-alism fails because it distorts assessment of the second-order risks of pol-itics. Focusing to excess – even obsessively – on particular target risks, precautionary constitutionalism overlooks collateral or countervailing risks, including risks generated by the precautions themselves. Critics of precautionary principles in subconstitutional matters of health, safety, and environmental regulation have argued that such principles produce imbal-anced risk assessment; those critiques echo, perhaps unknowingly, a line of argument developed in the constitutional setting at least two centuries before, and continuing to the present.

The "mature position" is the argument for balanced assessment of polit-ical risks advocated by Hamilton, Marshall, Story, Frankfurter, Jackson, and other critics of precautionary constitutionalism. A mature assessment attends to both target risks and countervailing risks, both the risks pre-vented by precautions and the risks created by them, and attempts to bal-ance the resulting considerations in a larger overall calculus of optimal constitutional regulation of second-order political risks. In order to tie together the threads of my argument for the mature position, I will con-clude by attempting to put it in the best possible light, in just the way Chapter 2 attempted for precautionary constitutionalism.

THE (NEGATIVE) VIRTUES OF OPTIMIZING CONSTITUTIONALISM

In modern terms, the mature position represents a commitment to opti-mizing constitutionalism. In other words, constitutional rulemakers, to the extent feasible, should design rules so as to achieve an allocation of second-order decision-making authority, that optimizes across all polit-ical risks, at least in expectation. The virtues of the optimizing approach to constitutionalism prove, I believe, even more impressive than the undoubted virtues of the precautionary approach.

Avoidance of political obsession. As I have emphasized throughout, the positive content of optimizing constitutionalism verges on the banal ("consider all relevant risks"). Its main virtue, however, is deliberately negative. Above all, an optimizing approach posits that *constitutional rulemakers should have no obsessions*. There should be no risk that constitutional rulemakers bend all their efforts to warding off by means of precautions, even to the point of overlooking other risks, costs, and harms. Under an optimizing approach, rulemakers assess all political risks for what they are worth, no more and no less, and attempt to achieve a unified, balanced perspective that gives all relevant considerations their due weight. This refusal to obsess is a corrective for constitutional "availability cascades" and the tendency to excessive focus on the most recent, salient political risks that loom large in moments of constitutional crisis, as discussed at the end of Chapter 2.

Contextualism and particularism. A corollary of the preceding point is that the optimizing approach makes particularistic and contextual recommendations. This is somewhat paradoxical, given that the approach advertises itself as pursuing a global assessment of political risks, rather than obsessing over particular target risks. In fact the two points are complementary. Precisely because it takes all relevant risks into account, the optimizing approach eschews sweeping claims about the importance, across the board, of preventing any particular risk, such as tyranny, agency slack ("abuses"), or majoritarian oppression. Rather, optimal risk assessments will push toward localized solutions that carefully calibrate competing and potentially offsetting harms.

Openness to facts. The optimizing approach is intrinsically fact-driven and open to the fresh air of circumstances. Rather than imposing general strictures and rigidly following out their logic, come what may, the optimizing approach looks at the particulars of the situation to see whether rules are being defined so as to create diminishing marginal benefits and increasing marginal costs. The key issue is how the set of constitutional rules will actually work.

Avoidance of extremes. The optimizing approach also holds that if there are multiple countervailing risks in the picture, it is generally a good idea to avoid extreme solutions ("corner solutions" in the economist's lingo). Given the multiplicity of political goods, it will often be best for rulemakers to opt for "some of each" rather than all of one and none of the others – a point I urged in Chapter 4. This is not a conceptual point, nor is it a systematic commitment; instead it is an entirely pragmatic observation that will sometimes hold, and sometimes not, and that is based entirely on a rough empirical judgment about the recurring circumstances of constitution-making. In the messy settings in which constitutional problems tend to crop up, rulemakers often face clashes between rival goods with indisputable claims, and they must consider rival causal theories that are all plausible. The best guess about the shape of the social welfare function in such cases will be, with some frequency, that the pursuit of given goods has diminishing marginal benefits, or that departing from some ideal has increasing marginal costs (a convex cost function). Where this is so, it will be best to depart from many ideals simultaneously, to some degree; this is the well-known problem or paradox of second-best.[1] By violating many ideals to some degree, the rulemaker achieves some of every good, even while failing to achieve all of any good. But given the shape of the marginal cost and benefit curves, attaining some of each good produces a maximum of achievable social welfare. The result is messy institutions that do no one thing perfectly, but that do several things tolerably well.

Flexibility. Finally, the optimizing approach is consistent with a wide range of commitments and allocations of institutional authority, as discussed in earlier chapters. From one standpoint this is a weakness; adherence to the optimizing approach does not necessarily entail any particular institutional arrangements. Optimal assessment of second-order risks might even yield the conclusion, in a particular domain, that the low capacities of decision makers created by the constitution, or the nature of the relevant political risks in a given threat environment, themselves counsel in favor of a precautionary approach in that domain. Yet that decision will itself be made not on precautionary, one-sided grounds, but on a mature and balanced calculus. At the highest level, the rulemakers' approach will not be precautionary or fearful, even if that approach may happen to yield local precautions in operation.

From another standpoint, the flexibility of the optimizing approach is a great strength. There is no constitutional structure or institutional allocation of power that just is generally and systematically best, regardless of the economic, social, and political environment, and regardless of

---

[1] *See generally* ADRIAN VERMEULE, THE SYSTEM OF THE CONSTITUTION (2011) (analyzing constitutionalism from the perspective of systems theory and the problem of second-best).

the nature of the second-order risks that constitutional rulemakers will confront. The optimizing approach recognizes this, while the precautionary approach has standing commitments and suspicions that bias rulemaking in particular directions, regardless of circumstances. Again, it may be best, all things considered, for rulemakers to build localized institutional skews into the constitutional system they fashion, but the rulemakers themselves should not think in a skewed fashion while doing the building; they should approach their task, to the extent possible, without preconceptions and without biases in favor of particular institutional arrangements.

CONSTITUTIONAL RULEMAKING WITHOUT A STYLE

The great chess player Miguel Najdorf commented that the even greater chess player Bobby Fischer had "no style," because "perfection has no style."[2] And Fischer's successor as world champion, Anatoly Karpov, said of himself: "Style? I have no style."[3] Najdorf's and Karpov's point was that the very best players strive to avoid abstract and general preferences, proclivities, or obsessions. They do not systematically enjoy either attacking or defending, either playing White or playing Black; nor do they systematically aim either to maximize the chance of victory, or to minimize the risk of loss. Of course all this is an overstatement; among the world champions, Garry Kasparov liked to attack, Tigran Petrosian to defend. Yet all were universal players, at least as compared to their inferiors. In general, the very best players are as concrete as possible, and minimize the relatively crude heuristics and generalizations on which lesser players rely.[4] The greatest masters of the game calculate all relevant costs and benefits of all possible courses of action as best they can, and then pick the best move in the circumstances.

Quite obviously, chess is a more limited and well-structured problem than constitutional rulemaking, but I have argued that an analogous point holds, with appropriate modifications. Constitutional rulemakers should, to the extent possible, rid themselves of standing commitments, fears, and obsessions. By contrast, precautionary constitutionalism elevates

---

[2]   *Chess Quotes – Style*, CHESSQUOTES.COM, http://www.chessquotes.com/topic-style (last visited Feb. 24, 2013).

[3]   *Anatoly Karpov Quotes*, BRAINYQUOTE.COM, http://www.brainyquote.com/quotes/authors/a/anatoly_karpov.html (last visited Feb. 24, 2013).

[4]   *See* JOHN WATSON, SECRETS OF MODERN CHESS STRATEGY (1999).

such biases – in the literal sense of leanings – to the level of principle. If precautionary constitutionalism is untenable, the conclusion is discomfiting, because we cannot rely on our standing dispositions and biases to guide us under conditions of uncertainty. Nonetheless, comfort is not the issue, and optimal assessment of political risks requires that, to the extent humanly feasible, constitutional rulemakers do their work without a style.

Acknowledgments

Many debts of gratitude are due; if they cannot all be paid simultaneously, at least they can be acknowledged. Thanks above all to my family – Yun Soo, Emily, Spencer, Auntie, and O-Ma – for their constant love and support. Don Herzog, Martha Minow, Cass Sunstein, and John Witt provided helpful comments on the whole manuscript, as did anonymous reviewers at Cambridge University Press. Many friends and colleagues offered helpful comments on pieces of the project in earlier stages, especially Jon Elster, Dick Fallon, Jake Gersen, John Goldberg, Jack Goldsmith, Frank Michelman, Matt Stephenson, and Mark Tushnet. The book was begun concurrently with a seminar on "Political Risk and Public Law," co-taught with Dean Minow at Harvard Law School in Fall 2011. Her penetrating questions, and the students' contributions, were invaluable in helping me to clarify and deepen my claims. The *Journal of Legal Analysis*, under the editorship of Mark Ramseyer and Steve Shavell, published a symposium on political risk and public law in which an earlier version of Part I was published; thanks for their encouragement for the overall project and for their helpful comments. Samantha Goldstein, Charlie Griffin, and Rachel Siegel provided excellent research and editorial assistance, while Ellen Keng kept the optimizing machine in trim.

I have incorporated heavily revised material from articles I have published elsewhere, as listed here. I wish to thank the journals and their editors for permissions and for their assistance.

"Recess Appointments and Precautionary Constitutionalism," 126 HARVARD LAW REVIEW FORUM 122 (2013);

"Introduction: Political Risk and Public Law," 4 JOURNAL OF LEGAL ANALYSIS 1–6 (2012);

"Precautionary Principles in Constitutional Law," 4 JOURNAL OF LEGAL ANALYSIS 181–222 (2012);

"Government by Public Opinion: Bryce's Theory of the Constitution," available at SSRN (http://papers.ssrn.com/sol3/papers.cfm?abstract_id=1809794);

"Contra 'Nemo Iudex in Sua Causa': On the Limits of Impartiality", 122 YALE LAW JOURNAL 384 (2012);

"Second Opinions and Institutional Design," 97 VIRGINIA LAW REVIEW 1435 (2011);

"The Parliament of the Experts," 58 DUKE LAW JOURNAL 2231 (2009).

Index